E-Commerce and Cultural Values

Theerasak Thanasankit
Monash University, Australia

IDEA GROUP PUBLISHING
Hershey • London • Melbourne • Singapore • Beijing

Acquisition Editor:	Mehdi Khosrow-Pour
Senior Managing Editor:	Jan Travers
Managing Editor:	Amanda Appicello
Development Editor:	Michele Rossi
Copy Editor:	Terry Heffelfinger
Typesetter:	Amanda Lutz
Cover Design:	Michelle Waters
Printed at:	Integrated Book Technology

Published in the United States of America by
Idea Group Publishing (an imprint of Idea Group Inc.)
701 E. Chocolate Avenue, Suite 200
Hershey PA 17033
Tel: 717-533-8845
Fax: 717-533-8661
E-mail: cust@idea-group.com
Web site: http://www.idea-group.com

and in the United Kingdom by
Idea Group Publishing (an imprint of Idea Group Inc.)
3 Henrietta Street
Covent Garden
London WC2E 8LU
Tel: 44 20 7240 0856
Fax: 44 20 7379 3313
Web site: http://www.eurospan.co.uk

Library of Congress Cataloging-in-Publication Data

E-commerce and cultural values / [edited by] Theerasak Thanasankit.
p. cm.
Includes bibliographical references and index.
ISBN 1-59140-056-2 (hard cover) — ISBN 1-59140-093-7 (ebook)
1. Electronic commerce—Social aspects. 2. Information society. I. Thanasankit, Theerasak.
HF5548.32 .E1825 2002
303.48'2—dc21

2002153245

British Cataloguing in Publication Data
A Cataloguing in Publication record for this book is available from the British Library.

E-Commerce and Cultural Values

Table of Contents

SECTION II: E-COMMERCE AND ORGANIZATIONAL CULTURE

SECTION III: BUSINESS TO CONSUMER E-COMMERCE AND CULTURAL VALUES

SECTION IV: E-LEARNING AND CULTURAL VALUES

SECTION V: E-COMMERCE INTERFACES

Preface

This book idea originated after talking with my academic colleagues around the world, who I met at numerous IS conferences. There are a number of academics who are interested in the role of culture and its influence on information systems in the areas of development, use, adoption and diffusion. The published work of these researchers is scatted in various publications such as conferences and journals. The idea of this book was to try to collect research in the area of culture and information systems, especially in e-commerce, as a starting point for other researchers who want to pursue or gain a better understanding in this topic. This book brings together 12 chapters about various aspects of culture values and e-commerce in the area of policy management, web interfaces, e-learning, consumer behaviour and technology diffusion.

The first section of this book is focused on Information Technology and E-Commerce policy. There are 4 chapters in this section. In Chapter 1, Corbitt establishes the relationship between globalisation, culture and e-business in the world economic environment. The chapter also investigates what globalisation means in different countries and in different cultures. E-business cannot be viewed as an isolated entity. The role of culture influences managerial styles, human interaction. Attitudes toward e-business are imbued with cultural practice that challenge any sense of uniformity or heterogeneity in the world of e-business.

In Chapter 2, Chieochan, Lindley and Dunn investigate the factors influencing e-commerce adoption in Thai Agricultural Cooperatives. The role of the cooperative's mangers were investigated and the authors found that the managerial role is important as their subordinates perceive them as knowledgeable and leaders in turning e-commerce technologies into success. The value of respect was investigated to support their argument of the role of the manager as a leader. Again, this study also shows the role of government leadership in providing clear policy and incentives about the adoption of information technology in Thailand. Other factors such as the manager's knowledge of IT, information intensity, the competitive environment and the social and cultural context of Thai society are also explored in this chapter.

In Chapter 3, Kong investigates the inhibitors to e-commerce adoption in Singaporean SMEs. He suggests that direction by and incentives given by the Singaporean government are important as SMEs in Singapore prefer clear direction and government assistance in their adoption of e-commerce.

Chapter 4 is a fascinating chapter where Kabalimu, Corbitt and Thanasankit investigate the influence of colonialism and its influence in the Tanzania government, especially in IT implementation. The chapter is concerned with how Tanzania has been socially and economically affects by post-colonialism at the policy level and describes how Tanzanians are reinventing themselves in the post colonialism period. The argument essentially is that progress is retarded somewhat by the influence of post-colonial practices.

The second section of the book focuses on the role of organisational culture and national culture and their influences in e-commerce projects. In the first chapter of this section, Chapter 5, Pan and Flynn investigate e-commerce project abandonment by applying the post-mortem analysis. This chapter argues that knowledge can be gained by understanding project abandonment. One of the new pieces of knowledge learned from this chapter concerns the conflict of organisational cultures between the Japanese and Singaporeans. The cultural conflicts are also caused by the differences in national culture levels between the two countries.

In Chapter 6, Sarkar and Cybulski investigate the organisational conflict in the development of web-enabled information systems. They investigate the cultural conflicts between different stakeholders during application developments. Stakeholders or organisations members participating in a common business process are varied in their computer competency, business knowledge, language and culture. These differences then may cause conflict between them and then impact on the development of web-enabled information system applications.

The last chapter of this section, Chapter 7, introduces the importance of stakeholders in the e-commerce relationship and compares a specific framework in both Singapore and Australia. The study contributes to existing literature in Electronic Commerce by identifying and emphasizing stakeholder relationships in Electronic Commerce, and how they can be used to differentiate B-to-C and B-to-B Electronic Commerce types. Clear understanding of the distinction of the two types of Electronic Commerce may assist organizations to formulate the appropriate business strategies when venturing into the dot com territory. In addition, this study allows strategies for integrating both types of Electronic Commerce (e.g. a retailer which integrates its virtual storefront with its backend Enterprise Resource Planning (ERP) system) to be developed. Electronic Commerce reduces face-to-face interaction between stakeholders, hence Electronic Commerce organizations will need to pay additional attention to stakeholder relationship issues in order to satisfy trading partners and customers better.

The third section focuses on B2C models and culture in e-commerce. In the first chapter of this section (Chapter 8), Peszynski explores the role of Mäori culture and its influences on Mäori shopping behaviour on the Internet, especially the role of trust. Mäori arrived in New Zealand from the Pacific approximately a thousand years ago and now they have become an integrated part in New Zealand society. Mäori tend to trust their immediate family members (*whanau*) and tribal elders (*iwi*), especially for recommendations about products and services. This also includes online shopping and the trustworthiness of websites. The values of *whanau* and *iwi* are part of the Mäori collective society, which then influences their society.

In Chapter 9, Intrapairot and Srivihok investigate the use of e-commerce in Thai SMEs, especially in the tourism industry. They found that lack of technology knowledge and infrastructure prevents Thai SMEs from the adoption of e-commerce. The government directions and incentives are also important factors for SMEs adoption of e-commerce. Online payment systems are also a factor as many Thais do not trust online payments as Thai society is still based on cash and face-to-face negotiation. Therefore, many web sites for e-tourism are mainly brochures rather than the incorporation of online payment and booking.

Chapter 10 continues this theme. Ekasdornkorn, Corbitt and Phalavonk, explore an alternative option for online payments on the Internet in the Thai context. The lack of trust about Internet security and the nature of Thai shoppers' habits have been two major factors in the low up take in online shopping in Thai web sites. They propose a micropayment method as an alternative payment system as that method can be used on the Internet with high security and, most importantly, in keeping anonymity of customers who want to keep their identity anonymous.

The fourth section in this book investigates the factors that influence the acceptance of e-learning in Thai universities. The adoption of e-learning in Thailand is still in a very early stage. This study (Chapter 11) is a very useful study in gaining an understanding of the factors that influence the slow uptake of e-learning in Thai universities. Tetiwat and Huff found that Thai culture and values have significant influences on the adoption of e-learning. A clear guidance from the top executive of the universities and Ministry of University Affairs are important, as Thai universities require clear direction and incentives from the government. The learning style of Thai university students also contributes to the slow up take of e-learning as Thai students have less of a sense of participation as an attitude towards learning. Face-to-face interaction between academics is the preferred method of learning and teaching rather than virtual interaction.

In the last section of the book, the final chapter (Chapter 12) investigates the use and design of Chinese e-commerce. Hsu suggests that e-commerce web sites that want to tap into Chinese lucrative market must be able to handle Chinese languages, as Mandarin is the official language for People Republic of China and Cantonese in Hong Kong. The author also explores the differences of western (America) and eastern (China) cultures in the area of collectivism, religion, colours, symbols and how these elements influence the design of e-commerce web sites.

This book is the first to collaborate and collect high standard scholarly work in the area of e-commerce and the influence of indigenous cultures and values. The book challenges the acceptance and interpretation of e-commerce in different societies. To be able to conduct more effective and efficient business and trade, businesses must utilise the Internet more; businesses are required to understand their trading partners, stakeholders and customers attitudes toward e-commerce and understanding their culture and values. The book does not aim to answer every question about culture and e-commerce but poses more questions for further research in this area.

Theerasak Thanasankit
Monash University
September 2002

Acknowledgments

Firstly, I have to thank all the authors who participated in this book. Without their efforts in writing their chapters, this book would never have been published. I would also like to thank Professor Brian Corbitt at Deakin University, Australia as my mentor, and for encouraging me to edit this book and explore the role of indigenous culture and its influence in information technology and systems.

Secondly, my special thanks also goes to the publishing team at Idea Group, especially Michele Rossi for her help and support throughout the whole process

Thirdly, I also have to extend my deepest gratitude for the reviewers for this book. The reviewers were very generous in providing their time in reviewing all of the chapters and provided the authors with a wonderful and constructive feedback for improving their chapters. However, the five reviewers would like to remain anonymous.

I have to thank my family (mum, dad, all of my brothers and sisters-in-law, my grandparents and my nieces and nephews) for their love and encouragement.

Theerasak Thanasankit, PhD
School of Information Management and Systems
Faculty of Information Technology
Monash University
Australia

SECTION I:

E-COMMERCE POLICY AND INDIGENOUS CULTURE AND VALUES

Chapter I

Globalization, Culture and E-Business

Brian J. Corbitt
Deakin University, Australia

ABSTRACT

This chapter argues that globalisation, culture and e-business exist in interesting ways that challenge accepted norms of interpretation about business practice in the new century. There appears to be a paradox of parallel business practice of defacto standards versus a culture of micro management. Discourse has been constructed that accepts the parallel existence and the co-existence of two layers operating within the business world. The international layer of standards, albeit defacto, co-existing with a layer of cultural difference supported by Guanxi *and cultural values and cultural practice. This chapter argues that the one doesn't challenge the other. Rather, the one compliments the other. They co-exist and create economies of scale, deliver efficiency, deliver cost effectiveness, deliver productivity savings, solve currency trade problems, solve logistics problems, solve tracking problems, and deal with the imperfections in the market place. The two levels, it is argued, encourage collaboration and foster necessary co-operation along the supply chain. The end result is a world of e-business that benefits international business.*

INTRODUCTION

This chapter is concerned with the way globalization, culture and e-business are interacting in the world economic environment to produce globalized trade and expansion of e-business not only across nations, but between organizations and across organizations internationally. This chapter is also concerned with the nature of globalization and gaining an understanding of what globalization means in various cultures. It will produce an understanding of why globalization is important in understanding e-business, how it impacts on e-business and how it has supported and promoted the changing nature of trade across the world.

This chapter will also address why understanding culture is important in the e-business realm. Electronic business cannot be isolated from the cultures in that it works. While there is a tendency towards a world view, or globalized view, of the nature of e-business, the managerial factors and human interaction within e-business are imbued with cultural practices that challenge any sense of uniformity or heterogeneity. We will also be concerned with how e-business development is related to the expansion of globalization thinking and of the way that we are changing our worldview as a whole.

The final section of this chapter will address the challenge of e-business integration and mix created by cultural differences. Only when we address cultural issues and globalization will we fully understand the significance of e-business. The integral nature of e-business has emerged as the world has embraced e-business methodologies and the importance of e-business technology as a means to increase efficiency within an organization and to understand how to trade better and smarter between nations.

In a 1999 paper, Corbitt emphasized that Singapore, Hong Kong and many other parts of Southeast Asia, clearly see the importance of e-business as they begin the trading relationships necessary to move from developing countries to industrialised and developed nations. Singapore has a long history of being an entrepot, positioned between old colonial powers and newly emerging tigers of Asia. As Singapore has become a developed country, it now wants to utilize the new methodologies of e-business to foster and strengthen its position as a hub for trade, not only in the traditional entrepot sense, but also as a focus for new trade and new business (Corbitt and Thanasankit, 2002b).

WHY GLOBALIZATION?

Globalization is important because it is one of the fundamental drivers of international trade in the 21st century (Castells, 2001). As new technologies associated with transport have emerged with larger ships, more efficient airplanes, more services to shift product from one place of the world to another, a clearer understanding of comparative advantage has developed where agricultural surpluses are converted into consumer goods imported into a country. Labor is seen as a valuable commodity that can be used to induce manufacturers of traditional developed-country goods like luxury cars, chemicals, or clothing and textiles. There is a sense of inducement to use that human capital to make those industries attractive in developing countries. The establishment of the Honda factory and the Mercedes-Benz factory in Thailand is as much to do with the use of the human capital in those countries to make those cars more efficient and more cost-effective. The fundamental nature of globalization, one of those a German company, and one of those a Japanese company is to see the benefits for their production process in establishing themselves in an alternative environment. It is part of the nature of globalization. Japanese can invest in Thailand. The Thais can invest in other countries. We see across the world cross-investment of production and cross-investment of capital gained from agricultural surpluses in one country, invested in other sorts of industries in another country.

In addition, globalization has awakened the world to the importance of not only information management, but also knowledge management. New knowledge is being created constantly, with increased and effective communication systems in the globalized world. New knowledge passes very quickly from one phase to another, from one nation to another and from one organisation to another. There is an increasing trend to see what can be produced as an agricultural surplus in one country can be traded very effectively and quickly with another. Communications to establish that trade can be very effectively done through large integrated organizations like the World Trade Organization or the United Nations.. In addition, there is a sense that countries realize that they cannot be producers of all goods, but concentrate on what they do best and build up the resources to do those things they need to do to change and to adapt.

On the island of Penang in Malaysia, there is the development of a "small Silicon Valley" using imported knowledge through large U.S. and European countries establishing IT facilities and manufacturing plants on Penang supported by local human capital. This represents the fostering of other forms of globalized trade, that the products that are accepted as standards across the world can now be produced in any part of the world as a means of developing and pushing forward the nature of trade.

The nature of the new Republic of Ireland in the decade of the 1990s was associated with the use of Euro money to utilize the human capital and skill set of Ireland, so Ireland could engage in the use of its own human capital and produce surpluses. In this case, they were manufactured surpluses, made to trade with the world in its unique skill set and products, utilizing new investment emerging out of a new economy.

In a sense, much of this has been driven by politics. The late 20th century saw the strong emergence of integrated collaboration, politically. We now have trade blocks, the strongest being the European Union, supplemented by in other places, for example, in Southeast Asia, the Asian Trade Organisation or the Free Trade Agreement that exists between certain countries, for example, Singapore and Malaysia, or the free trade agreement between Australia and New Zealand. Each of these is driven by political agendas that see globalization as beneficial to a country, and that see politics as the framework - that supports private development of globalized trade. In many instances, as in Malaysia and Thailand, the Government plays a very proactive role in promoting and developing trade in the globalized world (Corbitt, 1999; Corbitt and Thanasankit, 2002b; Thanasankit and Corbitt, 1999; Thanasankit and Corbitt, 2002). It is a political imperative. It provides the strength that those nations see as the means to move from countries dependent upon agricultural surpluses to countries who can start to produce surpluses from manufactured goods or service industries.

Governments see trade as a way of strengthening their position in the global context. They see this as a way of strengthening the nature of the country in that they operate. They see this as a way of establishing their government and their nation as a power in the globalized economy (Corbitt and Thanasankit, 2002b).

Paradoxically, the politics of trade have emerged in another format. While governments see e-business and globalized trade as a means of political and economic development, growth and expansion, governments also want to protect native industry, natural resources within countries, and local manufacturers from the impact of free trade agreements. The impact of the World Trade Organization meetings about trying to increase the amount of free trade across the world has had limited success, purely because there are political imperatives protecting local initiatives. This has as much to do with politics as it has with the politics of one nation versus another. Driving all of this is a sense that the adoption of information technology methodologies and e-business will strengthen those countries that are early adopters. That is, for political gain. It is about what is being played out: who is the dominant trader, who is the dominant entrepot, who is the dominant surplus producer and therefore, who is the dominant influence in a particular sub-economic region of the globalized world.

The Internet is the global tool for the development of trade and e-business. The Web is the tool that enables the methodologies of e-business, whether it is business-to-business relationships with the management of supply chains or logistics management to enable efficiencies to be focused in a particular node, so that economical and political strength can be gained from the trading process. It is through the stimuli of government that tools of e-business and the use of the Web come together to create a global environment in that the centers of attention are *political* nodes.

In 1960s Europe, the concept of growth poles was used as a means of strengthening the trading position of various cities in Europe. The growth poles of Paris, London, Frankfurt, Rotterdam, Amsterdam, and Copenhagen were centered on a political objective that by strengthening the nature and infrastructure of the city, that you could gain more and more strength in the bargaining process associated with trade. In the 21st century, e-business has replaced the growth poles of the cities with the notion of hubs at the national level. Globalization is no longer necessarily about cities alone; it is about nations and the way that they trade. It is enforced by a global imperative. It is enforced by the need to be aware of the impact of one nation's economic woes or strengths as they influence other nations' woes and strengths.

The dominant political process of the end of the 20th century was one of disintegration. Formerly large accumulations of nations had begun to disintegrate, for example, the USSR, Yugoslavia. What is emerging is strong nationalism that is driving the strength of importance of e-business in its relationship with trade.

With increasing use of logistics, better transport systems, the immediacy of the Internet as a communication tool, the use of globalized information systems such as global positioning technology, or the use of management technologies e-business is becoming integral in world trade. The implementation of knowledge management, customer relationship management and the implementation of integrated software systems such as ERP systems, suggests that integration of the economic tools with e-business technology will strengthen a nation as a hub. These ideas are being fostered politically and invariably they have been driven by information technology. Those countries that want to develop faster, and quickly gain strength induce trade into and out of countries that are adopting e-business technologies and fostering e-business technology through specific policy. This is being done simply to gain a trade advantage that may come as a result of adopting e-business. But nations alone cannot control this.

The meltdown in the Asian economies in 1997/98, continuing into 1999 and 2000, had as much to do with the impact of global factors as it did with internal factors within each of the affected countries. The technology crash of 2000 and the demise of the 'dot.coms' in the United States were as much as about global effects as they were about inefficient company organisation and companies that were hollow in terms of production of any value.

Global trends follow the world. No one factor determines what is happening in Japan as opposed to what is happening in the U.K., the U.S., Australia, New Zealand, Thailand or Tanzania. What happens in one part of the world affects and impacts other parts of the world because of interrelationships of trade. Countries at war still trade. Countries in political conflict still trade. A change of political system does not change the nature of trade. It may increase the propensity to trade more, but the reality is that countries are seeking stability and one of the ways that they can maintain that stability is to establish information technologies that foster trade. This trade encourages interaction in terms of commodity exchange and advances exchange beyond the impact of politics.

In 2002, there has been an increasing trend to dismiss IT workers. There has been an increase in this trend in the collapse in companies such as Enron and world 'dot.coms' in the United States. Very large companies have disintegrated. Part of that disintegration has come about because of a lack of understanding that the world does not evolve around large companies as it did in the latter part of the 20th century. In Australia, the collapse and demise of HIH Insurance and OneTel Communications Company in 2001, were indicative of the same problem of seeing themselves in an isolated environment devoid of the necessity to see e-business as a focal - strategy that can underpin the strength of a particular company. That strength comes about because in reality, the politics imbued within organizations and the politics affecting the way economic structures run, are determined invariably by humans. E-business technologies can remove or lessen the effects of that human interaction.

The new world of globalization and trade has in the sense, adopted the de facto leadership of the World Wide Web. Globalization and telecommunications, software and the World Wide Web are all now an integrated part of the nature of business. It is no longer the cost associated with buying technology. Technology or information technology is now an investment, an asset that companies can value, that audit, and that use to strengthen their position both within the country in that they work or in that they operate internationally. Those companies that are able to trade internationally through the use of technology, through instantaneous communication via the Internet or mobile devices, are able to have comparative advantage that strengthens their position relative to other countries in the trading process. Efficiencies gained from e-business are not necessarily those of cost reduction, but essentially are gained from assets in terms of value added, in terms of new knowledge supporting the strategic alignment and direction of intra-national companies, international companies and nations themselves. That leads to the second challenge: knowing that the world is operating in a global context, knowing that globalization is a fundamental part of what is going on in the world. How does the world deal with the impact of culture?

WHY CULTURE?

Culture is a national differentiator of the world. It challenges globalization. The work of Hofstede (1984, 1991), Trompenaars (1993), Thanasankit (2002), Intranond et al. (2002) and others would clearly demonstrate that what is accepted practice in one culture is anathema to practices in other cultures. In a sense, globalization and culture could be seen as opposites. Globalization seeks to see how nations and countries are interrelated. Culture is a means of describing how different they are from each other. How does the notion of a national culture sit within the newly globalized world established from the 1990s to the present time? In a sense, it represents the world of business. It presents the world of politics with a fundamental paradox.

Culture differentiates practices. Some countries are classified as being individualistic. Others are social or collective. In some nations, family collectivism and groups play an important role; in others they play less of a role. In the world of business, the nature of the individual and the practice of individualism are being challenged, whether it is an individualistic country or a collective country. The world has moved to the practice of forming teams. Teams are important. Virtual teams, face-to-face teams and hybrid teams are being formed internationally, globally, across nations, intra-nationally and intra-organizationally to achieve software implementation, software development or business process re-engineering, but the paradox remains.

Culture differentiates the way information is given meaning. Information in one country can be defined and redefined as it is socially constructed. Policy is socially constructed; therefore, the policy that frames IT policies across the world has been analyzsed. They too can be differentiated (Corbitt and Thanasankit, 2002). Web sites for e-businesses reflect their cultural differences (Corbitt and Thanasankit, 2002a; Kang and Corbitt, 2002; Kang and Corbitt, 2002). So how do we deal with the paradox? How does the world of e-business work when there is cultural differentiation, where there is a cultural challenge to the notion that business practices internationally are being seen as been more and more homogeneous?

The answer lies in a belief that the world now socially and culturally is operating at two distinct levels. There is the level of the nation in that cultural practices and values accepted nationally are being maintained. They framed what management does. They frame the way that businesses transact. They frame the way businesses negotiate. They frame the way that e-business is adopted and managed. However, at another level, there is an acceptance that the world itself is good for the nation. Globalization is that other layer. It represents another set of values, albeit uniform, that they accept and recontextualise within each nation to support existing national values and business practice.

Each nation/business has to accept that the logistics of moving people from one point to another, whether it is Singapore Airlines, Thai International, MAS, PIA, United Airlines, Japan Airlines, Qantas, Air New Zealand, British Airways, Lufthansa or SAS, all operate in essentially the same way. They do the same business. The micro-management processes, however, will be different. The way that they perform operations within the cabin, the food, the style of seating, the configuration of the aeroplane, at the micro level are all different but the business processes of an airline internationally are the same. Across the globalized world there is a globalized culture that is simply an acceptance of a form of standard process, whether it is an ERP system or a transport system or an e-business methodology or customer relationship methodology, and that then is managed at the micro level by differences created by national cultures. In this sense then, there are two layers of process happening: the layer of globalization process and the layer of cultural process. The two sit and work simultaneously; they drive and work off each other.

The adaptation of airline logistics transportation of goods across the world is impacted on at the national level by national values and culture. But internationally, freight is moved around the world efficiently. Pallets, bins, barcoding systems have almost become standard, but they are influenced at micro level by cultural practice. These do not impede the globalization process that is occurring. The world has moved to a position where the nature of trade as occurring according to two levels of standard. This standard is accepted globally and nationally. Interestingly, these international or global standards are invariably underpinned with e-business and IT, e-business technologies and information technology.

Practices at the national level are invariably underpinned by cultural values, cultural practice and accepted modes of behavior that are politically driven; socially constructed and culturally embedded into the way that nation operates (Shanks et al., 2000; Hanisch et al., 2001). E-business is almost a cultural icon. The methodologies and techniques of logistics management are being driven by automated agents, intelligent agents and smart agents that promote efficiency and effectiveness across a logistics management system or an e-business trading relationship. The essential components of e-business frame standards that have been adopted. These are *de facto* standards. Standards occur by *de facto* acceptance and as these standards become more defined, the relationship becomes more legitimized. The nature of that upper layer of globalized trade, globalized logistics and globalized e-business will continue to be sustained and even supported while there is differentiation at the national level as goods and services are logistically moved from one particular country to another. In essence, they remain simultaneous and the two operate together. It is an interesting challenge and paradox but one that has just emerged not by force, design or plan, but as the world has accepted the nature of globalization and at the same time has fought to maintain nationalism and nationalistic strength. While the world has nationally disintegrated, as large accumulations of countries have broken up into smaller or ethnically-based nations, the sense of globalization still exists.

On September 11th, 2001, the tragedy of the World Trade Center bombing by two airplanes was not in a sense, created by cultural difference, it was a political act. At the same time, its impact was global because of that existing layer across the whole world. The fact that it was nationalistically an attack on the United States affected that country deeply. But in one sense, the way people have reacted to it, the way that they have travelled, has been differential at various country levels, but the nature of globalization, the impact of e-business and the uptake of e-business has not been affected because the world has seen it amongst fear, national identity and national strength. National problems are seen at another level.

GLOBALIZED E-BUSINESS

Considering the paradox that exists and the fact that we have globalization and national culture existing parallel with each other and supporting each other and while there might be tensions between the practices of national culture and the demands of globalization, globalized e-business is a reality. It is flourishing and is working strongly in the development of many countries around the world. In this section of the chapter, we will deal with some examples of the way that globalized e-business is working and relate the structures, albeit a sample of them, to the paradox of globalization and culture.

International Exchanges

Across the world organizations that naturally trade with each other have seen the benefit of operating through e-business exchanges. These can be auction exchanges. They can be trading exchanges. They can be collaborative exchanges. They can be collectives of organisations doing collective buying and selling as a result of trying to improve efficiencies through the natural operation of the market. These international exchanges or market places are there to foster each international or globalization player in the world of business. They become a neutral territory in terms of dealing with national culture. They are imbued with a sense of globalization and the achievements of the benefits of globalized business practices. They are not concerned with being impacted upon or working with nationalistic cultures and practices.

One example is Lignum.com (www.Lignum.com). This further exchange was established to deal with the national problems associated with the ways timber is bought and sold. At that micro-management level of national influence, individual national cultures determine that timber can be bought by weight, length, width, timber type, quality of timber, or by the nature of the timber — whether it is a hardwood or softwood. This makes international exchanges very difficult and likewise, makes the trading relationship very difficult also. What e-business has offered is a solution based in neutral territory, where the goods that can be purchased in one country can be purchased in another by interchanging the criteria in that the timber is actually sold. Lignum is an independent globalized marketplace or exchange. It operates above the layer of national culture. It operates in a way that addresses the paradox or the apparent conflict between national culture and globalized trends. It illustrates quite clearly that the two can coexist in a business marketplace.

Logistics Management and Tracking

Dell Computers, Amazon.com, and many other companies trade internationally. Dell computers, CISCO systems, and Microsoft products are found in every country of the world. Microsoft Word can be used in Japanese, Chinese, Thai, Swahili, English, German or French.. At one level it reflects national culture. Being able to write Thai Script, Japanese Kanji, or Chinese Hanzi reflects the culture in that the technology is being used, but at the other level, there is a sense of globalization. It is still Microsoft Word and whether a person is using the Japanese or the German version, a Japanese or a German keyboard, there exists a standardized practice. The keyboard is standardized, Word software is standardized and the practice of Word is standardized.

There is at the global level a view that there is equity, equilibrium and a sense of saneness at the national level. This can be reinterpreted, recontextualised and reused in ways that fit the national culture. The apparent paradox is resolved by separating the process that is global and uniform from the interpretation and use that is nationalistic and imbued with culture and cultural practice. Logistics management across the world deals with the same problem. Transporting goods by UPS or FedEx is the same process whether it is from the United States to Africa or Chile or from Chile to Africa. While the languages differ, while the cultural practices of loading and storing and managing the logistics might be different, the fact is that process of logistics management across international boundaries is determined by a set of standards that is not imbued with politics, but that is accepted internationally and globally. The paradox again is challenged, the paradox of co-existence remains at one level. The way materials are combined together or packaged represents a cultural influence. On the other hand, the barcodes that are used to transport and track the goods from one country to another country is an international standard that everyone can read and understand. The barcode printout in Japan will be in

Japanese language, in the United States it will be in English. The uniformity at the global level parallels the cultural interpretation that differentiates one nation from another.

The Management of Trading Nodes

Across the world, trade has to pass through nodes. The world airline systems have established a modern set of nodes usually associated with key airports across the world: Heathrow Airport in the United Kingdom, Charles de Gaulle Airport in Paris, Schipol Airport in Amsterdam, Copenhagen Airport in Denmark, just to name a few nodes established in the modern world of airline systems. Each of those nodes is imbued with nationalistic practices. The way the airport operates in Bangkok is different than the way the Heathrow airport operates, but at the same time, there are standards that cut across national cultures. Standard processing of passports, customs and immigration are accepted processes for the traveller or for the person managing trade. The precise differentiation of the way that customs and immigration work varies from one country to another. The paradox is again challenged. The two processes of global practice and cultural difference coexist.

These new transport nodes developed in the new aeroplane era of the 20th century support and invariably parallel the original trading routes that were established in the 17th, 18th, and 19th centuries. Ports such as Singapore, Hong Kong, London and Amsterdam remain focal points for shipping trade; they remain focal points for land transportation such as rail and bus also. The nodes themselves have become larger and stronger and more economically viable. They have become entities in their own right, but they represent two things. They represent the international nodes of passing from one place to another. If one travels from Australia to the United Kingdom, every traveller or item that is exchanged must pass between either Singapore or Bangkok on their way to London. Any ship that leaves Australia with goods and services for the United Kingdom will travel a similar route and will know that the ports have always existed in the trading routes of the world, whether it is Cape Town, New York, or Rio de Janeiro. The ports still remain, and the nodes have sprung from them. E-business creates a sense that these nodes are just as important for each other in the trade relationships of the world; that tends to enable coexistence with the cultural differences naturally apparent at each port or airport.

Economics of Globalized E-Business

The world has accepted the coexistence of the cultural difference and globalized standardization across the world of e-business as the result of several factors. The first of these is the technology itself. E-business has enabled the world to gain efficiency, cost effectiveness, increased profitability and perhaps increased productivity as a result of choosing standardized forms of IT process or IT-driven processes that enable companies to interact between companies using standard processes (Castells, 2001). These processes are built into computer systems and software. They do not challenge business practice in the normal sense. They offer a standard means of communicating between companies, divisions within a company or between nations. They enable a standardized form of communication irrespective of language.

The world forms of e-business technologies and more recently integrated technologies such as enterprise resource planning (ERP) systems or customer relations management systems, enable people to be able to talk from country to country and culture to culture using a standardized set of software or hardware. This key issue has enabled the world of e-business to develop and strengthen and integrate into the process of business across the world. As a result, companies are able to gain economies of scale. Large internationalized multinational companies are able to trade and communicate within that one company gaining benefits from their size. Being able to trade in bulk enables economies of scale to be gained, enables communications to be more efficient and more effective. New mobile technologies such as standardized communication or email systems enable forms of communication. Communication becomes simpler because it is done in one way across one system, again gaining economies of scale. This also creates efficiency in communicating with translators from one nationality to another, from one national language to another national language. It also increases the speed of communication. One can communicate within a 24 x 7 framework that allows communications within business to enable constant operations, gaining not only economies of scale through time, but also efficiency. Business processes do not have to stop because the factory finishes or closes at 5 o'clock. The business can still continue. Some would argue that this increases productivity.

E-business technologies enable some mechanical business processes to be taken over entirely by machines. This has happened in the banking industry by the use of mobile banking across the world. This supposedly increases the productivity of repeated processes. Robots were introduced into the motorcar industry in the 1980s and earlier because of their efficiencies and ability to increase productivity in the assembly line. That has not changed with the introduction of e-business processes. They have become the robots of business transaction processing across the world.

E-business and standardized IT platforms enable the immediacy of currency transaction. The translation of goods and services traded from Australian dollars to Euro or from Euro to U.S. dollars or U.S. dollars to Japanese yen or Japanese yen to Hong Kong dollars, or Chinese renminbi can all be instantly translated on a screen. They have become instantaneous relationships. The exchange relationship between a company and a banking partner becomes immediate. Cash flows can be traced electronically. Audits and audit trails on transactions and purchases and orders can be done automatically through databases established under international standards established and utilized on the web. E-business provides a globalized world with a set of business and financial practices that are standardized and that can impact on the economics of a company. To some extent this may be used for multiple transactions, as in banking, to reduce cost per transaction. On the other hand, it can also increase the valued assets of an organisation.

One of the emerging trends in the world of IT is not to see IT as a cost, but IT as an asset in the same way that we value human capital now as an asset. The processes imbedded in software can in themselves be seen as an asset if they produce the economies of scale and efficiencies and productivity gains that are many claimed to have. Where the planning associated with the implementation of that software fails, many of the advantages that might be gained from the use of e-business standardized practices are lost. They are lost in the political squabbling that can invariably occur about failed software implementation, resulting from poor planning and strategy alignment as a result of political interference either at the organizational, regional, state or national level in terms of what the software is, was, or might be intended to do.. As a result of that, the world of e-business looks beyond just dealing with and solving one practice after another. In the late 1990s and into the 21st century, the world of e-business and globalization has moved one step further away from the disaggregation of one process versus another into a world of integration. It is to that we now move.

INTEGRATION AND THE CHALLENGES OF CULTURE

Throughout this chapter, the paradox of accessing globalization and the impact of culture has been addressed. Culture itself is a challenge. The world of e-business is global. The adoption of e-business technologies and e-business processes must meet the challenge of culture. One of the solutions to that in the 1990s was the development of a world almost obsessed with 'vanilla' solutions. There was a sense that every IT solution has some meaning in terms of 'one size fits all.' It became apparent by the end of 1990's and early into the 21st century that this no longer applied. Enterprise Resource Planning (ERP) systems that were originally very structured and rigid became very flexible. There was a sense that software written for e-business, whether it was an ERP solution or a customer relationship management solution, was developed in such a way that it could be fit into the various practices of an organization or fit into a culture in such a way that we were no longer seeking vanilla solutions, but seeking differentiated solutions. We were no longer accepting that 'one size fits all,' but seeking a variety of sizes applicable for small to medium enterprises (SMEs) versus medium enterprises versus large enterprises and seeing that solutions could, and probably needed to, be different in each e-business scenario. The market no longer was seen as perfect. The role of government intervention was again accepted. The fact that markets themselves could be manipulated by government practice was again considered acceptable where the outcome was for the good of the nation or the politics associated with the nation.

E-business is a technical solution, but culture can challenge and differentiate that. Does it break it down? Probably not. The worldwide evidence is that while there is an apparent paradox and existing parallel systems, the world can deal with the uniqueness of globalization in its homogeneity and at the same time, deal with the differential effects of culture of micromanagement levels and with microprocesses and the way that this disaggregates the processes apparent in e-business. How does the world cope with these two apparent processes? In the immediacy of the modern world, and instantaneous communication 24 x 7 access to 95 percent of the world has created an environment in which space shrinks or appears to shrink. Time and distance also shrink in terms of their impact. This has created a situation where people are able to accept much more complex solutions in the world of business. No longer is business seen as the simplistic relationship between a business organization and an existing culture. No longer is business seen as a geographical location. The existence of an electronic world, a virtual world, enables business to operate at different times at different speeds in different scenarios. Business is meeting the challenge of culture and accepting that fundamental business practice is essentially the same, no matter where the location.

How does e-business deal with the challenge that culture creates for globalization? In one instance, it is worth noting the impact. For most of the 19th century and certainly all of the 20th century, the role of relationships in business in Asia has been fundamental. The Chinese use the word *guanxi* to give a name to the nature of personal relationships, such as the person you have lunch with, the person you play golf with, the person you want to be your business partner. The meeting of one person with another, doing a favor for one person to another, all create *guanxi.* For many years throughout the 20th century and prior to that, *guanxi* was the fundamental way one did business with Asian organizations and countries (Corbitt and Thanasankit, 2001). Who you knew was more important than what you knew. Who you knew was more important than a business process, because it was based on trust and reliability.

At an organizational level, it is interesting to note that Honda uses the same suppliers year in and year out because of the established trust relationship, the *guanxi*, because of the quality issues associated with containing the *guanxi*. Another large automobile manufacturer, GMH puts to tender all of its suppliers on a regular basis looking for cost savings while maintaining quality. In the Asian context as with Honda, the idea is that a business builds the relationship and the trust, and that is how the quality process is maintained. If it costs more money, it is worth it for what a business can gain out of it. These business practices, whether it is statistics management, eCRM or e-business or the use of EDI is forever and will be challenged by *guanxi*. In fact the relationships that form at each end of each of those business processes is framed in, supported by, and concreted together, by *guanxi*. However, the processes that happen in between are something that is built on e-business technology. It is something built in the new world of the knowledge economy; it is accepted by the *guanxi* and coexists with the *guanxi*. While that might appear a paradox, it is fundamental to the way that the world has developed. It is fundamental to the new globalized economy and to an understanding of why e-business in its broadest sense has probably been very successful.

In conclusion, the paradox of parallel business practice of *de facto* standards versus culture of micromanagement represents a challenge that really does not need to be dealt with. Discourse has been constructed that accepts the parallel existence and the co-existence of two layers operating within the business world: the international layer of standards, albeit *de facto*, coexisting with a layer of cultural difference supported by *guanxi* and cultural values and cultural practice. The one doesn't challenge the other. Rather, one compliments the other. They coexist and create economies of scale; deliver efficiency cost effectiveness and productivity savings; solve currency trade problems, logistics problems, tracking problems; and deal with the imperfections in the marketplace. They encourage collaboration. They foster the necessary co-operation along the supply chain that makes the world of e-business beneficial to international business.

REFERENCES

Castells, M. (2001). *The Internet Galaxy: Reflections on the Internet, Business and Society*, UK: Oxford University Press.

Corbitt, B.J. (1999). Social construction of an IT policy – Singapore and Thailand. *Prometheus*, September, 17 (3), 309-322.

Corbitt, B. & Thanasankit, T. (2001). The challenge of trust and guanxi in Asian e-commerce, pp. 141-158. In Singh, M. & Teo, T. (Eds.) *e-Commerce Diffusion: Strategies and Challenges*, Heidelberg Press, Australia.

Corbitt, B. & Thanasankit, T. (2002a). A model for culturally informed web interfaces. In Haynes, J. (Ed.), *Internet Management Science: A Global Perspective*, Idea Group Publishing, Hershey, PA.

Corbitt, B. & Thanasankit, T. (2002b). Acceptance and leadership - Hegemonies of e- commerce policy perspectives. *Prometheus,* 20 (10), 39 –57.

Hanisch, J., Thanasankit, T., & Corbitt, B. J. (2001). Exploring the cultural and social impacts on the requirements engineering processes- highlighting some problems challenging virtual team relationships with clients. *Journal of Systems and Technology*, 5(2), 1-20.

Hofstede, G. (1984). *Culture 's Consequences* (abridged edition). Sage, Newbury Park, CA.

Hofstede, G. (1991). *Cultures and Organizations*. McGraw-Hill, UK.

Intranond, S., Corbitt, B., Thanasankit, T & Peszynski, K. (2002). Cultural differences, information and code systems, *Pacific Asia Conference on Information Systems, PACIS*, Tokyo.

Kyeong-Soon, K. & Corbitt, B. (2001). Effectiveness of graphical components in web site e-commerce application-a cultural perspective. *BITWORLD Conference*, Egypt.

Kyeongha-Soon, K. & Corbitt, B. (2002). Effectiveness of graphical components in web site e-commerce: Application-A cultural perspective. *The Electronic Journal on Information Systems in Developing Countries.* Vol. 7, EJISDC - ISSN 1681-48. Retrieved on from the World Wide Web: http://www.ejisdc.org

Shanks, G., Corbitt, B.J., Hu, B., Seddon, P., Parr, A. & Thanasankit, T. (2000). Differences in critical success factors in ERP systems implementation in Australia and China: a cultural analysis. *European Conference in Information Systems*, Austria, June, 537-544.

Thanasankit, T. (2002). Requirements engineering – exploring the influence of power and Thai values. *European Journal of Information Systems*, *11*, 128-141.

Thanasankit, T. & Corbitt, B. (1999). Cultural context and its impact on requirements elicitation in Thailand. *Electronic Journal on Information Systems in Developing Countries*, 1(1), 15-32.

Thanasankit, T. & Corbitt, B.J. (2002). Understand Thai culture and its impact on requirements engineering process management during information systems development. *Asian Academy of Management Journal,* 7(1), 103-126.

Trompenaars, F. (1993). *Riding the Waves of Culture*, Nicholas Brealey Publishing, London, UK.

Chapter II

The Adoption of Information Technology: A Foundation of E-Commerce Development in Thai Culture

O. Chieochan, D. Lindley, and T. Dunn
Charles Sturt University, Australia

ABSTRACT

E-Commerce can be developed after information technology is adopted. Before understanding the phenomenon of e-commerce in Thai culture, this chapter aims to discuss the adoption of information technology in that culture. Thai agricultural cooperative societies are selected as a case study to describe the understanding of the factors governing the adoption of information. Our work was done at a time when new government policies were introduced to improve Thai trading by introducing e-commerce.

This chapter argues that the first step in encouraging and managing information technology and e-commerce usage is to develop an understanding of the factors that influence its usage.

A multidisciplinary approach is used to examine factors affecting the use of information technology in Thai agricultural cooperatives. Empirical evidence defines universal factors which govern the adoption of information technology in Thailand such as the decision-making characteristics which distinguish adopters from non-adopters. In Thailand, business size is also important and larger organizations are more intensive users of information technology.

INTRODUCTION

Agriculture is important to the Thai economy, contributing about 17 percent to the Thai GNP. It accounts for about 34 percent of all exports (Mahidol University, 1998). Important activities include crop cultivation, rearing of livestock, fishery, and forestry. In 1991, about 62 percent of the Thai population, approximately 36 million people, was involved in agriculture (Office of Agriculture Economics, Ministry of Thai Agriculture and Cooperatives, 1992, p. 29).

Thai agricultural cooperatives play an important role and a study of them provides a window into Thai agriculture. For some Thai farmers, co-operatives provide access to information from the outside world; for others, they provide information about Thai agriculture. Particular cooperatives provide marketing information on agricultural produce that should improve the income of Thailand's farmers. In addition, Thai agricultural co-operatives can use e-commerce to improve their trading. A report in *The Nation* newspaper in 1998 (1998a) supported this view, saying that market information such as product prices, could assist farm planning and protect farmers from merchants' unfair trading practices. Merchants could also use such information to improve business planning and to evaluate investments.

It is further suggested that the Thai government could use information technology to better support the Thai farming community; that information technology could be used by agricultural cooperatives as a tool for communication with farmers; and that the government could be better informed of farmers' needs, and so provide better and more useful services. In a similar vein, Sirimance (1998) suggests that information technology could reduce the communication gap between rural communities and the cities [*The Nation* newspaper (1998b)].

Despite the apparent advantages, Thai agriculture, including agricultural cooperatives, have been slow to introduce and exploit e-commerce; this is basis of our research project as described in Chiecochan and Lindley (1999), Chieochan, Lindley and Dunn (2000a, b).

In these papers, diffusion and adoption theory was used to classify Thai agricultural cooperatives according to if and when they adopted e-commerce. The main conclusion is that Thai agricultural cooperatives are slow in adopting e-commerce. Chieochan, Lindley and Dunn (2000) show that only 60 percent of Thai agricultural cooperatives use information technology and only 5 percent access the Internet.

The Internet in Thailand is used mainly as a communication tool and websites for publishing organizational information, but is rarely used to conduct commercial transactions (King Mongkut's Institute of Technology, Thonburi, 2001). Therefore, understanding factors affecting the use of information technology in Thai agricultural cooperatives is the fundamental to understand the use of e-commerce in Thai agricultural cooperatives and Thai culture.

Al-Qirim and Corbitt (2001) support that factors inhibiting and encouraging e-commerce adoption are similar to factors inhibiting and encouraging information technology adoption in Thai agricultural cooperatives.

Five keys factors affecting the use of information technology in Thai agricultural cooperatives need to be examined:

- Thai agricultural cooperatives
- Information Technology and e-commerce
- National factors affecting the use of information technology and e-commerce in Thai agricultural cooperatives
- Organizational factors affecting the use of information technology and e-commerce in Thai agricultural cooperatives
- Implications to Thai government and Thai agricultural cooperatives

THAI AGRICULTURAL COOPERATIVES

Agricultural cooperatives are a type of cooperative society. They are commonly understood to be a business owned and controlled by the members who form them to provide good services to their own, usually at a lower price.

Thai agricultural cooperatives are registered with the Thai government and owned by Thai farmers. There presently 3,344 agricultural cooperatives in Thailand with a total membership of 4,659,070 farmers (Cooperatives Promotion Department, 1999, p. 1). A board of directors, elected by members, administers each cooperative. The board of directors appoints a manager and employees.

According to the Cooperatives Promotion Department of the Thai Ministry of Agriculture and Cooperatives (1993), Thai agricultural cooperatives provide these four main services for their members:

1. Providing credit for the purchase of agricultural supplies and farm machinery;
2. Supplying and selling agricultural necessities and consumer goods;
3. Marketing agricultural produce through local markets, provincial and national federations, and abroad; and
4. Providing agricultural extension services.

INFORMATION TECHNOLOGY AND E-COMMERCE

Woodall (1997) has commented that the term *information technology* can cause confusion since there is no generally agreed definition. Some include not only computing and telecommunication, but also microelectronic and digital electronic equipment that can manage information such as receiving, storing, analyzing and communicating. However, others include people and procedures. Cusumano (1991) has noted that information technology was used to denote people, procedure and equipment, based on microelectronic, computing and telecommunications, enabling people to record, store, retrieve and transmit information. This technology is used to manage many types of information, namely voice, pictures, text, and numbers. Andersen (1995) has stated that information technology combines three technologies: microelectronics, computing and telecommunications. He has also noted that IT is the equipment used to transform data into information, which is then communicated to people who require it.

E-commerce is the revolutionized business activities (Abell & Lim, 1996). They are used information and telecommunication technology as tools for organization in gaining competitive advantage and in accessing global markets (Poon & Swatman, 1995). E-commerce focuses on direct transactions between businesses and end consumers. This is the trading and transactional relationship between an organization's website and its end users over the Internet (Al-Qirim & Corbitt, 2001). Consumers are able to purchase goods and services at any time convenient to the customer. One of the key benefits of e-commerce is the convenience of day and night trading, 365 days of the year (Peszynski & Thanasankit, 2002).

NATIONAL FACTORS AFFECTING THE USE OF INFORMATION TECHNOLOGY AND E-COMMERCE IN A THAI AGRICULTURAL COOPERATIVE

Understanding the factors affecting the use of information technology across the whole nation needs to be considered before analyzing the organizational factors affecting the use of information technology in Thai agricultural cooperatives. This part of the chapter compares the Thai experience with that of other nations, particularly Singapore.

The selected national factors are taken from Chieochan and Lindley (1999), Chieochan, Lindley and Dunn (2000a, b) and include:

- National economic conditions
- Information technology policy
- Socio-cultural factors
- Human resources in information technology

National Economic Conditions

The lower the economic development of a country, the lower will be the financial investment in infrastructure, including information technology infrastructure. Furthermore, individuals and organizations in such countries tend to have a low level of income; hence the demand for services tends to be low. This results in a slow diffusion of the use of information technology and e-commerce within the country. That the level of economic development of a country is closely related to the availability of is a conclusion supported by Bazar and Boalch (1998), Janczewski (1992), and Watson and Mayers (2000) infrastructure and the level of demand for information technology, Internet service and e-businesses.

Rice production is critical to the economic welfare of Thailand and the government outlays little expenditure on it. The principal expenditure is on defense (95,601 million Baht), public order and safety (46,651 million Baht), education (159,053 million Baht), health (59,205 million) and social security and welfare (28,637 million Baht). The Thai government spends still less money on information technology infrastructure–the number of Internet users in Thailand is approximately 131,000 in a population of 60 million. These percentages are taken from Turner (2000, pp. 1523-1524) and cover the year 1996. The World Bank Group (2000) classifies Thailand as a lower-middle-income economy ($761-$3,030).

When compared with its neighbor Singapore, Thai information technology is six years in arrears (Thailand Development Research Institute Foundation, 1994, p. 74). In 1997 and 1998, Singapore was at the top of the World Economic Forum's global competitiveness report, which assesses countries on their potential for economic growth and their income levels. The World Bank Group (2000) classifies the gross national product (GNP) per capita in Singapore as high-income ($9,361 or more per annum). Turner (2000, p. 1389) notes that the Singaporean government spends more of its budget to build up a strong science and technology base to support high-tech industries and to innovate products and processes. The Singaporean government proposes to develop Singapore into a global city with total business capacity by using information technology and e-commerce to allow the economy to remain competitive. Additional evidence of the Singaporean government's success in promoting information technology, is that the number of Internet users is high–approximately 267,000 out of the population of 4 million.

From 1997 on, economic conditions in Thailand became difficult (Terdudomtham, 1998). The economic crisis affected government, infrastructure, and organizations. The educational sector was also affected. Turner (2000, p. 1522) notes that real GDP growth in Thailand was 7.8 percent in 1996 and 8.6 percent in 1995. In 1997 and 1998 it was estimated to be 1 percent and 8 percent respectively. The National Science and Technology Development Agency, Thailand (1997) notes the economic crisis affected not only government, but also the business sector. Sutharoj (1998) add that because of the economic crisis, the government cut the budgets for education for the whole nation and that the implementation of information technology at some university campuses could not proceed.

Sutharoj and Boonnoon (1998) report on the crisis in the Thai information technology industry. The local information technology industry was worth 18 billion Baht in 1998. This was a reduction of 37 percent from the previous year when it was worth 30 billion Baht. They also note that the information technology market in Thailand was tougher because of reduced purchasing in the local market. This applied to bank, finance, and insurance companies as well as to the government sector. In addition to Boonruang's point Potipattanakorn (1997) states that the retail sector in Thailand is a decade behind the United States and will fall further behind if the economy does not recover. The effect on business of economic conditions is important. Co-operatives, which are businesses, are also affected – including their adoption of IT.

Information Technology and E-Commerce Policies

Governments can direct the development of information technology and e-commerce development in a nation. Bazar and Boalch (1998) give significant arguments about government policy in those countries where there are liberal politics and regulations towards telecommunications and Internet services, the market environment tends to be more competitive. This environment is conducive to the diffusion of information technology, especially of the Internet.

The paper by Boonyamalik and Kanjanarunsinun (1996) analyzes the Thai national development five-year plans and concludes that the first five years (1988 – 1992) emphasized infrastructure development particularly transportation, the next five years (1993 – 1997) emphasized economic improvement, and the current plan (1998 – 2001) emphasizes human resources development. Corbitt (1999) notes that information technology is a support for the human resources development associated with existing national development goals established in the current five-year plan.

In Thailand, a national information technology policy places more emphasis on development inside the country especially social development such as providing equality of information access between rural and urban groups and the distribution of democratic information from the government to the people. Corbitt (1999) explains that the Thai national information technology policy focuses on relating progress in information technology distribution in Thailand to the social and economic development of its population. The needs are not immediate and the focus is on doing information technology in a Thai way. The policy pays little attention to the immediate and essential needs of business and trade outside of Thailand particularly e-commerce.

Koanantakool (1998) suggests that the information technology policy of Thailand should foster the widespread use of information technology and therefore holds promise to spread economic activity, democratic principles, wealth distribution, and social benefits across every region of the country, thus greatly stems the tide of social ills. In particular, Koanantakool (1998) notes the following five points:

- Information technology might help to reduce pollution and traffic, and could facilitate telecommunication from home or a nearby telecommuter center.
- Widespread and affordable rural communications networks could provide on-line information or serve as the vehicle to deliver public services such as distance learning and telemedicine to remote rural residents. Telephones, electronic mail and fax could, in addition to traditional postal service, be used to instantly gather citizens' opinions or problems.
- Information technology must be viewed as a tool for achieving broader national objectives, both social and economic. Information technologies are definitely not merely and end in it.
- Information development must be firmly aimed to reduce the substantial gap between the information "haves" and "havenots," not to further widen it. It is easy for the affluent and the better-educated segments of society to gain most from the use of information technology. The city poor and rural residents are more likely to be left even further behind.
- The application of information technology in support of national development can create more equal opportunity and provide benefits for all segments of society.

Corbitt (1999) concludes that in the 15 pages that make up the Thai national policy, there is only one reference to a view that such policy development is concerned with enhancing the Thai position as the hub of Southeast Asia. Unlike Singapore, there is no endeavor to promote Thailand as a center for information technology.

Corbitt (1999) compares the national information technology policies in Singapore and Thailand and argues that they are different in philosophy and concept. Yap, Thong and Raman (1994) conducted research investigating the effect of Singaporean government incentives on computerization in small business in Singapore, and they concluded that Singaporean government policy is a strong influencing factor in a decision to computerize. The government policies reduce the risk of computerization failure by making available good quality external expertise in the form of advisors and screened consultants.

National information technology policies in Singapore place more emphasis on encouraging the whole nation to have better information and telecommunication infrastructure in order to improve business competition inside and outside the country.

Corbitt (1999) notes that the Singapore national information technology policy focuses on information technology as a strategy for business development. The policy reflects a view that business must take the lead and initiate the economic effects of information technology.

Mansell and Jenkins (1992) support the view that the Singapore government's strategic approach toward the development of an electronic trading environment aims to create opportunities for businesses to benefit from the increasing globalization of trade. It is suggested that both universal access to advanced telecommunication services and a new generation of network-based institutions are necessary preconditions for the success of this strategy. Current trends toward the separation of physical from electronic networks of trade will have uncharted consequences. Singapore's experience in developing new institutional solutions in response to the challenge to create an advanced electronic trading environment in the ASEAN region as well as in the wider global economy is outlined.

Gurbaxani et al. (1990), and Gurbaxani (1990) note that in an attempt to make Singapore an economic power in the post-industrial information era, the Singaporean government is implementing a series of national computer plans designed to further the country's efforts to move up the value-added chain by driving information technology into all sectors of society. An analysis of the information technology policy of Singapore shows that the government has had a high level of involvement in the computerization and informatization of Singapore. The government has taken a large participatory role and a smaller (but significant) regulatory and coordinating role in the development and diffusion of IT. While production and use of IT started out as equal priorities, the emphasis has shifted to promoting IT use as a means of increasing the competitiveness of all sectors of the economy.

The Singaporean national information technology policy reflects:

- the entrepot, trading nature of Singapore;
- its internal focus;
- an immediacy that something has to be done now;

- an acceptance of doing e-commerce and implementing a national information technology policy that fits in with and works with Western systems and practices; and
- accepts that problems and issues associated with e-commerce and information technology are those of business trade.

Navarat (2000) compares Singapore and Sri Lanka and makes the interesting point that both of them are small islands. Forty years ago the performances of both countries were similar in terms of their economic situations. Singapore has been developed faster than Sri Lanka and has become the hub of Asia for transportation, trading, and business. Navarat explains that one possible reason is that Sri Lanka has more natural resources than Singapore but that the political situation in Sri Lanka is not stable and the government spends more money on the military. Singapore is more peaceful and stable. Sri Lanka is similar to Thailand in that the Thai government spends more money on military development. Turner (2000) supports this.

In other countries besides Thailand, government policy has great effect on the use of information technology in their societies. Here are some examples. Rodriguez (1994) and Sanchez-Vegegas (1995) report that government is one of the factors that inhibit the spread of information technology in Latin America. Other factors include unstable government, excessive concern for secrecy and security, frequent changes of priorities, constant threat of foreign intervention, centralization of political decision and minimal impact of the scientific approach at the highest decision levels.

Odedra et al. (1998) report that in many sub-Saharan Africa countries, government policies and strategies are not sufficiently clear to encourage organizations to use information technology. Oliver (1997) also supports the idea that governments in Africa are aware of the power of the Internet and other networks to spread embarrassing information. Moreover, governments often set up obsolete frameworks, over-regulate, and are required to pay high charges on imported telecommunications equipment.

Nature (1996) explains that the Chinese government has restricted international Internet access by domestic service providers to lines supplied by the ministry of post and telecommunications. The purpose of this is to control the flow information in and out of the country for security reasons.

Goodman and Green (1992) report that in the Middle East, regional politics have always impeded the regionalization of information technology. For example, in Syria, faxes are controlled in some places by higher-level politicians as if their power were in controlling and containing information, especially information that can cross borders. For another example, people in Saudi Arabia bought previously restricted satellite dishes to watch news during the Gulf War. At the end of the war, certain government officials felt they should register, monitor, or dismantle the dishes.

Watson and Myers (2000) conducted research on a comparison of the success of information technology industries in Finland and New Zealand. Their results showed that Finnish government has promoted IT very heavily compared to New Zealand government. Their research focused on government promotion in terms of national IT strategies, IT priority and the existence of government IT organizations.

Culture-Social

This section examines the effect of the Thai social culture on the adoption of information technology in the kingdom. Special emphasis is placed on language, particularly English. Thanasankit (1999) and Thanasankit and Corbitt (1999) agree that Thai values shape and control the direction of information technology usages. They influence the way Thai people think, tackle problems, and make decisions.

English is the dominant language for development of information technology and e-commerce. It is the second language in most Asian countries. Ang and Loh (1998), and Oliver (1997) note that language is one of the most serious barriers to the use of information technology in developing countries. Bazar and Boalch (1998) support this and note that English language is not only a problem for developing countries, but also for any non-English-speaking country using information technology, especially the Internet. The use of English is common in some countries, but the real penetration of the Internet into communities requires using Internet applications in the local language.

Gibson (1997) conducted research in Thailand on the confluence of culture and information technology in Thailand. His results show that the English barrier is directly related to Thai culture. He explains that Thailand is one of the Southeast Asian countries where most people speak and read only their native language. Thai people study English in middle school, but most can only read simple English words. While computer keyboards are available with Thai characters, programming commands and in-depth work with computers demand fluency in the English language. Thais have become nationalistic in the use of their own language, and naturally try to preserve it. The medium of instruction in schools at all levels is Thai.

Gibson (1997) comments that, in a way, Thai education has become a negative influence for acceptance and acquisition of modern ideas and technologies. He explains that because the Thai language is so influential, many people cannot comprehend English well enough to be able acquire new ideas and knowledge related to information technology.

In the same work, Gibson notes another problem with the way the Thai social culture inhibits the use of information in organizations. Top management is conservative and will not accept this new technology. For example, in government department offices every piece of paper needs to bear the logo of the department. The computer can create this logo in three sizes: small, medium, and large, but when employees submit work done on computers, some top management will not accept it. They complain about the kind of paper, and that the logo is not the same as the original. This is a problem where top management comes from an older generation and does not want any changes. They believe only in the way they used to work. Consequently, people will avoid using computers unless forced to do so.

On the other hand, the official language in Singapore is English. Singaporean residents can be multi-lingual with English and Mandarin as co-national languages with Malay and Tamil. This suggests that the focus of the Singaporean information technology policy is external and driven by a need to place Singapore in a world scene economically.

Corbitt (1999) explains that there are perhaps two main reasons for this contrast. The most obvious is the historical development and modernization process of both countries. Singapore has a colonial history based on trading. It is a nation developed into a post-modern state in which there is a real complexity or plurality in society. It is distinctly multi-cultural and supports a variety of cultures within a nationalistic view that sees the role of the state as dominant. Cultures are expressed independently of the state and encouraged by the state to maintain their different natures. In Thailand, the state has not moved from the modern to the post-modern. There is no impact of colonialism as there was none. Plurality is rare. There is a national language and a monocultural view of society. Government planning focuses on five-year plans abandoned long ago in Singapore. National culture then, is important; the adoption of English in the adoption of information technology cannot be over-emphasized.

Human Resources in Information Technology and E-Commerce

The TDRI (1995) and Malaiwong (1999a) report that one of the problems in the use of information technology in Thailand is the lack of quality human resources in the disciplines of information technology and telecommunication. Malaiwong (1999b) explains that the root problem for Thailand is the lack of good educational planning and inefficient information technology training. He (1999c, p. 39) concludes that the recent problems of Thai education are emphasis on producing numbers of students at the expense of quality, the lack of the academic perspective, the lack of research and development and the central belief that learning depends on teachers rather than students. Gibson supports this conclusion (1997) that Thailand lacks general education and the more intensive skills required to effectively use the tools of information technology. Furthermore, Ang and Jiwahhasuchin (1998) add that research and development in Thailand is behind that of other countries when the Thai universities' lack of skill in conducting research and developments is considered. Almost all graduate schools in universities emphasize course work rather than research.

The Spell Out (TDRI) (1994) explains the differing experiences of Singapore by suggesting that Singapore has no natural resources, but good human resources. The Singapore government supports the development of human resources in the discipline of information technology. The National Computer Board, Singapore, cited by the TDRI (1994, p. 15) reports that in 1980 there were only 850 people in the discipline of information technology. This increased to 4,000 in 1984; then 8,300 in 1988; and finally 14,300 in 1991. The TDRI (1994) compares human resources in the discipline of information technology between Thailand and Singapore. Data in Thailand was collected in 1993 and data in Singapore was collected by the National Census Bureau (NCB) in 1988. The TDRI concludes (p. 74) that development of information technology in Thailand is six years behind Singapore.

Numbers of professional software workers in Thailand are less than in Singapore. The TDRI (1994, p. 75) reports that 65 percent of employees were using software in Singapore in 1988 whereas there were only 45 percent in Thailand in 1993. It is to be noted that the lack of human resources in information technology, especially in professional software development, is a major problem in Thailand. Thailand uses more human resources at lower levels of information technology. TDRI (1994, p. 76) reports that Thailand employs 66 percent at vocational and technical levels whereas Singapore uses only 45 percent.

According to the TDRI, there are three possible reasons to explain why information technology development in Thailand is six years behind Singapore:

- Singapore has more advanced and effective training than Thailand. People who did not graduate in the discipline of information technology can be trained to work in information technology.
- Singapore has a strategy in technology transfer from overseas into Singapore such as encouraging overseas experts to work in Singapore. The TDRI (1994, p. 76) reports that in 1988 in Singapore, 15 out of 100 permanent residents from overseas and employment passport holders worked in the discipline of information technology; in 1991, the number increased to 20. Moreover, 20 percent of Singaporeans graduate from overseas in information technology and related disciplines. Twenty percent had graduate doctorates

and master's degrees and 35 percent had graduate bachelor degrees. In contrast, 9 percent of Thais had graduated from overseas and that only 11.7 percent were from graduate postgraduate levels.

- TDRI (1994, p. 55) notes that staff in information technology in Thailand lacks experience. Forty percent of human resources in information technology in Singapore have been working less than three years and 50 percent of employees in Thailand have been working less than three years. The specific comparison is of concern to Thai agricultural cooperatives and small businesses.

Human resources are important in information technology for both cooperatives and for the nation.

ORGANIZATIONAL FACTORS ENCOURAGING THE USE OF INFORMATION TECHNOLOGY AND E-COMMERCE IN THAI AGRICULTURAL COOPERATIVE

Thai Agricultural Cooperative Managers' Knowledge of Information Technology and E-Commerce

This section examines the effect of managers' knowledge of information technology and e-commerce on the adoption of information technology in Thai agricultural cooperatives.

The decision maker-characteristics of managers especially the manager's knowledge of information technology are the main keys in distinguishing Thai agricultural cooperatives using information technology from those not using it (Chiecochan & Lindley, 1999; Chieochan, Lindley & Dunn, 2000a, b). The finding that decision-maker characteristics of CEOs of small businesses in Singapore are the main keys in distinguishing small businesses using information technology from those not using it, is supported by Thong and Yap (1995).

Rogers (1983) argues that leadership is the degree to which an individual is able to influence other individuals' attitudes or overt behavior informally in a desired way with relative frequency. There are two main theories about why knowledge of information technology or innovation influences the decision-maker to adopt that technology or innovation. Rogers (1983) presents the first theory and the Attewell (1992) presents the second theory.

According to Rogers' (1983) innovation theory, knowledge of technology is the first stage in his model of the innovation-decision process. In Attewell's (1992) theory of lowering the knowledge barrier, he argues that the diffusion of complex organizational technologies is better understood as a process driven by decreasing knowledge barriers than as a process driven by communication and social influence. There is some evidence from other types of organizations in other nations that a decision maker's knowledge of information technology is the main factor in adopting information technology in their firms.

Larsen (1993), Boynton, Zmud and Jacobs (1994) found that managerial information technology knowledge is a dominant factor in explaining the high level of information technology use in organizations. Similarly, Cragg and King (1993) note that the strongest factor inhibiting firms from adopting it is the owners' lack of knowledge. Öhlmér (1992) studied the effects of information technology on the data needs in farm management and found that a manager's lack of knowledge of information technology is the main obstacle to using automated data collection at the farm. Igbaria, Zinatelli and Cavaye (1998) studied information technology success in small firms in New Zealand and found that computer education and self-training played major roles.

Chau's (1994) research in Hong Kong found that owners or managers of small businesses who have a higher information literacy tend to emphasize more technical factors. Those who have more experience in using and purchasing packaged software tend to give more weight to the importance of the vendor's technical and non-technical capability. Moreover, he found that owners of small business in Hong Kong tended to look at technical factors more seriously, while managers tended to emphasize more non-technical factors such as price and popularity of the software package when making the selection decision.

Baker (1990) conducted his research in New Mexican agribusiness on the characteristics of computer users and determinants of microcomputer success by agribusiness. He found that the agricultural business mangers with a higher level of education are more likely to adopt information technology.

More recently, Seyal, Rahim and Rahman (2000) investigated the use of information technology in small and medium business organizations in Brunei. They found that CEO computer literacy contributes towards the use of information technology.

Some Thai agricultural cooperatives do not adopt information technology. This might be explained by the fact that managers of Thai agricultural cooperatives are lacking not only in computer literacy, but also knowledge and experience about managing their businesses. Managers of Thai agricultural cooperatives might not perceive the importance and benefits of information technology. Sawatanon (1996,

p. 227) shows that only 20 percent of managers of all Thai agricultural cooperatives are professional in running agricultural businesses.

This problem is also addressed in agricultural cooperatives in America. The United States Department of Agriculture Rural Business Cooperative Service (1990) reported a similar problem – that cooperatives are subject to the same "people problems" as any business, but have additional problems stemming from being owned by those who use them. Some of their members and directors are misinformed; some have little realistic knowledge about business activities or how effectively their cooperative is operating or what it can be expected to accomplish. Directors and managers at times neglect their responsibilities or take advantage of their positions, resulting in poor performance or failure of the cooperative. Not all farmers in an area believe alike and thus not all will join or trade at a given cooperative. Likewise, leaders among farmers and cooperatives do not always agree on objectives, policies, and approaches, often leading to intense competition and duplication of services and facilities between cooperatives serving the same area. This situation can limit their efficiency, market power, and members' benefits. Directors of cooperatives are frequently faced with the difficult choice between building the financial strength of the cooperative through retained patronage refunds, or increasing returns to farmer members. The frailties of human nature may result in decisions that do not build cooperatives to their full potential. This problem is found similarly in the forestry cooperatives of New San Juan in Mexico. Tenenbanum (1996) reports that the cooperative, were mismanaged and disorganized. Other difficulties were attributed to corruption, insufficient technical knowledge, poor social cohesion, and lack of government support.

The decision-maker characteristics of managers of Thai agricultural cooperatives, especially the manager's knowledge of information technology, are the main factors distinguishing Thai agricultural cooperatives using information technology from those not using it.

Attitude of Managers of Thai Agricultural Cooperatives

Thong (1996) explains that as information technology is new to a CEO, he or she has no way of knowing whether it will be superior to existing methods of operation. A degree of uncertainty exists as adoption of information technology is risky, and each CEO will perceive the degree of risk or uncertainty associated with the information technology differently. If a CEO perceives that the benefits of information technology usage outweigh the risk, then the business is more likely to use information technology. There is some evidence from other types of organizations in other nations to explain that decision makers who have positive attitude towards the use of information technology tend to use it in their in their organizations.

Lakhanpal (1994) found that a middle manager's attitude towards microcomputer usage had a relatively positive influence on the adoption of microcomputers. Thong and Yap (1995) assert that CEOs who possess a positive attitude towards information technology are more likely to adopt information technology in their business. Baker supports this finding (1990). He conducted his research in a New Mexican agribusiness concerning the characteristics of computer users and the determinants of microcomputer success by agribusiness. He found that the agricultural business managers with more favorable attitudes toward innovation are more likely to adopt information technology.

Rogers (1983) explains that formation of a favorable or unfavorable attitude toward an innovation takes place before a decision to adopt is made. Attributes of an innovation are important during the formation of attitude. If information technology is perceived as being better than the manual systems it supersedes, it is consistent with needs of the potential adopter, it is easy to understand and use, it allows experimentation, and the results of usage are easily observed and communicated, it is more likely that a favorable attitude from managers of Thai agricultural cooperatives toward the innovation will be formed. The attitude of the manager in adopting information technology in Thai agricultural cooperatives is important.

Manager Innovativeness

In his 1976 theory of innovativeness, Kirton concludes that everyone is located on a continuum ranging from an ability to do things better to an ability to do things differently. He calls the two extreme ends of the continuum *adaptors* and *innovators* respectively. Thong (1996) explains that small business adoption of information technology presents a radical innovation that not only requires a large outlay of financial resources, but also involves complex technology. Information technology usage would be regarded as a risky venture that not many small businesses would be willing to undertake, since potential losses would be substantial in terms of both tangible and non-tangible losses. It is quite likely that the less innovative CEO who is the main decision-maker will look for other less radical and less risky solutions. Only a CEO who is more innovative would be willing to do things differently by taking the risk of adopting information technology in their organizations. Thong and Yap (1995) and Thong (1996, 1999) found that firms are more likely to adopt information technology when their CEOs are more innovative.

Some Thai agricultural cooperatives do not adopt information technology. This can be explained as some managers of Thai agricultural cooperatives are less innovative, less creative in ideas and less competitive compared to commercial and industrial businesses. In the model of cooperative activities, there are seven main activities including providing funds, credit, marketing, purchasing, processing, service and land improvement and agricultural promotion. Sawatanon (1996) reports that some Thai agricultural cooperatives have failed in their business because some activities are not undertaken – especially processing agricultural products. Therefore, cooperatives get fewer profits. The profits belong to the middleman. On the other hand, if cooperatives process their products – for example processing and packing milk – they might achieve more profit.

Sataporn (1996) explains that cooperative activities need input factors such as men, money, materials and management, which factors are called limited resources. Men in cooperatives are members (farmers, board-directors), management and administrative officers (managers and officers). Management processes such as planning, organizing, staffing, directing, coordinating and controlling are used to process input factors. Cooperative activities support the management process such as providing funds and credits for farmers, marketing and processing agricultural products from them, and educating and introducing new techniques to them. The last products of the cooperative activities are efficiency, effectiveness, economy and satisfaction. These are the economic and cooperative objectives.

The United States Department of Agriculture Rural Business Cooperative Service (1990) also reported this problem. In the United States, not all cooperatives acquire the leadership and financial ability to deal effectively with other firms in the marketplace. Because of a lack of vision, leadership, managerial ability, capital, or for other reasons, some cooperatives do not or cannot vertically integrate their operations, either individually or jointly with other cooperatives in federated associations. They do not acquire strength at the processing or manufacturing level where the real market power may be found in the industry.

If managers of Thai agricultural cooperatives are more innovative, there is more likelihood their cooperatives will adopt information technology in order to improve their business. Innovativeness of members of Thai agricultural cooperatives is not included in this research project. However, there is evidence that positive innovativeness by members of agricultural cooperatives can help mangers in running businesses efficiently. Positive innovativeness by members of agricultural cooperatives can affect the decision making of managers to use information technology in their operations.

Members are sometimes lacking their spirit of cooperation. Credit is one of the major businesses in Thai agricultural cooperatives. Tapsawat (1999) explains that the main purpose of farmers in becoming members is to borrow money from cooperatives. They are not involved in the process of developing and improving cooperatives. The Cooperative League paper (1992) argues that members (farmers) are unmotivated in developing their cooperatives and helping themselves because they think government should help them at all times. On the other hand, based on American experience, Anonymous (1996) and Somjee (1996) report that the Farmland cooperative system has grown to become the largest farmer-owned agricultural cooperative in the U.S., with sales in 1995 totaling $7.3 billion and business conducted in all 50 states and with more than 70 countries. Farmland is more like a large agribusiness than it is like other producer-funded associations where producers and the board might make marketing decisions. These directors hire the president/chief executive officer – who has the responsibility to run the day-to-day operations of Farmland – and vote to approve a strategic plan, which gives Farmland's management staff its direction. The individual board members are not involved in developing specific marketing strategies.

Farmland is a success in its operation because members (farmers) are involved in cooperative development. The United States Department of Agriculture's Rural Business Cooperative Service (1990) argues that successful cooperatives often develop leaders among directors, managers, other employees, and members, by participating in business decisions on a democratic basis, become more self-reliant and informed citizens in their communities.

Business Size

Business size can distinguish Thai agricultural cooperatives that use information technology intensively from those that use it lightly (Chieochan, Lindley & Dunn, 2000b). Larger organizations are more likely to use information technology intensively. Rogers (1983, 1995) notes that business size of an organization has consistently been found to be the best predictor of organizational innovation. He notes that size is a variable that is easily measured, and presumably with a relatively high degree of precision. So size has been included for study in almost every organizational innovativeness investigation.

There is some evidence from other types of organizations in other nations to explain that business size influences the use of information technology in the organization.

Thong and Yap (1995) found that business size is the most significant discriminator in determining the use of information technology in Singapore. Wierenga and Ophuis (1997) note that the size of organizations is positively related to innovation. Baker (1990) in his research in New Mexican agribusiness found that the agricultural businesses that have more members are more likely to adopt information technology.

One explanation by Thong (1996) and Raymond (1990) is that larger organizations usually have more organizational and financial resources and greater professional expertise. In Thai agricultural cooperatives with a large number of members (farmers), the size of the organization is increased; organizational structures become more complex and coordination of work activities more complicated. Increasing the size leads to economies of scale, which enhance the feasibility of adopting information technology. The large volume of information processed by large organizations gives them the advantage of scale. For this reason, Thai agricultural cooperatives have an opportunity to start using information technology. After that organization's gain, it accumulates experience and clearly sees the benefits.

The advantage of using information technology intensively is perceived in cooperative operations. On the other hand, Yap (1990) explains that small organizations have more difficulty justifying investment in information technology. They face a number of problems arising from limited financial and human resources. Thong (1996) reports that small business in Singapore suffers from resource poverty such as financial constraints, lack of professional expertise, and susceptibility to external forces due to operating in a highly competitive environment. They watch their cash flow carefully, do not have the necessary in-house information technology expertise, and tend to have a short-range management perspective with regard to information technology implementation. Yap (1986) says that small businesses also tend to choose the lowest-cost information technology, which may be inadequate for their purpose and to underestimate the amount of time and effort required for information technology implementation. Thus, inadequate planning for information technology increases the risk of implementation failure.

Small Thai agricultural cooperatives are concerned with different kinds of problems in relation to their use of computers because they do have internal technical support in their organizations. Gibson (1997) explains that in developing countries like Thailand, computer equipment and accessories tend to be far more expensive than in more developed countries. In addition, there is also the high cost in establishing, adapting, developing, and maintaining information technology systems. These can double the outlay as the overall sale is rather limited. Finally, hiring expert employees can be rather costly. Only large organizations or government agencies can afford these costs. Some Thai agricultural cooperatives especially smaller ones suffer from resource poverty such as financial constraints. Sawatanon (1996, p. 234) presents the figures that 50 percent of the income of Thai agricultural cooperatives is from investment business, 30 percent is from agricultural products trading and 5 percent is from other businesses.

Because Thai agricultural cooperatives lack finance, they tend to employ generalists rather than professional expertise to operate their businesses, including using and maintaining computers. Consequently, information technology is adopted in Thai agricultural cooperatives with employees who are more knowledgeable about information technology because they can reduce their budgets for computer training and maintenance. Moreover, a Thai agricultural cooperative employee's salary is less than an industry or company employee's salary. Some employees work in agricultural cooperatives to gain some experience, especially in using information technology and then move to working in industries or companies because their salaries are more attractive. As the result, if the cooperative has no employees who are knowledgeable about information technology, the replacement of computer officers needs to be of concern. On the other hand, if cooperatives have more employees who are more knowledgeable about information technology, other officers can replace the computer officer's vacant position immediately.

Thong (1996, 1999) finds that employees who have more knowledge of IT are more likely to use IT in their firms. Gibson (1997) conducted research on the topic of confluence of culture and information technology in Thailand. He (1997, p. 728) explained that one of the problems in Thailand is that employees' lack of computer knowledge makes them afraid of the technology.

Gibson (1997) extends his explanation by suggesting that the problem is rooted in lack of appropriate training. Trainers only teach how to run the computer, the meaning of some terms, and other basic computer ideas. Additional training is needed, leaving most users confused. Moreover, the Thai computer industry lacks experts who are over 30 years of age, with enough experience to provide leadership and direction. This is important for Thai companies, which have well-established patterns and norms for working together in their organizations. Employees need to act with respect, believe in, and obey their bosses, if they want to be promoted or show any career advancement. They learn how to stand or sit properly when talking and listening to their supervisors. This practice may have negative effects on the use of information technology because it will not allow experienced information technology professionals (who tend to be younger and more knowledgeable about information technology) to serve in higher management positions. It is a reminder that in Thai society, younger people must show respect to older people, or those having a higher social rank. As a result, the computer industry will not have enough experienced thinkers to steer the country in the proper directions for good information technology development. Business size then is important in forecasting the likelihood and extent of the use of information technology in Thai agricultural cooperatives.

Competitive Business Environment

This section examines the effect of competitive business environment on the adoption of information technology in Thai agricultural cooperatives and suggests that the environment of Thai agricultural cooperatives does not provide the opportunity for adopting information technology.

The New South Wales (NSW) Department of Fair Trading Consumer Protection Agency (1998) argues that the cooperative form of enterprise is specially suited for meeting the collective needs of members, be they producers, consumers or workers. The basic objective of a cooperative is member service and satisfaction, unlike in a company, which is driven by the need to maximize profit.

The debate from economic and social viewpoints is presented in order to support the theory that a competitive business environment does not influence the use of information technology in Thai agricultural cooperatives.

From the economic and marketing viewpoint, based on Canadian and United States experiences Lang (1995) argues that agricultural cooperatives enhance the ability of farm operations to survive on a relatively small scale by achieving scale economies in output and input operations. But history gives us little reason to believe that this will occur as technology makes larger operations more competitive. Lang (1995) asserts that technological change, the changing structure of agriculture, and growing individualism are key threats to the future of cooperatives. This gives the impression that, in his view, the industrialization of agriculture so limits the ability of producers to add value through cooperatives that investor-owned firms will prevail.

I would agree that the most classical organizational performance is measured by profits. Sataporn (1996) and Sawatanon (1996) note that a cooperative is a type of business in which the main objective is not only economic (profits), but also better serving member objectives. Thai agriculture has an extra goal: organizational performance is not only measured by profits but by the social benefits such as the moral satisfaction of their members.

The United States Department of Agriculture Rural Business-Cooperative Service (1990) explains that benefits of cooperatives are difficult to measure. Most benefits are evaluated in economic terms but some also may be social. Randall et al. (1997) argues that from a sociological perspective there exist some conceptual and practical dilemmas that occur within the theory and practice of the cooperative movement and cooperative organizations that define differing orientations between the social and economic philosophies of cooperation. From the social viewpoint, Thai agricultural cooperatives are still considered as a benefit to rural development. If there are no agricultural cooperatives, farmers have nowhere to borrow money. Anonymous (1998) calls an agricultural cooperative a socio-economic organization. Therefore, Thai agricultural cooperatives are not aggressive in marketing. The Cooperative League (1992) argues that Thai agricultural cooperatives have less competition compared to other types of business.

The main product for agricultural cooperatives is rice; they share the same market. Moreover, all Thai agricultural cooperatives operate similar businesses because they are regulated by the Thai government, which controls cooperative activities such as providing funds, credit for members, marketing, purchasing, processing, services and land improvement and agricultural promotion (Sataporn, 1996). Sawatanon (1996) supports the finding that some Thai agricultural cooperatives have failed in their business because some activities, especially processing agricultural products, are not undertaken. Therefore, Thai cooperatives get fewer profits. The profits still belong to the middlemen. On the other hand, if cooperatives developed their products, for example by processing and packing milk, they might be able get more profits than they do by simply collecting milk from farmers and selling raw milk to the middlemen. Moreover, Chieochan, Lindley and Dunn (2000b) show that only 40 percent of Thai agricultural cooperatives provide consultation and agricultural education services to members. Twenty percent of Thai agricultural cooperatives do not operate collecting and selling agricultural products from members.

Nashima (1996) supports this finding. He reports on behalf of the Japanese agricultural ministry-affiliated National Research Institute of Agricultural Economics that agricultural cooperatives should maintain their status as organizations for farmers because no other financial institutions would lend money to farmers, whose income tends to fluctuate from year to year. Randall et al. (1997) explain that cooperatives are the places to provide training in democratic practice.

Cooperatives are considered as rural worker's organizations. Egger (1992) asserts that rural workers' organizations must be established and consolidated by and for rural development, and this implies three consequences. In the first place, the organization must not be modeled on the traditional trade union structure but must develop naturally from activities associated with rural development–it should contain elements of the trade union, the cooperative and the service organization, possibly enriched by local traditions. Secondly, it must be involved as deeply as possible in all decisions affecting rural development, at several levels. Lastly, indirect support for the creation of an environment favorable to the expansion of grassroots organizations is just as important as direct support.

However, in order to survive, Lang (1995) suggests that many cooperatives must add more value to their products as they compete in more refined consumer markets with many different partners and in a global marketplace. As a crossroads in cooperative marketing development, this differs greatly from those situations faced in the past. At this juncture, cooperatives have many more development options that appear as different possible partners, consumer products, markets, and services. Rational selection among these options requires strategic planning, strategic choices, and commitment by cooperative members to succeed in one of many choices they make. This requires an offensive, flexible mentality that has not characterized most cooperatives in the past. To this he adds that the ability of cooperative leaders to convince their members to structure themselves as required competing on multi-commodity, value-added, and global bases. This requires more aggressive marketing than most cooperatives have pursued in the past. Whether they act accordingly will depend upon cooperative leaders' abilities to convince members to become truly proactive, exploiting opportunities rather than choosing among limited options and acting only out of necessity. To do so, they will have to convince members that their best private interest is served by such efforts.

Interestingly, this agrees with the findings of Thong and Yap (1995) and Thong (1996, 1999). Thong and Yap explain that in small businesses in Singapore the competitiveness of environment did not really provide any direct "push" for business to adopt information technology. They note that competitiveness of environment might have indirect effects on adoption of information technology through the CEO's attitude toward information technology adoption. Thai agricultural cooperatives however do not provide a competitive business environment and do not advance the adoption of information technology.

Information Intensity

Thai agricultural cooperatives have similar information processing needs and that information concerning agricultural products alone, and members' records, does not warrant computerization. It can be another reason to explain why Thai agricultural cooperatives are failures in using information management. Thai agricultural cooperatives might not adopt computers for the purpose of information management. Interestingly, this agrees with the findings of Thong and Yap (1995) and Thong (1996, 1999). They explain that, in small business in Singapore, information intensity had no direct effect on the decision to adopt information technology, though it may have indirect effects through the CEO's attitude toward information technology. A CEO's attitude towards information technology is positively correlated with information intensity. They also explain that it is speculated that an information intensive business sector may influence the CEO's perception about the adoption of information technology adoption.

There is another possible reason to explain why information intensity does not influence the use of information technology in Thai agricultural cooperatives. Primozic (1991), cited in the National Institute of Development Administration, Thailand (1997), classifies the level of using information technology in organizations. There are five beneficial levels of information technology usage in organizations and Primozic calls them "waves of innovations." The five are: reducing cost, leveraging investment, enhancing products and services, enhancing executive decision-making, and reaching the consumer.

In line with the waves of innovations model, the TDRI (1997), and Malaiwong (1999a, b) report that the main purposes of using computers in Thailand are for producing documents and creating databases. However, there is a lack of the use of computers for the purpose of analyzing information for higher level of administrative and management and for reaching the consumer. The TDRI (1994; 1996) supports the finding that the Thai government still uses traditional technology – such as messengers, telephone, telegraph, courier service – rather than using information technology for their communications. Moreover the TDRI (1994) adds that because of the lack of cooperation in not only the same government sectors, but also different sectors, there is fragmented application development for creating and maintaining databases. Problems occur such as uncontrolled data redundancy, inconsistent data definition, and inconsistent data manipulation. Thai agricultural cooperative might not know how to organize and use information technology to organize and manage their information.

CONCLUSION

The adoption of information technology is fundamental in e-commerce development. Information technology and e-commerce has been used in both developed and developing countries to support operational, tactical, and strategic processes within organizations (Abdulgader & Kozar, 1995). Chau (1994) adds that it has been argued that organizations can improve their organizational performance and increase their competitiveness with information technology.

Baker (1990) supports the belief that in recent years information technology has become practical for all businesses. Agricultural businesses have been no exception. The price of microcomputers has fallen to a level that system cost is no longer a major limitation for most businesses. Additionally, the increased "user friendliness" of software, and the number of business applications available for agribusinesses, have led many agribusinesses to consider purchasing a microcomputer for the first time.

Some organizations are faster to introduce information technology than others (Thong & Yap, 1995). However, Thai agricultural cooperatives are slow introducers of information technology and e-commerce.

The factors that encourage and inhibit the use of information technology in Thai agricultural cooperatives can be useful to encourage Thai agricultural cooperatives to use information technology and apply e-commerce in their operations as well as the whole nation. This understanding can apply to improve e-commerce development in Thai culture in the future. These, factors from studies from Chieochan, Lindely (1999), Chieochan, Lindley and Dunn (2000a, 2000b) and shows that national factors (e.g., national economic conditions, information technology and e-commerce policies, social cultural factors and human resources in information technology) as well as organizational factors (e.g., business size, competitive business environment and information intensity) are important for Thai agricultural cooperatives. In addition, the most significant factor in deciding to use information technology in Thai agricultural cooperatives is the decision-making characteristics of managers, particularly their information technology knowledge. It is the main key in distinguishing Thai agricultural cooperatives using information technology from those not using it.

IMPLICATIONS

Implications for Thai Government

This chapter has argued that for the better information technology usage in the whole Thai kingdom, information technology policy from the government is as important as English language.

Thai government information technology and e-commerce policy places more emphasis on development inside the country, particularly social development. Thai government information technology and e-commerce policy also supports the modernization process associated with the existing national development goals established in the current eighth national development five year plan. However, Thai government information technology policy and e-commerce lacks encouragement for the whole nation to have better information and telecommunication infrastructure as a strategy for business development in order to gain business competition inside and outside the country. Therefore, the Thai government should place emphasis on providing better information technology and e-commerce policies to business development as well as social development in the whole kingdom.

It is important to note that some of the success of the development of information technology and e-commerce in Singapore is due to the encouragement that the government gives to foreign information technology experts to work in Singapore. English is the official language in Singapore. It is agreed that English language is the dominant language for information technology and e-commerce.

English is not an official language in Thailand. The Thai government should give more encouragement to Thai people to use more English. It might help Thailand to better acquire information technology development and transfer. In addition, the government might attract foreign information technology experts to work in Thailand.

Implications for Thai Agricultural Cooperatives

This chapter has shown that beside the characteristics of managers of Thai agricultural cooperatives particularly the manager's information technology knowledge, employees' information technology knowledge is also important in driving Thai agricultural cooperatives to adopt information technology.

Information technology and e-commerce training for Thai agricultural cooperatives are needed. MacLeod and Chiware (1993) summarized some common problems in information technology training that are found in developing countries such as less practical experience of full information technology among senior staff, no practical experience of information technology and few keyboard skills among junior staff, different staff expectations and learning methods. Those problems are similar in Thai agricultural cooperatives.

Another considerable problem discussed by Hopey (1998) is that managers and employees of Thai agricultural cooperatives are considered as mature students. Adults are motivated to learn when they can see that the time and effort devoted to learning will pay off. Adult learners have a wide range of learning goals, and they are not likely to waste time on learning tasks that are not clearly leading to the achievement of their goals.

Therefore, before employees and managers of Thai agricultural cooperatives are ready to learn new skills and information for performing their tasks, they must be educated about the logic behind the changes being imposed (Katz & Katz, 1996; MacLeod & Chiware, 1993). The skill of the trainers, and quality of the trainees, are also equally important in this stage (MacLeod & Chiware, 1993). In addition, Baker and Welsby (1997) believe that it is important to encourage managers and employees of Thai agricultural cooperatives to have more confidence in using information technology and adopting e-commerce.

Following learning the new software's features and how to apply them to their jobs, employees and managers of Thai agricultural cooperatives must have a basic understanding of how to use the hardware and the software-operating environment (Katz & Katz 1996; MacLeod & Chiware, 1993). Baker and Welsby (1997) explain that once managers or employees have mastered the basics of computer knowledge and learned some essential vocabularies of computers, it becomes easier to advance the educational process. The continuation can often be done through the use of tutorials offered with most packages at intermediate and advanced levels.

After the training, Baker and Welsby (1997) suggest that it is necessary to measure if training is adequate such as establishing feedback mechanisms and training evaluation. McMurrer and Van Buren (1999) give the example of the experience of the state of training in Japan. It is evaluated with respect to:

- expenditures
- non-financial measures
- delivery and evaluation
- resources
- innovative practices

In addition, good training can be lifetime training. McMurrer and Van Buren (1999) documented the experiences of training in Japan. The success of training in Japan is that employers in Japan are well-regarded for their significant and long-term commitment to developing the skills of their workers. Consequently, not only the Ministry of Thai Agricultural Cooperatives but also academic institutions offering IT education should be involved in lifetime information technology training for Thai agricultural cooperatives.

Baker and Welsby (1997) and Wilson (1997) explain that the Ministry of Thai Agricultural Cooperatives should provide opportunities for managers and employees of Thai agricultural cooperatives to further their information technology skill and knowledge development. MacLeod and Chiware, (1993) agree that training should be considered to be a continuing process and extension of training beyond those areas that are necessary for immediate job performance. Messmer (1999) gives some suggestions for the Ministry of Thai Agricultural Cooperatives such as that the ministry should encourage computer-related and software course enrollment for managers and employees of Thai agricultural cooperatives, consider tuition reimbursement for continuing education, provide free or low-cost training offered by colleges and universities.

Moreover, managers and employees of Thai agricultural cooperatives should provide the opportunity for the cooperative to network knowledge. Tobin (1998) explains that managers and employees of Thai agricultural cooperatives can share their knowledge in not only cooperative businesses, but also information technology knowledge.

REFERENCES

Abdulgader, A.H., & Kozar, K.A. (1995). The impact of computer alienation on information technology investment decisions: An exploratory cross-national analysis. *MIS Quarterly,* 19(4), 535-559.

Abell, W. & Lim, L. (1996). *Business Use of the Internet in New Zealand: An exploratory study.* http://www.scu.edu.au/ausweb96/business/abell/paper.htm.

Al-Qirim, N., & Corbitt, B.J. (2001). Determinations of innovation adoption in small to medium-sized enterprises in New Zealand: An electronic commerce capability model. 6th *Annual Collector Conference on Electronic Commerce*, Coffs Harbour, NSW, Australia, December, 1-27.

Anderson, H. (1995). *Information Technology in Business: People, Systems and Procedures* (2nd ed). VCTA publishing: South Melbourne.

Ang, A.Y. & Jiwahhasuchin, S. (1998). Information systems education in Thailand: A comparison between the views of professionals and academics. *Journal of Global Information Management*, *6*(4), 34-42.

Ang, P.H. & Loh, M.C (1998). *Internet Development in Asia*. Internet Society Retrieved from the World Wide Web: http://info.isoc.org:80/isoc/whatis/conferences/inet/96/proceedings/h1/h1_1.htm.

Anonymous. (1996). What is the Farmland cooperatives system? *Agri Marking*, 34(6), F-G.

Anonymous. (1998). Economie, social developpement: Les cooperatives, mutuelles et associations dans les pays en developpement. *International Labour Review*, *137*(1), 112-114.

Attewell, P. (1992). Technology diffusion and organization learning: The case of business computing. *Organization Science*, *3*(1), 1-19.

Baker, D. & Welsby, J. (1997). *Library Training Guides: Training for IT*. London: Library Association Publishing.

Baker, G.A. (1990). Characteristics of computer usage and determinants of microcomputer success by agribusiness. *Agribusiness*, *6*(2), 109-119.

Bazar, B. & Boalch, G. (1998). *A Preliminary Model of Internet Diffusion within Developing Countries*. http://ausweb.scu.edu.au/proceeding/boalch/paper.html.

Boonyanalik, K. & Kanjanarunsinun, K. (1996). The development of Thai rural area in the era of globalization. *The Journal of Community Development*, 30-33.

Boynton, A.C., Zmud, R.W., & Jacob, G.C. (1994). The influence of it management practice on it use in large organizations. *MIS Quarterly*, 299-318.

Chau, P.Y.C. (1994). Selection of packaged software in small business. *European Journal of Information Systems*, 3(4), 292-302.

Chieochan, O. & Lindley, D. (1999). Factors affecting the use of information technology in Thai agricultural cooperatives: A work in progress, *Proceeding of CITA99: Conference on Information Technology in Asia, the Asian Regional Conference on IFIP Working Group 9.4 on the Social Implication of Computers in Developing Countries,* Kuching, Malaysia, Harris, R. (ed.), 136-148.

Chieochan, O., Lindley, D. & Dunn, T. (2000b). Factors affecting the use of

Information in Thai agricultural cooperatives: A work in progress. *The Electronic Journal on Information Systems in Developing Countries*, 2, 1-17.

Chieochan, O., Lindley, D. & Dunn, T. (2000c). Factors affecting the use of information in Thai agricultural cooperatives: A preliminary data analysis. *Proceeding of PACIS2000: Fourth Pacific Asia Conference on Information Systems, Conference on Electronic Commerce and Web-Based Information Systems 2000*, Hong Kong, Thong, J. (ed), 389-407.

Commentary: And life after Thaksin. (2001). *Bangkok Post*. Retrieved from the World Wide Web: http://www.bangkokpost.com/newindex/today/260101_news02.html.

Cooperative League (1992). *The Report of the Conference of Thai Ministers Who Response for Cooperatives in Thailand During 26- 28 August.*

Cooperatives Promotion Department, Ministry of Thai agriculture and cooperatives (1993). *Cooperatives in Thailand.*

Cooperatives Promotion Department, Ministry of Thai agriculture and cooperatives. (1999). *Annual Report of Cooperatives in Thailand in 1999.*

Corbitt, B.J. (1999). Exploring the social construction of IT policy - Thailand and Singapore. *Prometheus*, *17*(3), 309-321.

Cragg, P.B. & King, M. (1993). Small-firm computing: Motivators and inhibitors. *MIS Quarterly*, 47-60.

Cusumano, A. (1991). *Information Technology in Business: People, System, Process*. VCTA publishing: Collingwood, VIC, Australia.

Department of Fair Trading, NSW Consumer Protection Agency. (1998). *A Guide to Co-operatives*. Retrieved from the World Wide Web: http://www.peg.apc.org/~coopsnsw/guide.htm.

Eagger, P. (1992). Rural organizations and infrastructure projects: Social investment comes before material investment. *International Labour Review*, *131*(1), 45- 60.

Gibson, R. (1997). Confluence of culture and information technology in Thailand. *Proceeding of PACIS1997: Third Pacific Asia Conference on Information Systems, Conference on the Confluence of Theory and Practice,* Gable, G. G. & Weber, R.A.G. (Eds), 725-731.

Goodman, S.E., & Green, J.D. (1992). Computing in the Middle East, *Communications of the ACM*, *35*(8), 21-25.

Gurbaxani, V. (1990). Diffusion in computing network: The case of BITNET. *Communications of the ACM*, *33*(12), 65-75.

Gurbaxani, V., Kraemer, K.L., King, J.L., Jarman, S., Dedrick, J., Raman, K.S. & Yap, C.S. (1990). Government as the driving force toward the information society: National computer policy in Singapore. *Information Society*, 7(2), 155-185. London.

Help for Farmers, Byteline: Information technology Thailand. (1998), *The Nation*. Retrieved from the World Wide Web: http://www.nationamultimedia.com/byteline/byteline/stories/0951/st1.html.

Hopey (1998) *Technology, Basic Skills and Adults' Education: Getting Ready and Moving Forward.* Columbus, OH: Eric Clearinghouse on adult, career and vocational education center on education.

Igbaria, M., Zinatelli, N., & Cavaye, A.L.M. (1998). Analysis of information technology success in small firms in New Zealand. *International Journal of Information Management*, *18*(2), 103-119.

IT comes to rural community, Technology. (1998b). *The Nation.* Retrieved from the World Wide Web: http://www.nationamultimedia.com/news/ruraln.et2.html.

Janczewski, L.J. (1992). Factors of information technology implementation. *In under-developed countries: Example of the West African nations, computerization in West Africa. The Global issue of information technology management*. Palvia, S., Palvia, P. & Zigli, R.M. (Eds). Hershey, PA: Idea Group Publishing.

Katz, C, J. & Katz, P.L. (1996). Ask the right questions to ease computer learning. *HR Magazine*, *41*(2), 67-70.

King Mongkut's Institute of Technology, Thonburi (2001). *Thailand's IT-2010: Towards a Knowledge-Based* Society. Retrieved from the World Wide Web: http://www.nitc.go.th/seminar/it-2010.

Kirton, M. (1976). Adaptors and innovators: A description and measure. *Journal of Applied Psychology*, *61*(5), 622-629.

Koanatakool, T. (1998). *National IT Project in Thailand: IT Project into the Future*. National Electronics and Computers Technology Center. Retrieved from the World Wide Web: http://www.nectec.or.th/it-projects/index.html.

Lakhanpal, B. (1994). Assessing the factors related to microcomputer usage by middle manager. *International Journal of Information Management*, *14*, 39-50.

Lang, M. G. (1995). The future of agricultural cooperatives in Canada and the United States: Discussion. *American Journal of Agricultural Economics*, *77*(5), 1162-1165.

Larsen, T.J. (1993). Middle managers' contribution to implementation information technology innovation. *Journal of Management Information Systems*, *10*(2), 155-176.

MacLeod, R.A. & Chiware, E.R.T (1993). Lessons to be learned: Information technology training in a developing country academic library. *Library Management, 14*(6), 24-30.

Mahidol University. (1998). *Agriculture in Thailand.* Retrieved from the World Wide Web: http://www.mahidol.ac.th/Thailand/economy/agricult.html.

Malaiwong, K. (1998a). *The Future of Thai Students on Information Technology During IMF Era.* Bangkok: Multimedia Section, Information Technology Education Division, National Science and Technology Center, National Science and Technology Development Agency, Ministry of Science, Technology and Environment.

Malaiwong, K. (1998b). *The Use of Information Technology for Recovering Economic Crisis in Thailand.* Bangkok: Multimedia Section, Information Technology Education Division, National Science and Technology Center, National Science and Technology Development Agency, Ministry of Science, Technology and Environment.

Malaiwong, K. (1998c). *Thai Government Officers and IT: What the Best Choices.* Bangkok: Multimedia Section, Information Technology Education Division, National Science and Technology Center, National Science and Technology Development Agency, Ministry of Science, Technology and Environment.

Mansell, R. & Jenkins, M. (1992). Networks, industrial restructuring and policy: The Singapore example. *Technovation*, 12(6), 397-406.

McMurrer, D. P. & Van Buren, M.E. (1999). The Japanese training scene. *Training & Development, 53*(8), 42-46.

Messmer, M. (1999). The growing role of technology. *Management Accounting, 81*(6), 10-12.

The Ministry of Thai Agriculture and Cooperative. (1998). *The Study of the Satisfactions of Thai Agricultural Cooperatives on Activities from the Department of Auditing, the Ministry of Thai Agriculture and Cooperative.*

Nashima, M. (1996). Agricultural financial institutions face much-needed overhaul. *Japan Times Weekly International Edition, 36*(12), 10-11.

National Institute of development Administration, Thailand (1997). *The Study on the Use of Information Technology in Thailand.*

Nature (1996). Late developers log on. *Nature,* 380, 379-380.

Navarat, N. (2000). Why Thailand is not a developed country. *Thairat Newspaper.* May.

Odedra, M., Lawrie, M, Bennett, M., & Goodman, S. (1998). *Information Technology in Sub-Saharan.* International Perspective, CACM. Retrieved from the World Wide Web: http://cygnus.sas.upenn.edu/African_Studies/Comp_Articles/Information_Technology_11712.html.

Office of Agricultural Economics (1992). *Agriculture in Thailand: A Commemorian Edition on the Occasion of The Centennial Anniversary 1 April 1992*.

Oliver Coeur de Roy (1997). The African challenge: Internet, networking and connectivity activities in a developing environment. *Third World Quarterly,* 18(5), 883-898. London.

Öhlmér, B. (1992). Effects of information technology on the data need in farm management. *Swedish Journal of Agricultural Research*, 22(4), 181-188.

Peszynski, K.J. & Thanasankit. T. (2002). Exploring trust B2C e-commerce: An exploratory study of Mäori culture in New Zealand. *School Working Papers Series 2002*, School of Management Information Systems, Deakin University. Retrieved from the World Wide Web: http://www.deakin.edu.au/mis/research/working paper.htm.

Poon, S. & Swatman, P. (1995). *The Internet for Small Businesses: An Enabling Infrastructure for Competitiveness*. Retrieved from the World Wide Web: http://inet.nttam.com.

Potiattanakorn, S. (1997). *Crisis Costs Retailers "10 years delay"*. Retrieved from the World Wide Web: http://203.146.51/nationnews/1997/199709/19970930/17438.html.

Primozic, K., Primozic, E. & Leban, J. (1991). *Strategic Choices: Supremacy, Survival or Sayonara*. New York: McGraw-Hill.

Randall E.T. Bruce J.R., & Thomas W.G. (1997). Evolution of cooperative thought, theory and purpose. Paper presented at the Conference on Cooperatives. *Cooperatives: Their Importance in the Future of the Food and Agricultural System.* Food and Agricultural Marketing Consortium, Las Vegas.

Raymond, L. (1990). Organizational context and information systems success: A contingency approach. *Journal of Management Information Systems, 6*(4), 5-20. Idea Group Publishing, Hershey, PA.

Rodriguez, K. (1994). Barriers to information technology in Latin America and the Caribbean: Some option. *The Electronic Library, 12*(1), 29-35.

Rogers, E.M. (1983). *Diffusion of Innovation* (3rd Ed.). New York: The Free Press.

Rogers, E.M. (1995). *Diffusion of Innovation* (4th Ed.). New York: The Free Press.

Sanchez-Vegas, S. (1995). David meets Goliath on the information superhighway: Venezuela in the Electronic Communication Networks. *Information Technology and Libraries*, 1, 32-35.

Sataporn, P. (1996). *Cooperative Managements.* Bangkok: Odeon Store Pub.

Sawatanon, P. (1996). *Cooperative Economics*. Bangkok: Chulalongkon University.

Seyal, A.H.; Rahim, Md., M.; & Rahman, M.N. (2000). An empirical investigation of use of information technology among small and medium business organizations: A Bruneian scenario. *The Electronic Journal on Information Systems in Developing Countries*, 2, 1-16.

Sirimance, S. (1998). *The Information Technology Revolution: What about the Developing Countries*, International Development Information Center. Retrieved from the World Wide Web: http://www.acdi-cida.gc.ca/xpress/dex/dex9604htm.

Somjee, A. H. (1996). Who shares? Co-operatives and rural development. *Pacific Affairs*, 69(4), 558-559.

Sutharoj, P. (1998). Govt sector fails to spend enough on IT projects. *The Nation*. Retrieved from the World Wide Web: http://www.nationmultimedia. com/byteline/stories/0915/st6.html.

Sutharoj, P., & Boonnoon, J. (1998). Local IT industry to shrink with economic crisis. *The Nation*. Retrieved from the World Wide Web: http://203.146.51.4/nationnews/1998/199801/ 19980127/21335.html.

Tapsawat, N. (1999). *The Analysis of the Problems in Thai Society*. Bangkok: Thamasat University.

Tenenbaum, D. (1996). Entrepreneurship with a social conscience. *Technology Review*, *99*(4), 18-19.

Terdudomtham, T. (1998). The bubble finally burst: Economic review year end 1997, *Bangkok Post*. Retrieved from the World Wide Web: http://www.bangkokpost.net/ecoreview97/ review9701.html.

Thailand Development Research Institute Foundation (1994). *The Possibility of Information Technology Human Resources Development in Thailand.*

Thailand Development Research Institute Foundation (1996). *The Analysis of the Feasibility of Information Technology Improvement in the Royal Thai Government.*

Thanasankit, T. (1999). *Exploring Social Aspects of Requirements Engineering - An Ethnographic Study of Thai Systems Analysis*. PhD thesis. The University of Melbourne.

Thanasankit, T. & Corbitt, B.J. (1999). Cultural context and its impact on requirements elicitation in Thailand. *Electronic Journal on Information Systems in Developing Countries, 1*(1).

Thong, J.Y.L. (1996). *Information Systems Adoption and Implementation in Small Businesses in Singapore*, Ph.D. thesis, National University of Singapore.

Thong, J.Y.L. (1999). An integrated model of information systems adoption in small businesses. *Journal of Management Information Systems, 15*(4), 187-214.

Thong, J.Y.L., & Yap, C.S. (1995). CEO characteristics, organizational characteristics and information technology adoption in small business. *Omega-International Journal of Management Science, 23*(4), 429-442.

Tobin, D.R. (1998). Networking your knowledge. *Management Review, 87*(4), 46-48.

Turner, B. (2000). *The Statesman's Yearbook: The Politics, Cultures and Economies of the World* (136th ed.). London: Macmillan.

United States Department of Agriculture, Rural Business- Cooperative Service. (1990). *Cooperative Benefits and Limitations: Farmers Cooperatives in United States*, Cooperatives information report 1 section3. University of Wisconsin Center for Cooperatives. Retrieved from the World Wide Web: http://www.wisc.edu/uwcc/index.html.

Watson, R. & Myers, M.D. (2000). A comparison of IT industry success in Finland and New Zealand. *Proceeding of PACIS2000: Fourth Pacific Asia Conference on Information Systems, Conference on Electronic Commerce and Web-Based Information Systems. Hong Kong*, Thong. J. (Ed.), 414-427.

What Thailand Needs to Survive (1997). *The National Science and Technology Development Agency*. Retrieved from the World Wide Web: http://www.nstda.or.th/newsroom/pr/pr241097a.html.

Wierenga, B. & Ophuis, P.A.M.O. (1997). Marketing decision supported systems: Adoption, use, and satisfaction. *International Journal of Research Marketing, 14*, 275-290.

Wilson, L. (1997). Tops at training. *Computerworld, 31*(13), 100-103.

Woodall, J. (1997). *Total Quality in Information System and Technology*. St Lucie Press: Delray Beach.

The World Bank Group. (2000). *Development Data: Classification of Economies*. Retrieved from the World Wide Web: http://www.worldbank.org/data/databytopic/class.htm.

Yap, C.S. (1986). *Information Technology in Organizations in the Service Sector,* Ph.D. thesis, The University of Cambridge.

Yap, C.S. (1990). Distinguishing characteristics of organizations using computers. *Information & Management, 18*(97), 97-107.

Yap, C.S., Thong, J.Y.L. & Raman, K.S. (1994). Effect of government incentive on computerization in small business. *European Journal of Information Systems, 3*(3), 191-206.

Chapter III

The Implementation of Electronic Commerce in SMEs in Singapore

Wei-Chang Kong
The University of Melbourne, Australia

ABSTRACT

This chapter aims to understand the reasons for adoption or non-adoption of Electronic Commerce in Singaporean SMEs as well as explain the importance of issues affecting adoption. The Singapore Government has consistently focused on promoting informatization and information industry development as a key thrust in the economic development strategy of the island economy (IMCM, 1998). This chapter, in using a qualitative research method and in-depth interviews with five SME participants, identifies both the success factors that encourage adoption of Electronic Commerce and barriers to/against adoption in Singapore. In conclusion, this study shows that the aforementioned factors are inherently linked with the policy process.

INTRODUCTION

This chapter analyzes why small to medium enterprises (SMEs) in Singapore have or have not adopted electronic commerce, and explains issues affecting its adoption. In recent years, the Singapore government has spearheaded the implementation of e-commerce in Singapore. SMEs still have not heeded the government's call. In a survey conducted by AC Nielsen, commissioned by the National

Computer Board of Singapore, it was found that of 13 percent of 1,500 randomly selected adults, only 6 percent made a purchase using the Internet (NCB, 1998). The reasons for Singapore's SMEs' uniform and widespread unwillingness to adopt e-commerce despite the government's push, are still largely unknown. Research published on the Singapore Government's e-commerce web site (http://www.ec.gov.sg) (also Singapore 2000, 1998a, b), has information only on surveys showing that Internet users are still rather unsure of e-commerce, especially towards Internet commerce. What is required is information from the SME's viewpoint. Already certain "seminal" advantages exist in adopting e-commerce, such as: cost savings, improved productivity and streamlined business processes. This research will obtain relevant information from selected SMEs in Singapore, to better understand issues that have led to the current e-commerce situation in Singapore.

The Singaporean Government has consistently focused on promoting informatization and information industry development in the economic development strategy of the island economy (IMCM, 1998). Among developing countries, Singapore has achieved one of the highest rates of diffusion of information technology (Wong, 1996; Wong 1998; Corbitt & Thanasankit, 2002). Singapore has also been regularly rated as maintaining among the best telecommunications infrastructure in the world, according to the annual World Competitiveness Report (International Institute for Management Development, 1996).

The "electric commercialization" of Singapore started in 1996 with the National Computer Board (NCB) and with the e-commerce Hotbed Program (ECH) to jumpstart the pervasive use of e-commerce and position Singapore as a hub for e-commerce. An e-commerce committee established six guiding principles to promote e-commerce in Singapore:

- The private sector should take the lead
- Government should create a framework that provides certainty and reliability
- Government should provide a secure and safe environment
- Joint venture pilots and experiments between Government and the private sector are needed to expedite e-commerce growth and development
- Innovative, transparent and liberal policies should be proactively pursued by Government
- Consistency with international regimes, international cooperation and interoperability are necessary for e-commerce to thrive (National Computer Board, 1998)

The borderless nature of e-commerce and the unique characteristics of the Internet meant that there had to be proper legal, regulatory and enforcement procedures in place to complement the above six principles. An Electronic Transactions Bill (1998) ensured that a commercial code is in place to support e-commerce transactions. This Act also empowers the public sector to accept electronic filing and provides for public key infrastructures using certification authorities. Besides enforcing the rule of law, the Act protects the interests of network providers, in that it does not hold liable an Internet Service Provider for third party content outside his or her control. Due to the increased use of networks and computer systems to engage in such transactions, the Computer Misuse Act (1998) has been updated and intellectual property laws reviewed (e-commerce Policy Committee, 1998).

Infrastructure services for e-commerce are essential for cyber traders, merchants and buyers; thus, several secure on-line services are currently spearheaded by the National Computer Board under the e-commerce Hotbed Program and Singapore ONE to provide the industry with a host of e-commerce enabling services. Examples of such include electronic payment services, electronic supporting services, technical standards, developing logistical support for e-commerce activities locally and internationally, and enhancing overseas linkages (e-commerce Policy Committee, 1998). Singapore ONE is a nationally initiated high speed network that delivers a new level of interactive, multimedia applications and services to homes, businesses and schools throughout Singapore (1-Net, 1998).

The government also has a vision of Singapore becoming the hub for international e-commerce (Corbitt, 1999; Corbitt & Thanasankit, 2002). The Singapore government is also spearheading the implementation of e-commerce with the use of various grants and incentives, such as the LECP (EC) funding program, for Small and Medium Enterprises (SME). This program scheme offers financial incentives of up to S$20,000 for SMEs to adopt e-commerce.

THE ADOPTION OF E-COMMERCE

This exploratory study is concerned with understanding the impact of the Singapore Government's policy on adoption of e-commerce by SMEs in Singapore. Such policy process, it is argued, reflects underlying ideologies and values (Kogan, 1975) that direct and dictate decision-making. Concepts such as power, control, legitimacy, privilege, justice and equity affect the perceptions and ideological judgments underpinning the policy and perceptions of its meanings to those who the policy is directed at. Thus, the policy process cannot be divorced from the economic and political ideologies, conflicts and interests which are an integral part of it (Corbitt, 1999). Understanding the nature of political action in policy becomes crucial because the political sphere has the resources to make policy development and implementation more successful (Corbitt, 1999:3). Factors such as fear of redundancy, fear of challenging an existing record, the 'vested interests' of bureaucrats, routine, uncertainty, and the organizational costs of change have a dramatic effect on what is intended in the solution of a policy problem.

Implementation takes place in a fluid setting. Implementation problems are never "solved." Rather, they evolve through a multi-staged (McLaughlin, 1987), iterative process (Corbitt, 1997). Analyses of policy implementation problems occur at both the macro and micro levels. According to McLaughlin (1987:178), the former operates at the level of the system, stressing regularities of process and organizational structures as stable outlines of the policy process and frame individual action in terms of position in a relational network; while the latter provides limited guidance to policymakers faced with system-wide decisions. This review of implementation literature will suggest the importance of having a well-rounded implementation policy, which invariably determines the success factors that encourage e-commerce adoption, or the barriers against adoption. Concepts derived from an understanding of the social, political and economic context of policy can assist the researcher in better understanding how reality is created in society, and how it is sustained.

McLaughlin (1987) claims that implementation success depends critically on two broad factors: local capacity and will. However, there are other factors that play an important role in ensuring success. Belief may also be nurtured from action. For example, if interested merchants receive grants or incentives from the Singapore Government to set up e-commerce facilities, and they can see for themselves that it is business as usual even with this new method of trading; then they might be convinced or develop a belief that e-commerce works. Even motivation or will is influenced by factors beyond the reach of implementation: environmental stability, competing centers of authority, contending priorities or pressures and other aspects of the social-political milieu can influence implementor willingness profoundly (Yin, 1981).

Experience (McLaughlin, 1987) has proven that successful implementation generally requires a combination and balance of pressure and support. Pressure by itself may be insufficient when policy objectives contain their own implementation directions (Corbitt, 1997). Pressure per se cannot effect those changes in attitudes, beliefs and routine practices typically assumed by reform policies. Furthermore, support is a limited strategy due to competing priorities and demands that operate with the implementing system. Moreover, vague mandates and weak guidelines provide opportunity for dominant coalitions or competing issues to shape program choices. Balance is needed because pressure is required to focus attention on a reform objective while support is needed to enable implementation. In settings where there is uneven consensus about the merit of a policy or where policy aims at weak beneficiaries, pressure can provide necessary legitimacy for program officials. Policy effects are indirect, operating through and within the existing setting.

Corbitt (1997) undertook a case study of the implementation, which focused on the struggle for control and power, at the micro-political level, within the implementation process. An analysis of that implementation process showed that at certain times the power of the state was crucial and central, yet, at other times the power of the state was decentred and significantly reduced, with power and control of policy being refocused at the institutional/organizational level. Ball (1990) argues that implementation breakdown results from the effects of influence, pressure, dogma, expediency, conflict compromise, intransigence, resistance, error, opposition and pragmatism. Communication of ideologies and arguments can be deliberately distorted by misinformation to influence process and gain power (Forester, 1989). Furthermore, Corbitt's research study highlighted the iterative nature of conflict about the relative importance of one policy versus another. This brought about action by the state to alter the organizations' activities by bureaucratic and authoritarian action (Corbitt, 1997).

Implementation and development is essentially political and non-rational (Self, 1981). It is influenced by pluralistic inequality associated with sectional interests, power and factions. The realities of influence, political dogma, sectional interests, conflicts, factionalism, pragmatism, self-preservation, financial constraints, errors and misinterpretations all create a complexity in the policy process that denies simplification and generalization.

Therefore, we would suggest that the success of implementation depends on the balance of power between the parties' involved. The authority responsible for e-commerce implementations in Singapore, the government (state) and other stakeholders have to strike an agreement with each other and with certain parties charged with well-defined roles, and an agreement to abide by the rules and regulations. This is because the implementation process is influenced by, and influences, human behavior. Individuals can subvert and/or avoid attempts at regulation. Unintended, unanticipated or unacknowledged consequences often result from human behavior within policy (Wallace, 1991).

The failure of information systems implementation has been linked with the absence of an IS champion or change agent, lack of management support (Ginzberg, 1981; Kydd, 1989; Corbitt, 2000), strain on already restricted managerial time (Cragg & King, 1983), poor attitudes towards information systems (Corbitt, 1997), absence of education and training (Cragg & King, 1983), organizational problems (Markus, 1984), technical problems (Cragg & King, 1983), and perceived gaps between expectations of IS supporters and those expected to use the system (Nichols, 1981; Kydd, 1989). On the other hand, research has shown that success in implementing IS in business organizations is more common than failure (Kydd, 1989).

Success in implementing intraorganizational information systems is attributable to a number of success factors (Grohowski & McGoff, 1990), such as, organizational commitment, the existence of an executive sponsor within the organization (Raymond, 1985), the existence of an operating sponsor within the organization to provide quick feedback across the organization (Montazemi, 1988) and the existence of dedicated facilities within the organization. Furthermore, software and hardware support by suppliers and frequent access to software and hardware developed by users, fast iteration of software changes throughout the organization, the existence of training, outputs from the new system meeting managerial expectations, and a positive evaluation of the costs and benefits of the information process being used can assist in attaining success. Cragg and King (1993) suggest that the implementation of IT in small businesses occurs most successfully where there is demonstrated relative advantage in terms of time saved, benefits accrued or discomfort decreased, and where competitive pressure could be addressed as IT was seen as an enabling technology that could make the firm flexible and profitable.

Corbitt (2000) suggests that there are two types of influences, internal and external, which may be out of the control of an organization, in identifying the barriers to both development of an e-commerce strategy, and its adoption and implementation. Furthermore, uncertainty about what e-commerce was and how it could help was a contributing factor. Misguided conceptions that e-commerce would deliver efficiencies, reduce costs, and improve service delivery all at the same time, was another mistake. Lastly, expectations of senior management perceived as being economically rationalist, quality driven, rather than effectiveness, was another negative force. Parr, Shanks and Darke (1999) and Duchessi, Schaninger and Hobbs (1989) support this central importance of the role of management.

In another study, Corbitt (1997) suggests that two common issues indicate the success or motivating factors, and those factors which appear to inhibit the implementation of, in this case, e-commerce in business organizations. These two themes are uncertainty and equivocality. Uncertainty refers to the absence of information and equivocality refers to the existence of ambiguity and the existence of multiple, conflicting interpretations about a given organizational situation (Kydd, 1989). The resolution of uncertainty depends on knowledge and information as this equips the manager or potential user of an e-commerce form with the power to deal with and or understand that process. Equivocality suggests that some state of confusion exists and that as a result, solutions require discussion and debate suggesting "social interaction so that intuition, judgement, and beliefs can contribute to the enactment of a shared interpretation" (Kydd, 1989). Daft and Lengel (1986) suggest that the interaction of equivocality and uncertainty in organizations can provide a useful model to understand the important role of information in the adoption and implementation of IT.

Corbitt, Behrendorff and Brown-Parker (1997) suggest that motivators are essentially addressed by demonstrated relative advantage in terms of time saved, benefits accrued or discomfort decrease, and where competitive pressure could be addressed by IT, which is seen as enabling technology that makes the firm flexible and profitable. Cragg and King (1993) further suggest that the owner should be enthusiastic towards the technology. Poon and Swatman (1999) suggest that it is possible that governments perceive global competitive pressure and are using Internet commerce "as enabling technology" to make their economies "flexible and profitable." On the other hand, in addressing the inhibitors, knowledge and information must be existent to managers and potential users. This knowledge and information equips them with the power to deal with and understand organizational processes, discussion and debate. Thus intuition, judgement and beliefs can contribute to the enactment of a shared interpretation, eliminating equivocality.

Adopter and driving factors can be identified under a number of categories. Internal influences are those which occur within the organization, and exist in the form of misguided conceptions, lack of knowledge, and even political motives. The latter influence originates from outside the organization, and sometimes they are uncontrollable. In order to move a step forward, as much uncertainty and equivocality should be resolved within the organization. One way is to demonstrate the advantages and benefits gained, addressing the motivating factors. Most importantly, both government policy and management action and response play significant and valuable roles in influencing implementation success. They have to be there to provide support, both technical and emotional, to staff in the implementation.

RESEARCH METHODOLOGY

The aim of this study is to develop an enhanced understanding of the factors that affect e-commerce policy adoption in Singapore and attempts to identify apparent shortcomings in government policy. The drawing of implications, concepts and themes from the resultant data requires a philosophical and qualitative perspective.

Qualitative research is used to answer questions about the nature of phenomena with the purpose of describing and understanding the phenomena from the participant's point-of-view (Leedy, 1997:104). Qualitative research studies may be done via various methods including the case study. Orlikowski & Baroudi

(1991), Benbasat et al. (1987), and Myers (1997) argue that this method is particularly appropriate for the study of information systems development, implementation and use within organizations. Case study research can be used in various ways from within different research perspectives using a variety of data collection and analysis methods, producing diverse types of research outcomes (Cavaye, 1996). It should be used where an understanding of interactions between information technology related innovations and organizational contexts is needed. Darke, Shanks and Broadbent (1997) argue that case study research can be used to provide descriptions of phenomena, develop theory and test theory. Furthermore, case study research has frequently been related to description and with theory development, where it is used in the justification and substantiation process of hypothesis generation and for exploration of areas where existing knowledge is limited (Cavaye, 1996).

Yin (1994:13) defines case studies as "an empirical enquiry that investigates a contemporary phenomenon within its real–life context, especially when the boundaries between phenomenon and context are not clearly evident." Case studies are especially effective for studying the subtle nuances of attitudes and behaviors, and for examining social processes over time. Thus, the chief strength of this method lies in the depth of understanding that it may permit. Its flexibility means that the research can be modified at any time. Case studies are appropriate for studying topics where attitudes and behaviors can best be understood within their setting. It is especially appropriate for studying social processes over time (Babbie, 1979:206).

Interpretivist researchers tend to see the world as an emergent social process which is created by the individuals concerned. Social reality, insofar as it is recognized to have any existence outside the consciousness of any single individual, is regarded as being little more than a network of assumptions and inter-subjectively shared meanings. The ontological status of the social world is viewed as extremely questionable and problematic as far as theorists located within the interpretive paradigm are concerned. Such philosophers and sociologists seek to understand the very basis and source of social reality. They often delve into the depths of human consciousness and subjectivity in their quest for the fundamental meanings which underlie social life (Burrell & Morgan, 1985:28-31). Since this study is contextual in nature, an interpretivist approach is appropriate here. Such data collection requires the development of textual data and in this study that was collected by interview.

Informal, partially-structured interviews were conducted with five SME CEOs in the development and implementation of this study. These included executives who were involved directly or indirectly with the implementation of information technology and/or strategic planning services in the company. According to Walsham (1993), limited numbers of observations may not inhibit one in generalizing the findings. Furthermore, large amounts of generalization do not necessarily lead to *more meaningful* generalizations. Generalization from individual or many cases does not necessarily depend on statistical validity, but the plausibility and cogency of logical reasoning used in describing and drawing conclusions from them (Walsham, 1993). Three criteria were used to assist in the selection of potential participants in this research: size, designation, organization type and industry.

The interviews were taped, then transcribed and handed back to the respective respondents for confirmation. Upon receiving confirmation, a matrix was developed to enable both within and across case analyses. This form of data analysis enables the researcher to seek out and verify themes within text. This study used a reiterative analytical technique of taking the literature review and applying it to the data collected. From such a hermeneutic analysis of text (Lee, 1994) meaning and interpretations were derived until conclusions or theorizing suggests further reinterpretation.

Although the companies being researched are SMEs, such companies vary in size. It was decided to select managers of organizations that were of varied sizes, as each organization had different levels of spending power and personnel with different qualification levels. For instance, TelYP was a subsidiary of a government-linked corporation, while Malleables was seen to be a more traditionally run, family-based company. It was decided that one company each from the manufacturing, trading, telecommunications, farming and transport industries was to be chosen. Different organization types were chosen so that varied opinions could be sought from as many industries as possible to gain increased understanding on a nationwide scale and not on an industry-specific scale. No firm conclusion is presented as the sample is too small to make any such propositons. However, the data suggests some trends that will frame a further study of a large sample of SMEs in Singapore.

RESEARCH FINDINGS

Electronic Commerce and Inhibitors and Adopters for SMEs

Two of the companies in this study have adopted B2C e-commerce. In Busco's[2] case, external influences affecting the adoption included the Internet's increasing popularity and the rising number of Internet users. As the number of users increase, with the popularization of the Internet, it creates a demand for B2C services. Within the organization, management perceived it as a form of productivity gain – a benefit. To the customer, Busco's model of B2C, was a conduit for faster feedback and allowed the company to offer special services to the registered customer, thus promoting the notion of customer service.

> *I think the Internet is getting popular. There are more and more such Internet users in Singapore. It's growing. It is also one of the ways where the consumer is able to... where we can look at some form of productivity gain over at our site. Today we have to employ customer service agents to key in the information. If we are able to do a full B2C transaction, then we can do away with some workload at the back-end, at the control centre (operations). So this is one of the benefits that we are looking at. Of course, the Internet provides the opportunity for us to get quicker feedback from the customer. (Mr. Tan, Busco Holdings Pte, Ltd.)*

> *...with the account number, we can track more closely, in terms of the usage. We are also thinking of personalizing the service, in one of the earlier plans that we had. Once the person has registered, we can go to the extent to offering him some extra services. Maybe on his birthday we can offer discounts, [or] things like this. (Mr. Tan, Busco Holdings Pte, Ltd.)*

In TelYP's case, adoption was focused more towards the external situation in Singapore, where Singaporeans have to be educated on when and how to use e-commerce for trading via Business-to-consumer (B2C) or Business-to-business (B2B). Mr. Han suggested that this was because of the current attitudes and consumer behavior of Singaporeans and their attitude towards e-commerce. Mr. Han said that research had discovered that the ages of online shoppers in Singapore were between 18 – 30+. According to Mr. Han, he attributes that as acquiescence with a fad or new lifestyle. This is important because when people regard e-commerce as a fad or lifestyle change, it is a sign that e-commerce may be more accepted/adopted amongst other people, as it is human nature to be fashionable. For example, local banks, such as the Development Bank of Singapore (DBS) are taking the initiative by setting up clearinghouses (IBEXCo, http://www.ibexco.com) for B2B e-commerce transactions. They are offering to place selected customers on the Internet because they realize that Singaporeans trust banks. At the same time, merchants have to be convinced that there is profit to be made and the need to build up a pro-e-commerce culture among Singaporeans. This has to be done using certain merchants offering free delivery to customer's homes so customers can see the benefits of purchasing via B2C e-commerce. This view was expressed by Mr. Han of TelYP Pte, Ltd. Notwithstanding that, the good name of the merchant enhances the building up process. 'Pure play' merchants help foster a culture from the inherent flexibility in their business.

Mr. Han also suggested that Singapore's financial, transportation and communication infrastructures can be exploited to attract overseas buyers and gain their trust. Mr. Han argued that the government may also extend 'double taxation'[3] to companies who advertise on approved web sites.

The literature on adopters focuses on organizational aspects. Many of the factors identified in that literature do not apply to two of the cases studied, Busco and TelYP. For instance, there was little or no mention of an operating sponsor within the organization providing quick feedback across the organization, the existence of dedicated facilities within the organization or the existence of training. This is an area where further research is needed. Instead, Busco's willingness to adopt e-commerce was evident through demonstrated relative advantages. For example, productivity gain (time saved) and other benefits accrued, such as an enabling technology, making the firm more flexible and profitable.

> *In fact for our business, if you strictly look at public transport alone, then I would (say) things that is important is that we can provide real-time information for our passengers, where they are able to get up-to-date information regarding our services. (Mr. Tan, Busco Holdings Pte, Ltd.)*

Similarly, TelYP's experience shows that training must be in existence. A positive evaluation on the costs and benefits will encourage more adopters. Again, there must be demonstrated relative advantages such as time-saving and discomfort decrease. An example of discomfort decrease is the merchant's ability to help organize the customer's life as seen in the quote below:

> *So I think in terms of usage wise, the merchants themselves as well as the intermediary bodies, like us, who are half pure play and half, in terms (are) retailers, media owners at the same time, we have to promote. Promotion wise, you inculcate, drum in them the habit of using (e-commerce). (Mr. Han, TelYP Pte, Ltd.)*

However, from the information gathered from the interviewees, it is apparent that the government has covered much of the initiation process in terms of legislation and the establishment of a safe and conducive environment. The government can play a role in this by advocating the convenience and security of using the Internet to purchase certain government services, while merchants may need to advertise on the print and television media that same convenience and security provided in using the Internet to purchase or sell goods of interest. Such problems in changing the mindsets were mentioned by Mr. Han.

> *So in a nutshell, basically as we move from print to electronic modes, we will find that there's actually in our culture here, the problem of trying to get the people who are print-oriented to the electronic orientation; that's one of the challenges and issues we face. (Mr. Han, TelYP Pte, Ltd.)*

Non-adopters had similar responses. Again, management had to perceive a need, a demonstrable advantage, before the adoption process could begin. Pontif Industrial Products and Grand Lakes Fisheries have decided to focus on the customer relations, if they adopted e-commerce.

> *I would say more on our, not so much on our supply chain side but more on our customer side. An online inventory checking, so we'll just link up inventory systems, and pricing. Lots of times, customers call up just to request for price, things like that. So, it'll be good, if, let's say customers can just come in through the Net, check out the latest pricing, log in their order, check on availability, that would save on a lot of our paper work also. (Mr. Lim, Pontif Industrial Products Pte, Ltd.)*

> *Eventually, you have to provide very good service by giving them a lot of information, and that can be done through the Net. A lot of business transactions, you can get it done through the Net to save cost and time. So the speed of transaction is very fast, you definitely have to keep this in mind. In the next millennium, there is going to be a change in how we do business and I don't consider myself as trader, but of things is we buy in things, we add value and then we sell. In order to give our customers better service – more information – we just have to go into the Net and create some things for them to rely on our service. That's more immediate because they can see and they can place orders. The most important thing, once they are*

used to your system, you can actually lock in a customer. For them to move to another supplier with a similar level of service, it's quite difficult. Most probably, they will stick with you. (Mr. Yeap, Grand Lakes Fisheries Pte, Ltd.)

An interesting response from both SME managers was that they felt B2C e-commerce will be successful if they were engaged in selling merchandise to end-users or that if the merchandise was 'dead.' The latter merchandise refers to goods where value need not be added to them before being sold to the end-consumer, for example, paper cups. The manufacturer or merchant can conduct a direct sale to the customer, without having to go through an intermediary in the supply chain. Cost savings and time saved in transacting business were mentioned as demonstrable advantages by Mr. Yeap.

Barriers to the adoption of B2B e-commerce were mainly attributed to the lack of business partners and other companies taking it up, and also the current attitudes and confidence levels of Singaporeans towards e-commerce. This is evident in B2C e-commerce where, although the number of credit card owners is quite high, not many people see the benefits of using them as a mode of payment for e-commerce.

Although the number of people having credit cards is, I'm not too sure if I'm right, quite high in Singapore, but this mode of payment over the Internet is not something that is common, here. So if you're talking about performing a transaction over the Internet, then consumer behavior and the confidence level of these people using some of these payment modes must be there. (Mr. Tan, Busco Holdings Pte, Ltd.)

Busco decided to put current resources into the upgrading of present information technology systems. This served as a temporary barrier. While the adopters saw a need, the non-adopters perceived none. Loss of business flexibility in terms of trading with specific customers was another major factor.

...although you can have password, dealer planning, but then again, certain things are sensitive and there are cases that you know, (we) have to give different prices to different customers and it's not a straight forward case. You know some customers get bulk discounts, things like that, so it's not nice for the customer to know... (Mr. Lim, Pontif Industrial Products Pte, Ltd.)

Many still prefer the traditional way of putting in an order. This was attributed to a 'fear of change' mentality. The current legal framework is not comprehensive enough to deal with discrepancies in international transactions. Security problems were equally applicable to a corporate and individual user of the Internet.

> *But currently if I (on behalf of my company or myself) were to buy something off the Net, in say, South America, and if the goods don't arrive, there's something wrong, there's nothing I can do about it? Because ... is that the case? That transaction is not being recognized through the Internet. (Mr. Lim, Pontif Industrial Products Pte, Ltd.)*

Lack of technical know-how, an inexpensive infrastructure for SMEs to use, and lack of trained personnel were other important factors. In addition it was said that not all clients can migrate over to the e-commerce market, as their services may not be fit for it at this time.

Peculiar to Mr. Yeap's business are his products—live animal species. These require special precautions to be taken while in transit. His market is mainly outside of Singapore, in Europe. However, certain European countries are still ignorant about the use of the Internet for trade. Even to maintain a B2B connection to the US, an Internet savvy country, is not cost effective for Mr. Yeap. The sluggishness in deregulating the banking industry in Singapore only means that banks are reluctant to introduce products to support merchants interested in e-commerce. Transportation and logistics costs are not a major factor compared to other bigger overseas countries. While merchants hope to increase their level of customer service via e-commerce, a possibility exists that if fish are sold over the Internet, there will be no one to explain how to keep and protect the fish and this would have a detrimental effect. Finally, cultural and language problems exist for certain countries.

> *If each country creates their own Internet based on their own language, then you still face a cultural problem, a cross-cultural problem. So you cannot say the border will not disappear. (Mr. Yeap, Grand Lakes Fisheries Pte, Ltd.)*

These issues in themselves raise questions of uncertainty for the merchants undertaking e-commerce and result in them being equivocal about whether e-commerce is really an effective business tool for them.

Electronic Commerce Policy Adoption – Uncertainty and Equivocality

Policy implementation has been subject to many interpretations. We have argued in this chapter that policy does not have a fixed "beginning" and "end," and that it is not a straight-forward linear process (Stroeken & Coumans, 1998). Instead where appropriate, organizations may skip certain stages, highlighting the inappropriateness of linear thinking (Woolgar, 1998). Moreover, empirical studies have shown that failure in policy adoption was discovered in the initiation, diffusion or control stages of the process. From the case studies, it was apparent that the initiation process by the government had created sufficient foundations. Despite this, SMEs are still ambivalent about adopting e-commerce and this implies that the diffusion process was deficient. In addition, the government has no idea how to overcome this inertia from the private sector and so implies that the control process is also deficient. Since the crux of implementation failure, in this case, lies in the diffusion process, it only substantiates the fact that that stage is non-linear and it is continually iterative.

Both uncertainty and equivocality were evident where the Singapore Government favored research and development projects and required companies to employ external consultants. Thus, while the government is encouraging SMEs to adopt e-commerce, the SMEs find that accepting the policy comes with numerous terms and conditions, which are not favorable to the latter. Moreover, the government cannot expect merchants to adopt e-commerce when other merchants and consumers have not. As such, the policy process did not allow local capacity to be easily built-up within the organization and this affected the organization's willingness to adopt. Equivocality is evident because SMEs are faced with conflicting interpretations about government policy.

> *Oh yes, (the) Singapore Government is quite proactive in all these areas. There are quite a number of schemes available but some of the schemes have conditions that we have to meet before we can qualify for it. Most of the sponsorship schemes that they have or some of the conditions are meant for projects that are R &D related. This makes it difficult for an organization like us to make use of it, or qualify for it. If you are more in the R &D areas, then your chances of actually getting the grants or qualifying for the scheme is higher. (Mr. Tan, Busco Holdings Pte, Ltd.)*

The lack of confidence and technology mentioned by the SMEs suggests that uncertainty is also evident.

> *...if you are talking about (the) consumer, certain kinds of services that we are going to provide over the Internet, it also depends on the confidence level of the people, and also the technology available. (Mr. Tan, Busco Holdings Pte, Ltd.)*

The study has also shown that the apparent lack of immediate success of policy implementation is related to the effects of influence, pressure, and dogma on the part of government, and resistance and opposition from the SMEs. Financial constraints within SMEs was another reality which apparently affected adoption. Process innovation or product innovation, such as the suggestion of a cost-effective e-commerce infrastructure for SMEs to use, may improve the likelihood of adoption. Mr. Yeap suggests:

> *But I myself cannot live in a world they (the government) are thinking about, my customers also have to do that... Unless you provide them with a good solution as to how to transact over that and also respective countries, the setting up of this kind of infrastructure, it's cheap enough for them to jump in; or else it takes a lot of time to persuade them. (Mr. Yeap, Grand Lakes Fisheries Pte, Ltd.)*

The slowness in policy implementation can be attributed to a mixture of internal and external influences. For instance, internal influences were evident in that people had various expectations, sometimes preconceived, of what e-commerce may or may not deliver. There were other interests within the organization influencing senior management about information direction and limitations within the organization about technological levels of structures and processes. For instance, the information direction within Busco Holdings was evident in their desire to upgrade their current information technology systems first. Mr. Han mentioned that the "acrobatics" behind implementing e-commerce systems created a phobia amongst SMEs, which shows that they have limited technological levels of structures and processes. On the other hand, external influences were evident in the apparently perceived inadequacy of the Electronic Transactions Act 1998 and the lack of understanding of what should be done to counteract the inertia among SMEs. Mr. Lim's expectation that his customer base is not ready for e-commerce and there are indications that e-commerce is not high on his list of priorities seen in the usage of "this e-commerce thing."

Why didn't we adopt that (e-commerce)? Firstly, we don't see any need at this point in time for EC. (The) reason being we do not think our customer base will take on...they're not ready for this e-commerce, to take on this e-commerce thing at the moment. As and when the need arises, we will (be) more than willing to try out the e-commerce thing. (Mr. Lim, Pontif Industrial Products Pte, Ltd.)

Mr. Lim was also concerned that the ETA 1998 is unable to provide sufficient legal recourse in case of disputes or discrepancies with an overseas merchant.

But the government, they want to set up an Act for it, is it within Singapore, the context of Singapore, or global? Because, I know there is no way you can, there's no way to govern the Internet. (Mr. Lim, Pontif Industrial Products Pte, Ltd.)

Another instance of an internal influence was evident in Mr. Tan's company, where current resources had been committed to other projects, thus influencing information direction.

Perhaps, our resources have been put into upgrading our present IT systems. It's not so much impeding factors, but we have other priorities. Perhaps, when we have completed the other project which is so resource-intensive, we can have some resources to look at this in the organization. (Mr. Tan, Busco Holdings Pte, Ltd.)

Mr. Lim was asked to comment on his knowledge of cost of set up: was it factual or was it his impression? His reply signified that he had preconceived expectations about cost.

Author: This issue on cost, is that an impression you have or is it factual information that you have read up on?

Mr. Lim: A bit of both.

There was some divergence from existing theory. This was evident in the responses from the adopters. The reasons given for adoption had little to do with organizational commitment, or with the existence of an executive sponsor within the organization. Instead, the reasons identified tended to relate more towards demonstrable relative advantages, and addressing competitive pressure via information technology.

> *We are also thinking of personalizing the service, in one of the earlier plans that we had. Once the person has registered, we can go to the extent to offering him some extra services. Maybe on his birthday, we can offer discounts, things like this. (Mr. Tan, Busco Holdings Pte, Ltd.)*

> *An online inventory checking, so we'll just link up inventory systems, and pricing. Lots of times, customers call up just to request for price, things like that. So, it'll be good, if, let's say customers can just come in through the Net, check out the latest pricing, log in their order, check on availability, that would save on a lot of our paper work also. (Mr. Lim, Pontif Industrial Products Pte, Ltd.)*

The interviewees suggested that a lack of access to government grants and incentives, could be a reason why there is lack of adoption of e-commerce among SMEs. Although the interviewees acknowledged that the Singapore Government was highly proactive in promoting the adoption of e-commerce, Mr. Tan from Busco Holdings and Mr. Yeap from Grand Lakes Fisheries suggested that certain conditions that their e-commerce projects had to satisfy made it difficult for companies like them to qualify for them due to government's perception of legitimacy, privilege and equity. It is evident from the TelYP web site that many SMEs are quite receptive in using such intermediary services to promote their products and yet the government does not appear to be addressing the needs of this rapidly growing area. In another study Chua, Ng and Tan (1999:44) did not recognize this as a barrier to e-commerce adoption. 'Security of payment' emerged as the number one ranking barrier. This was followed by, in descending order: the 'uncertain future of e-commerce' and the 'lack of expertise' available.

One respondent, Mr. Yeap, expressed concerns about international trading issues. The Electronic Transactions Act (1998) was enacted to put in place the legal framework, which provides for certainty, predictability, and clarity of the rights and obligations of the transacting parties within the domestic arena. However, it fails to address the needs and concerns of international trade done electronically. The security of cross-border transactions is easily compromised without a separate piece of legislation guaranteeing the rights of the overseas merchant and local client. Moreover, both parties have to abide by it, and problems where international law is concerned may need to be addressed first.

CONCLUSION

The barrier factors identified in this study focus on a mixture of technical problems, absence of education or training, organizational problems, poor attitudes towards e-commerce, strain on restricted managerial time, lack of management support, and an absence of an Information Systems champion or change agent. Despite the government's action, e-commerce is still not fully understood within organizations, as is evident when merchants are waiting for the environment to build itself up. This is supported by another study (Chua, Ng & Tan, 1999:46) which showed that most respondents tended to be in the 'neutral' range where there willingness to adopt e-commerce was concerned. This may be attributed to the various expectations people have about what e-commerce may or may not deliver. As Busco had put resources into upgrading their current information technology, it could be seen as other interests within the organization influencing information direction due to the various expectations that Busco's management may have had. The Electronic Transactions Act (1998) appears as if it may not be comprehensive enough to cover disputes in international transactions. Thus, it might be suggested that uncertainty and equivocality about adoption of e-commerce exists within the studied organizations. The government appears to have a lack of understanding about what should be done to counteract the apparent inertia in adopting e-commerce in SMEs. There is a general lack of self-confidence and an unwillingness to move out of a "rural comfort zone" among the management of those SMEs interviewed.

While the Singapore government has been spearheading the implementation of e-commerce with various incentives, there is still a lack of adoption among most SMEs. The analysis in this research suggests that this may be attributed to a deficient diffusion process on the part of government. However, an alternative reason could be the focus on resolution of the Y2K problem among SME companies in Singapore.

The problems identified in this policy process can possibly be attributed to a poor or incomplete diffusion process (Stroeken & Coumans, 1998). Either the Singapore government has failed to reiterate the purpose and benefits of implementing e-commerce within the organization, or factional interests (Self, 1981) within the organization influencing information direction may impact on the diffusion process. Furthermore, other research argues that implementation problems are never "solved," because they evolve through a multi-staged (McLaughlin, 1987), iterative (Corbitt, 1997) process. These case studies report SMEs either beginning or about to begin adoption of e-commerce. The details in the data collected in this study and reports from the National Computer Board (1999) demonstrate that the government's diffusion of propaganda on the benefits e-commerce is evolving through a series of stages and is a continuous process. This process will continue until the SMEs consider it to be a norm.

It can be suggested that the policy process is wrought with underlying ideologies and values (Kogan, 1975), directing and dictating the thrust of decisions. The Singapore Government has adopted deliberative and purposeful policy to meet their stated objective of making Singapore a 'hub' for e-commerce. Within this policy those perceptions of power, control, legitimacy, privilege, justice and equity are established as ideological judgments within the policy. However, acceptance of policy handed down in such form will affect the person(s) to whom the policy is directed. Such judgments made about policy are subjective in their meanings and adoption can be delayed by real concerns, especially when business outcomes can be affected. This was apparent in the interviews with the SME managers who participated in this study.

The study has shown that the policy process cannot be divorced from the economic and political ideologies, conflicts, and interests. Singapore may have achieved one of the highest rates of diffusion of information technology, but it certainly has not achieved high rates of policy diffusion in this area. In fact, the government has not properly addressed the post-diffusion process of control. A possible reason[4*] for the latter is that most organizations in Singapore are concerned in addressing the Year 2000 (Y2K) problem which is plaguing information technology systems. It is not evident what support the government is willing to offer those companies who have accepted the grants. It might be suggested that the government's action in Singapore is a form of over exertion of power and control on the part of government and this undermines the initiation process. The case studies in this research have demonstrated that individuals will seek to subvert the legislation process if government exercises overt power and control over a group(s) of people, supporting previous research by Corbitt (1997) and Ball (1994).

The central concern of this study has been with gaining some understanding of the policy implementation process of the Singapore Government with respect to e-commerce. This study has attempted to uncover some understanding of the associated adopter or inhibitor factors in Singapore SMEs. The study told the story of policy implementation in a nationwide setting from the perspective of the five SME interviewees and survey respondents. The most significant issue to emerge from the study was the amount of proper planning and tenacity involved in the policy process. The Singapore government has left the development of e-commerce largely up to the private sector, with the government constructing the foundations.

ENDNOTES

1 This is a rewritten and updated version of a paper originally presented at the Bled E-commerce Conference in Bled Slovenia, June 2000.

2 These are pseudonyms. Throughout this research project, names of people and the SMEs involved have been given alternative names.

3 To encourage adoption of e-commerce, Mr. Han's suggestion is that the government gives a 'double tax' back to the SME(s) who advertise on approved web sites.

4 Pers. Com Mr. Benji Ng, 21 July 1999.

REFERENCES

1-Net (1998). *Overview: Singapore ONE Defined*, http://www.s-one.gov.sg/html/overview/s1def01.html.

Ball, S. (1990). *Politics and Policy Making in Education*, London, Routledge & Kegan Paul.

Benbasat, I., Goldstein, D.K., & Mead, M. (1987). The case research strategy in studies of information systems, *MIS Quarterly*, Minneapolis, September, 11(3), 369-387.

Burrell, G. & Morgan, G. (1985). *Sociological Paradigms and Organizational Analysis*, Gower Publishing Company Limited.

Cavaye, A.L.M. (1996). Case study research: A multi-faceted research approach for IS, *Information Systems Journal*, 6, 227-242.

Chan, C. & Swatman, P.M.C. (1999). B2B e-Commerce implementation: The case of BHP steel, *Conference Paper*, RMIT University, Melbourne, Australia.

Chua, K.H., Ng, C.H. & Tan, S.M. (1999). Adoption of electronic commerce by the small and medium enterprises for business-to-business dealings, Paper, Nanyang Business School, Nanyang Technological University.

Corbitt, B. (1997). Implementing policy for homeless kids in schools: Reassessing the micro and macro levels in the policy debate in Australia, *Journal of Education Policy*, 12(3), 165-176.

Corbitt, B. (1999). Developing an Intraorganizational Electronic Commerce Strategy – Understanding the Internal and External Demands in Implementing in an Australian Corporate Finance Institution, *Working Paper*, Department of Information Systems, University of Melbourne, Australia.

Corbitt, B. (1999). Exploring the social construction of IT policy – Thailand and Singapore. *Prometheus,* 17(3), 309-321.

Corbitt, B.J. (1997). Uncertainty and Equivocality in the Adoption of Electronic Commerce by SMEs in Australia, *Working Paper*, Department of Information Systems, University of Melbourne.

Corbitt, B.J. (2000). Developing intraorganizational e-Commerce strategy: An ethnographic study, *Journal of Information Technology*, 15, 119-130.

Corbitt, B. & Thanasankit, T. (2002). Acceptance and leadership – Hegemonies of e-Commerce policy perspectives, Prometheus, 20 (1) 39-57.

Corbitt B., Behrendorff, G. & Brown-Parker, J. (1997). SMEs and electronic commerce, *Management*, April, 12-13.

Cragg, P. & King, M. (1983). Small-firm computing: Motivators and inhibitors, *MIS Quarterly*, 17(1), March, 47-60.

Daft, R.L. & Lengel, R.H. (1986). Organizational information requirements, media richness and structural design, *Management Science*, Providence, May 1986, 32(5), 554-572.

Darke, P., Shanks, G., & Broadbent, M. (1997). Successfully Completing Case Study Research: Combining Rigour, Relevance and Pragmatism, *Working Paper*, School of Information Management and Systems, Monash University and Gartner Group Pacific.

DeLone, W.H. (1988). Determinants for success for computer usage in small business, *MIS Quarterly*, 12(1), March, 51-61.

Duchessi, P., Schaninger, C., & Hobbs, D. (1989). Implementing a manufacturing planning and control information system, *California Management Review*, Spring, 75-90.

Electronic Commerce Policy Committee (1998). *Recommendations*, http://www.ec.gov.sg/Sum4_08Apr98.html.

Emmelhainz, M.A. (1992). *EDI: A Total Management Guide*, 1st Ed., International Thomson Computer Press, London.

Forester, J. (1989). *Planning in the Face of Power*, California, University of California Press.

Ginzberg, M.J. (1981). Early diagnosis of MIS implementation failure: Promising results and unanswered questions, *Management Science*, Providence, April, 27(4), 459-477.

Glaser, B.G. & Strauss, A.L. (1967): *The Discovery of Grounded Theory: Strategies for Qualitative Research*, Weidenfeld & Nicholson, London.

Institute for Media & Communications Management, (1998). University of St. Gallen, Switzerland, http://www.electronicmarkets.org/netacademy/publications.nsf/all_pk/194.

International Institute for Management Development. (1996). World *Competitiveness Report*, Lausanne.

Kogan, M. (1975). *Educational Decision Making*, Allen and Unwin, London.

Kong, W. (1998). Electronic Transactions Act 1998 and the National Information Infrastructure – A New Scene for Doing Business in Singapore, *Working Paper*, Department of Information Systems, University of Melbourne.

Kydd, C.T. (1989). Understanding the information content in MIS management too, *MIS Quarterly*, Minneapolis, September, 13(3), 277-381.

Lee, A.S. (1994). Electronic mail as a medium for rich communication: An empirical investigation using hermeneutic interpretation, *MIS Quarterly*, June, 18(2), 143-161.

Leedy, P.D. (1997). *Practical Research Planning and Design*, 6th Edition, Prentice-Hall, Inc.

Mason, R.M. (1997). SME adoption of electronic commerce technologies: implications for the emerging national information infrastructure, *Systems Sciences*, Proceedings of the Thirtieth Hawaii International Conference on Information Systems, 495-504.

McLaughlin, M.W. (1987). Learning from experience: Lessons from policy implementation, *Educational Evaluation and Policy Analysis*, Summer, 9(2), 171 – 178.

Montazemi, A.R. (1988). Factors affecting information satisfaction in the context of the small business environment, *MIS Quarterly*, 12(2), 239-256.

Myers, M.D. (1997). Qualitative research in information systems, *MISQ Discovery* (2), http://www.misq.org/discovery.

National Computer Board. (1998). *Main Guiding Principles*, http://www.ec.gov.sg/Sum3_08Apr98.html.

Organization for Economic Co-operation and Development (1997). *OECD Policy Brief – Electronic Commerce*, http://www.oecd.org/publications/Pol_brief/9701_Pol.html.

Orlikowski, W.J. & Baroudi, J.J. (1991). Studying information technology in organisations: Research approaches and assumptions, *Information Systems Research,* March, 2, 1-28. Cited in Myers, M. D. (1997). Qualitative research in information systems [Online]. Available: http://www.auckland.ac.nz/msis/isworld/ [1997, November 21].

Parr, A.N., Shanks, G. & Darke, P. (1999): Identification of necessary factors for successful implementation of ERP systems, *New Information Technologies in Organizational Processes: Field Studies and Theoretical Reflections on the Future of Work*, Kluwer Academic Publishers, Boston/Dordrecht/London.

Poon, S., & Swatman, P.M.C. (1999). An exploratory study of small business Internet commerce issues., *Information & Management*, January, 35, 9-18.

Raymond, L. (1985). Organizational characteristics and MIS success in the context of small business, *MIS Quarterly*, March, 9(1), 37-52.

Roberts, B. (1995). *Report for BT Supply Management EDI Implementation Review*, http://infosys.king.ac.uk/isschool/staff/b.roberts/edi_implementation_rev.html.

Self, P. (1981). Planning: Rational or political?, In Baehr, P.R. & Wittrock, B. (Eds.) (1981). *Policy Analysis and Policy Innovation: Patterns, Problems and Potentials*, Sage Publications, London, 221-236.

Shanks, G., Rouse, A. & Arnott, D. (1993). *A Review of Approaches to Research and Scholarship in Information Systems*, March, Department of Information Systems, Monash University.

Singapore Government (2000). Singapore Launches Electronic Commerce Master Plan, http://202.42.217.232/masterplan.html/.

Singapore: Electronic Commerce Policy Committee, Recommendations (1998a). At http://www.ec.gov.sg/Sum4_08Apr98.html.

Singapore: National Computer Board, Main Guiding Principles (1998b). At http://www.ec.gov.sg/Sum3_08Apr98.html.

Stroeken, J., Coumans, J. (1998). The actual and potential use of information technology in small and medium sized enterprises, *Prometheus*, 16(4), 469-483.

Teo, T.S.H. Lim, V.K.G. & Lai, R.Y.C. (1997). *Users and Uses of the Internet: The Case of Singapore*, International Journal of Information Management, 17(5), 330-331, Elsevier Science, Ltd.

Wallace, M. (1991). Contradictory interests in policy implementation: The case of LEA development plans for schools, *Journal of Education Policy*, 6(4), 385-399.

Walsham, G. (1993). *Interpreting Information Systems in Organizations*, Wiley, Chichester, UK.

Wong, P.K. (1996). Implementing the NII vision: Singapore's experience and future challenges, *Information Infrastructure and Policy*, 5(2) 1996, 95-117.

Woolgar, S. (1998). A new theory of innovation? *Prometheus*, 16(4), 441-452.

Yin, R. (1981). Life histories of innovations: How new practices become routinized, *Public Administration Review*, January/February, 21-28.

Yin, R. (1994). *Case Study Research: Design and Methods*, 2nd Edition, Sage Publications, Newbury Park.

Chapter IV

Implementing IT Policy and the Bedevilment of Post Colonialism-A Case Study of Tanzania

Joseph Kabalimu
Victoria University of Wellington, New Zealand

Brian Corbitt
Deakin University, Australia

Theerasak Thanasankit
Monash University, Australia

ABSTRACT

This chapter is concerned with how Tanzania has been socially and economically affected by post-colonialism at a policy level as well as at an ordinary (public) level during the IT policy development process in the country. An IT policy according to Corbitt (1999:309) "is a reflection of the society in which it is formed and is socially constructed within the ideologies which frame that society." Corbitt (1999:312) goes on to describe the implementation phase of the policy:

> *Policy is implemented in an environment influenced by ideologies which spawn values and beliefs, some of which are known, recognized and obvious to the actors involved, whilst other influences are not recognized, nor obvious.*

This chapter examines the post-colonial influence, which comprises both directly and indirectly, observed implications within the IT policy development process in Tanzania. The discussion focuses on challenges which face decision and policy-makers in the country. The chapter also proposes an IT policy model which might be developed or designed using a different approach from the traditional policy-making model.

INTRODUCTION

Tanzania needs to emphasize the use of information technology (IT) as a vital tool for strengthening her social and economic development activities. Tanzania's economy is natural resources rich. If those resources had been mobilized using modern ITs effectively and efficiently under an appropriate policy, the country could have moved ahead economically and been providing better social services. (Sheya & Koda, 1987; Wangwe, 1987; Sekimang'a, 1992; Wagao, 1992; Materu-Behitsa, 1994; Mgaya, 1994; Shila, 1994; Kilemile, 1995; Kabalimu, 1996; MSTHE, 1996; Inganji, 1997; Nkhoma-Wamunza, 1997; COSTECH, 1999; Mnyanyi, 1999; Adjibolosoo, 2000; Machumu, 2000b, 2001; Mkwayu, 2000c; Mdoe, 2001; Sabas, 2001b; Ubwani, 2001)

SCIENCE AND TECHNOLOGY DEVELOPMENT

Science and Technology (S&T) are considered to be essential instruments that can give strength to socio-economic development activities in Tanzania (COSTECH, 1991, 1996; MSTHE, 1996; Inganji, 1997; Esselaar et al., 2001; Tanzania Government, 2001b; eSecretariat, 2002). However, even though Tanzania has realized the importance of S&T, various factors especially lack of human and financial resources have hindered the development and promotion of scientific and technological activities in the country (COSTECH, 1999).

Science and Technology Policy (STP)

According to MSTHE (1996), Tanzania established The National Science and Technology Policy (STP) in 1985, which was reviewed in 1996. In the reviewed policy, MSTHE (1996, p. 5) describes the importance of the STP:

> *A national science and technology policy is needed in order to consciously orient the use of science and technology towards the economic, social and political objectives of the society. Thus, one primary function of National Science and Technology Policy is to establish relative priorities of programs for generating new knowledge and to determine strategies for the application of science and technology for development.*

This statement indicates the government's aspirations that reflect Tanzania's awareness regarding the use of S&T for enhancing socio-economic development activities. Thus, the general objective of Tanzania's STP according to MSTHE (1996, p. 8) is to develop and manage science and technology in a manner consistent with physical and human endowments of the country. Specific objectives of the STP are aimed to support sectoral objectives. MSTHE (1996) describes these sectoral policies in relation to STP strategy as follows:

Food and Agriculture: Generally, the policy in this sector is to achieve self-sufficiency in food and food security through increased food and livestock production as well as increased production of commodities for export. The Food and Agricultural Policy places emphasis on food production and underscores the need to develop the agricultural sector using science and technology. Science and technology will aim to maximize productivity through introduction of improved methods of farming, seed varieties, livestock production and better methods of food and crop processing, preservation and storage. It would also enhance the development of agricultural mechanization and irrigation technologies (MSTHE, 1996, p. 11).

Industry: The overall policy on the industrial sector is to create economically efficient, financially solvent, and profitable enterprises in order to utilize existing capacity fully and expand to take advantage of new production and export opportunities. It also aims at improving the business climate for the public and private sectors, increasing domestic competition to integrate domestic producers more into the world market and at restructuring public industrial enterprises (MSTHE, 1996, p. 16).

Energy: The energy sector's policy is to ensure adequate and sustained energy supplies for continued economic growth and development. The energy policy places emphasis on development and efficient utilization of indigenous energy resources in order to reduce dependence on imported energy and demand pressure on our natural forests. It also aims at self-reliance in energy science and technologies (MSTHE, 1996, p. 20).

Natural Resources: The policy on the natural resources sector focuses on the optimisation of the rational utilization of the country's resources based on scientific understanding of nature and the dynamics of the resources. For living resources such as wildlife, fisheries, and forestry, rational utilization of resources must take into consideration the importance of the environment, as well as the socio-economic needs of the local people (MSTHE, 1996, p. 23).

Environment: The environment policy focuses on the conservation and protection of the environment, and rational and efficient utilization of the natural resources. The aim of the environmental policy is to ensure that proper environmental management accompanies economic development so that Tanzanian natural resources and natural heritage are passed on undiminished to future generations. The policy recognizes the essential links between sustainable development and sound environmental management (MSTHE, 1996, p. 25).

Health, Sanitation and Population Planning: The aim of the policy of the health sector is to utilize scientific and technological know-how to minimize and overcome the health problems relating to communicable diseases, maternal and child-health, poor personal hygiene, poor environmental health, malnutrition and non-communicable diseases. Population policy shall lay special emphasis on regulating growth rate, enhancing population quality and improving the health and welfare of women and children (MSTHE, 1996, p. 27).

Transport and Communication: The overall goal of the transport policy focuses on the strengthening of all existing modalities of transportation versus national, intra-regional, inter-relational and international transportation systems. Communications policy will aim at establishing and/or strengthening telecommunication networks, including television networks, as well as the improvement of mass media facilities (MSTHE, 1996, p. 29).

Science and Technology Education and Manpower: The policy on this sector states that Tanzania needs trained and a well-prepared critical mass of human resources and a mechanism for controlling brain drain if there has to be an effective and successful application of science and technology for socio-economic development. This calls for the projection of long-term manpower needs, spelling out what school enrolment is needed, what disciplines should be encouraged and how talents should be developed and harnessed (MSTHE, 1996, p. 32).

All these sectoral policy objectives are essential to Tanzania's current socio-economic development strategic-planning because S&T are major contributors to various socio-economic development activities (COSTECH, 1999; eSecretariat, 2002). Moreover, formulation of science and technology policy (STP) is meaningful if it is effectively implemented. According to MSTHE (1996, p. 35), factors that have contributed to ineffective implementation of STP objectives include:

- poor science and technology education
- low level of support to science and technology system
- low level of expenditure on research and development activities
- weakness in co-ordination and operational instruments
- lack of support and appreciation of the role played by scientists
- technologists in national development by decision-makers.

These factors coincide with Mudenda's (1999) report regarding a new approach of formulating technology policy in Africa – including Tanzania. Factors that cause ineffective implementation of technology policy, according to Mudenda, (1999, p. 4) are mainly due to:

- Poor understanding of the relationship between technology and economic and industrial development.
- Unrealistic understanding of the nature of the dynamic industries and their technological requirements.
- Dependent economies and structural imbalances.
- A serious absence of strategic indigenous programs of action for overcoming underdevelopment.

The factors revealed by both the MSTHE (1996) and Mudenda (1999) reflect post-colonialism since the former colonizes (ICs) appear to want these obstacles to S&T development in developing countries (DCs) like Tanzania remain unresolved to give them an opportunity to continue to be the only scientific discoverers and technological innovators. The former colonized countries (DCs) remain dependent and only customers of their products (Mudenda, 1999; Esselaar et al., 2001). There is always a lack of funds in this sector. As a result no effective research or other related scientific activities are conducted (COSTECH, 1999; Esselaar et al., 2001). This implies that if scientific and technological activities remain undone, this situation will demoralise available scientists who will remain research dormant for long periods and finally may tend to find jobs in other countries. In such an environment, public institutions that are stakeholders will not be able to participate in the implementation of the policy as required. Thus, private institutions have to be given room to contribute their efforts in the implementation of STP. Without effective implementation of STP, no new knowledge will be generated and Tanzania cannot expect to move towards a knowledge economy. If STP remains ineffectively implemented, this could be interpreted as an obstacle to the IT policy development process in Tanzania in the sense that post-colonial factors that have been revealed would continue to persist.

The Tanzania Commission for Science and Technology (COSTECH)

In an effort to ensure effective implementation of Science and Technology Policy (STP) and also to reduce a gap of socio-economic development between Tanzania and industrialized countries (ICs), the government of Tanzania established The Tanzania Commission for Science and Technology (COSTECH) in 1986 (COSTECH, 1999; Tanzania Government, 2001b). COSTECH (1999, p. 1) states that being a main institution for research and science and technology in Tanzania was established by an Act of Parliament No. 7 of 1986 to repeal and replace the Tanzania National Scientific Research Council (NSRC). According to COSTECH (1999, p. 1), the main functions of this commission are to:

- Advise the Government on all matters relating to scientific research and technology development.
- Initiate, formulate and implement science and technology policies and priorities.
- Mobilize funds from Government and other sources for support and promotion of research and technology development.
- Co-ordinate and allocate funds to national research institutions.
- Monitor and co-ordinate research and technology development.
- Acquire, store and disseminate scientific and technological information and popularize science and technology at all levels of society.

These functional objectives are important in relation to S&T promotion in the country and indicate where the preconditions of IT policy formulation may derive from and/or where the process towards IT policy adoption may be initiated.

COSTECH's Advisory and Policy Making Activities

COSTECH had responsibility for performing both advisory and policy-making activities prior to the establishment of parent Ministry of Science, Technology and Higher Education (MSTHE) in 1990. However, the Ministry (MSTHE) is currently insisting that it does the task of the policy formulation; thus, COSTECH remains responsible for dealing with research (COSTECH, 1999; Tanzania Government, 2001). This means COSTECH has to implement policies formulated by the Ministry (MSTHE). COSTECH, however, is insisting that the Parliamentary Act No. 7 of 1986 still gives them the mandate to perform both activities (COSTECH, 1999).

This "tug of war" between the Ministry (MSTHE) and the Commission (COSTECH) indicates that the government appears to be in favor of maintaining the tradition of bureaucracy being the initiator of the policies. If the Act remains the same, COSTECH will remain independent and be able to both formulate and implement policies regarding scientific and technological development activities in the country. The traditional governing structures and powers are "inherited" from former colonizers. Decisions have to be directed from the top down.

As the technological advancements move quickly, governing styles and structures change to account for new emerging technologies (Esselaar et al., 2001). Thus, the government of Tanzania will be expected to decentralize technical as well as administrative activities including policy formulation to its bodies such as COSTECH and universities in order to enable these institutions to feel more responsible for contributing to national development activities. If such an attitude of responsibility is adopted among institutions dealing with IT use and development in the country, this may accelerate the process towards IT policy adoption. In the S&T sector, the government remains responsible for overseeing and co-ordinating S&T activities. However, it appears that the government of Tanzania is still influenced by its colonial legacy in terms of too much bureaucracy, its law, policy formulation procedures, and how it deals with changes – especially technical changes caused by IT advancements (COSTECH, 1996 & 1999; Shayo, 2000; Lyimo, 2001b).

In order to reduce the problem of lack of funds, which seems to be permanent, the IT policy to be established in Tanzania may include suggestions on how the government can plan to increase its income for boosting the IT sector in order to avoid what Esselaar et al. (2001, p. 6) have termed "a donor dependency syndrome." However, it is not easy to eliminate this post-colonialism in the sense of DCs-ICs' financial dependency. Rather, it may take long time for DCs like Tanzania to achieve this objective.

TANZANIA'S POSITION IN THE ELECTRONIC COMMERCE REVOLUTION

Electronic commerce (e-commerce) in simple terms refers to the automation of commercial transactions using computer and communication technologies (Westland & Clark, 1999, p. 10). Although this seems to be an acceptable definition, e-commerce today has a broader meaning from different perspectives. Purcell (2002, p. 6) supports the idea that e-commerce is defined according to goals. She argues that:

> *Some people view e-commerce as "doing business electronically" or "buying and selling goods and services over the Internet." Others view e-commerce as "the sharing of business information,*

> *maintaining business relationships and conducting business transactions by means of telecommunications networks."*

E-commerce then is considered to include more activities and processes than buying and selling transactions. Missoke (2001a, p. 1) suggests that:

> *Discovery and introduction of the Internet is to some people a development equal to the industrial revolution, which took place in the 18th century. This is because the computer or the Internet is today applied in every field of life. As a result of the technology, the business and trade sector is not left behind as now someone can trade using the Internet.*

However, the "digital divide" still persists. Hamelink (2000, p. 82) argues in terms of availability, accessibility and affordability of equipment and services as well as the mastery of technical and managerial skills there are great disparities between affluent and developing countries, but also between different social groups within all countries. While industrialized countries (ICs) such as the United States, United Kingdom, France, Germany, Australia and Japan have adopted e-commerce fully in most business transactions, in most developing countries (DCs) including Tanzania, e-commerce will not grow unless obstacles that face IT use and development are eliminated (Missoke, 2001a; Okuttah, 2001). This is because ICs are technologically highly developed while DCs are technologically poor and the IT industry is still undersized.

In the case of Tanzania, the most critical challenges hindering the majority of Tanzanians from benefiting from e-commerce are: first, ***language barriers*** - because most people do not use English to get information or gain knowledge directly as most of the material is available in this language (Mdee, 1990; Blommaert, 1996). Second, ***the lack of IT skills*** - since most Tanzanians have no access to computer training (Machumu, 2000b; Machumu, 2001; Michael, 2001; Mkinga, 2001; Njau, 2001). Third, the ***negative mindset*** of policy-makers – the majority of top-most decision-makers in the government lack IT knowledge and skills and thus, tend to fear to lose jobs if they encourage fully IT exploitation in the country (Mkwayu, 2000c; Lyimo, 2001b). And fourth, ***poverty*** – due to the fact that a large number of Tanzanians are too poor to buy computers or are unable to afford Internet service charges (Machumu, 2000b; Mihayo, 2000; Mkinga, 2001). Other outstanding problems that have been discussed before which also hinder e-commerce growth in Tanzania include an **unreliable power supply** to operate the computers, **a lack of well-functioning telephone networks** to transmit data, and a **lack of foreign currency** to import the technology (COSTECH, 1999; Esselaar et al., 2001; Tanzania Government, 2001b; eSecretariat, 2002).

These factors derive from existing policies and laws under the current government set-up, which, as mentioned earlier, seems to be still influenced by the colonial government structure and style of administration. It may also be argued that they do little to avoid differentiation of uptake of IT and e-commerce.

Perhaps e-commerce in Tanzania may take place only in urban areas if measures to develop the infrastructure in rural areas – i.e., strengthening power supply, telecommunications services, or transportation services are not undertaken. The digital divide, which at present separate rural and urban areas in Tanzania, is likely to continue causing the rural "uninformed society." However, Missoke (2001a, p. 2) argues that:

Tanzania, being a developing country, cannot afford to be left behind for too long due to globalization of business across the world. Being a new technology, e-commerce is poising a number of challenges to business sector like security of information, taxation issues, advertising and marketing, electronic signature and security of electronic transaction.

This means Tanzania must adjust from being an information-poor country into the center the of e-commerce revolution because this country is part of the networked world. The government of Tanzania has to be fully involved in the e-commerce revolution for the benefit of her citizens.

THE ROLE OF INSTITUTIONS IN THE IT POLICY ADOPTION PROCESS

IT policy (if adopted) can stimulate Tanzania's economic growth as well as directing provision of better social services. However, IT policy can contribute effectively to national development only when various public and private institutions such as enterprises, universities, research institutions, financial institutions, information services providers (ISP) and other institutions involved in creating IT experts and promotion of IT use are all fully co-ordinated to work together (Inganji, 1997; ECA, 1999a; Mudenda, 1999; Esselaar et al., 2001; eSecretariat, 2002). This is the task of the government to organize and assist all institutions dealing with IT use and development in the country to make sure that they play their role properly and effectively. For instance, in order for universities as training institutions to perform their role of producing IT experts effectively, they need adequate funds and other resources. With enough funds, universities can plan and take steps to achieve objectives of producing IT human resources, which in turn will boost IT use and development in the country. Thus, decision-makers in the government need to realize that funding universities for this purpose means to invest in IT as a vital tool, which will lead to enhanced socio-economic development activities in Tanzania (COSTECH, 1999).

The government of Tanzania is expected to encourage and involve universities and other research institutions to participate in the process of IT policy adoption by examining the preconditions that need to be considered in the process. Using research as a strategy, these institutions may interact with the potential IT users and the public at large and establishing factors that may help in the process towards establishment of IT policy. The policy adoption-implementation is a continuous process (Career View, 1994) that needs joint efforts of both the government and institutions. Both are stakeholders who have to work together throughout the process.

In addition, institutions in Tanzania can facilitate IT adoption by encouraging investment in production and promotion of the transfer of foreign technology into the country (Mfanga, 2001). This means institutions are expected to focus on IT investors and users so as to stimulate and/or increase their demand by providing them with appropriate information and knowledge. Institutions in any sector can generate and disseminate information to the public by providing, for example, research reports containing scientific and/or technical knowledge required by IT investors or users through libraries or the Internet (Machumu, 2000b; Mkinga, 2001). Thus, institutions in Tanzania can promote IT use as according to Mkwayu (2000b) some have already shown interest in performing encouraging activities related to the IT use and development in the country including investing in IT.

Although institutions in Tanzania (both public and private) are willing to operate according to their capacities, they are not given a full mandate to establish their own policies for progress because of too much government bureaucracy that derives from the existing law (COSTECH, 1999). Moreover, conditions that are imposed on private organizations are too tough to enable them to achieve their objectives (COSTECH, 1999; eSecretariat, 2002). In this case, there is a need to change the regulations that cause too much bureaucracy and the outdated law, which are believed to derive from the colonial legacy. Thus, the government needs to take advantage of the country's social and economic strengths, including the institutions' willingness, so as to move into the knowledge economy through IT exploitation.

Institutions need to establish strategic plans to attract the attention of the public as the progress to achieve their objectives. It has been observed that there are a number of institutions in Tanzania that have been performing below their capacities because of not being well known to the public (Gasper, 2001; Michael, 2001). According to Gasper (2001), a good example is Tanzania's Global Distance

Learning Center (TGDLC), which was established in mid-2000. Gasper (2001, p. 1) reveals that the TGDLC is regarded as one of the nodes in the Global Development Learning Network (GDLN) utilizing the power of information and communication technologies (ICTs) to enable decision-makers and professionals share knowledge and skills worldwide. The main objective of TGDLC is to enable decision-makers and IT practitioners to access information and share the knowledge gained among themselves or with other people in various parts of the world through communication facilities including video-conferencing, Internet, video, CD-ROM and print (Gasper, 2001). However, this Dar es Salaam-based center still remains a "white elephant" project (Gasper, 2001), Gasper (2001, p. 1) argues that:

> *The utilization of the center, intended to foster for developing countries' (DCs) initiatives to bridge the digital divide between them and the First World, is still very minimal compared to its capacity. It operates below 20 percent of its capacity...because of the general public's ignorance of its existence. The main problem currently facing the center is the fact that TGDLC is not well known to its potential clients and the general public at large. This underscores the need to popularize the existence of the center.*

Gasper (2001) reveals that the decision-makers from the government or institutions who are supposed to be potential users of TGDLC are not using the facility as expected. This implies two things about the potential users of TGDLC: they may lack IT skills or they may be ignorant of the importance of IT in the current socio-economic development.

The major role of institutions in Tanzania in the process towards establishing an IT policy is to examine how IT policy has to be effectively adopted. Institutions need to focus on requirements of both IT stakeholders (i.e. the government and other institutions or organizations dealing with the promotion of IT use) and IT users (i.e., the public). Institutions need to identify the concerns and factors of which such a policy might be implemented effectively including: first, the role of stakeholders, their crucial requirements, demands, aspirations or desires, interests and preferences; second, obstacles facing the promotion of IT use and development and how to overcome them; and third, the digital-divide that exists between rural and urban areas in the country and how it might be reduced. Since institutions employ potential experts in various fields such as science, technology, IT, economics, commerce, financial budgeting and control, education and training, political science, sociology, etc., they are expected to address policy issues that will stimulate and facilitate broader use of IT in various sectors in the country. Under the direction of an IT policy, the broader IT use will lead to an information-based economy for national development in Tanzania. These plans and strategies are expected to reduce the post-colonial impact currently existing because one of institutions' tasks will be to overcome obstacles facing IT use and development including those that derive from post-colonialism.

IT AND BUILDING AN INFORMATION SOCIETY IN TANZANIA

It is a long, difficult journey for Tanzania from being an *information-poor society* to becoming an *information society*. Plans, strategies, commitment, time, efforts, loyalty, getting down to work hard, and the like, are all needed to work together side by side in this long journey. To organize people to work hard, aiming to achieve their objective requires an appropriate guide and that is a policy. As mentioned earlier, an IT policy would be a "trigger" or a starting point of the process to stimulate the IT use in Tanzania. The broader use of IT can lead to build an information society in Tanzania. It is unlikely that Tanzanians are going to benefit from IT revolution without establishing a policy to enhance IT use and development in the country. An IT policy can also promote IT investments for future social and economic benefits (Esselaar et al., 2001; eSecretariat, 2002). Although the government of Tanzania has declared that it is committed to strengthening the information and communications technology (ICT) sector, Inganji (1997, p. 5) argues that:

> *The information activities being carried out at the national level were too rudimentary to qualify Tanzania as part of the Information Society. Tanzania should improve the methods of collecting, processing and dissemination of information, using modern information technology. Once Tanzania has the capacity to participate in the global economy using modern and appropriate information and communication technology, and once the regulations at national level will have been changed to facilitate free access to information, then Tanzania would be considered as part of the Information Society.*

There are many benefits for the country being part of the global information society including access to knowledge and information sharing. According to Mkwayu (2000), Tanzania has already made progress through establishing Internet links which have placed the country one step forward on the networked world. For example, "CATS-NET limited" is one of many companies which are providing Tanzanians with the most reliable, secure and fastest possible Internet services (Mkwayu, 2000b, p. 1). However, together with these efforts, Inganji (1997, p. 6) argues that:

> *Tanzania falls far behind the global information society, and as such, urgent effort is needed both in terms of redefining the function of the information and communication sector in a changing global and national, political and economic scenario. In the same vein, media institutions, both public and private, should realize that their survival depends on professional and technological mobility, which implies a sustained awareness of the need to change, be more creative, diversity and create a climate conducive to competition and the creation of quality products and services.*

This implies that Tanzania has a long way to go in the process of building and achieving its objective of becoming an information society. One strategy for building an information society is probably to strengthen the education sector, because it may be easier for the people to solve their social or economic problems through various means including effective policy implementation if they are knowledgeable. Similarly, Tanzanians who are knowledgeable are likely to participate more actively in the IT policy development process than illiterate because they are expected to be aware of the importance of IT use for their development.

GOVERNMENT PLANS AND INITIATIVES IN BUILDING AN INFORMATION SOCIETY

The Tanzanian government has recently announced its intention to formulate an ICT policy that will account for the current IT advancements (Machumu, 2000b, 2001). In fact, the proposal for Tanzania's ICT policy formulation framework is already published, seeking more inputs from experts and the public at large (eSecretariat, 2002). Further, the government intends to involve the private sector as its partner to exploit IT opportunities in all sectors in the country, for example, integrating IT into educational curriculum at all levels of education (Machumu, 2001; Mujuni, 2001).

However, there has always been a large mismatch between government intentions and implementation regarding IT development in the country mainly due to the existing bureaucratic system and an unwillingness of some decision-makers to fulfill a government commitment perhaps "fearing" IT revolutions (Mkinga, 2001). As the administrative systems in the country are still manual, some of the top-most decision-makers in the government of Tanzania are IT illiterate and thus seem to be "satisfied" with the existing situation, depending on foreign IT experts, especially from industrialized countries (ICs). This dependence element is the result of colonial legacy (Chabal, 1996; Esselaar et al., 2001; Mkinga, 2001). Thus, in the current information era, there is a need to go beyond mere government statements, and instead, seriously plan how to involve and equip people with IT use. This means, the government through the media has to educate the public about the essentiality of IT for their development (Esselaar et al., 2001).

While ICs have built information societies through IT exploitation, Tanzania is still far from taking advantage of this IT opportunity (Inganji, 1997). One of the major retarding factors is that the majority of the Tanzanians are IT illiterate (Mkinga, 2001) and it is very difficult to build an information society if many people in the country are IT illiterate. Mkinga (2001, p. 1) reveals that:

> *Most of the training being done in the country was theoretical rather than practical...there was a need to adopt the available software to fit the Tanzanian situation, a move that required skilled professionals.*

The current situation indicates that it is essential to train the Tanzanian population with IT skills. Companies that have shown interest in promoting IT use and training have to be given full support by the government by encouraging them to go into rural areas where there is little information access. Inganji (1997, p. 6) suggests that:

> *The rural/urban imbalance in information and communication flow should be readdressed by establishing regional broadcasting stations, newspapers and telephone systems. Investors should be encouraged to take part in this development effort through incentives.*

Such projects will be effective if they involve the local population because these are the intended audience–that is, the local people in the area are potential users of the facility. Thus, IT policy would be expected to include suggestions that focus on information dissemination in rural areas. Technical issues related to mechanisms for the co-ordination of various information systems, services, programs, and activities as well as the legal issues have to be included in the IT policy (eSecretariat,

2002). Such projects will succeed if institutions engaged in IT use and development are co-ordinated and their efforts are put together rather than working in isolation as it is currently happening (Inganji, 1997; eSecretariat, 2002). Relevant institutions may include the Tanzania Communications Commission (TCC), the Tanzania Broadcasting Commission (TBC), the Tanzania Commission for Science and Technology (COSTECH), the Tanzania Telecommunications Company Limited (TTCL), the Tanzania Library Services (TLS), Universities and Internet Service Providers (ISP).

This chapter argues that the establishment of an IT policy is the starting point in the process of building an information society. This is because that policy may ensure the broader use of new emerging ITs in the country. Also, while focusing on knowledge as the major tool for Tanzania's economic growth, this country will likely move towards building an information society. To achieve this, negative or retarding factors that derive from post-colonialism need to be resolved to strengthen the IT policy development process in Tanzania.

CHALLENGES FOR DECISION AND POLICY-MAKERS IN TANZANIA

The development of a policy is a continuous task which may involve the government, communities, institutions or groups of people, influenced by various socio-economic activities in a country (Career View, 1994; Hall & Jenkins, 1995; Parsons, 1995; Corbitt, 1999, 2000, 2001; Marcelle, 1999). Tanzania can design and develop policies in relation to national development objectives that reflect social and economic activities taking place in the country. Thus, the overall challenge for policy-makers in Tanzania is to identify social and economic needs of the people and thus create an environment that can provide opportunities for their benefit (Goodman, 1996; Menda, 2001), by using IT and adopting e-commerce.

However, the IT industry in Tanzania is still small, mainly because the IT infrastructure is weak, IT investment is low and the majority of the population lack IT skills and because the population is too poor to utilize IT opportunities (e.g., to pay for Internet services) to gain knowledge for their socio-economic development (Machumu, 2000b; Mihayo, 2000; Esselaar et al., 2001; Mkinga, 2001). The rate of IT use in Tanzania is very low and this affects the people's participation in the IT policy development process. This is the most challenging factor which policy-makers need to look into to determine what has to be done to create an environment which can enhance the growth of the IT industry in the country including how to promote IT services provided by IT investors and thus increase the demand for IT use (Esselaar et al., 2001; eSecretariat, 2002).

Under the umbrella of trade liberalisation, while developing countries (DCs) like Tanzania are requesting for increased national development aid from industrialized countries (ICs), ICs are planning for strategies to improve their markets in DCs (Mwambande, 2001). This situation represents as a kind of "tug of war" between DCs' economic planning against that of ICs. What is planned in Tanzania is probably determined by ICs through large donors including international suppliers of IT equipment (Sundaram, 1999; Kivamwo, 2001; Ubwani, 2001). The challenge facing Tanzania is how to enhance economic development activities within the current globalization process that is determined by World Trade Organisation (WTO) interests (Sundaram, 1999; Adjibolosoo, 2000; Handelman, 2000; Chege, 2001; Ubwani, 2001). The supply of various industrial products including IT equipment and services from ICs to DCs, as mentioned earlier, derives from the colonial objective of treating DCs as the marketplaces of ICs' products (Sundaram, 1999). Since Tanzania is not an IT manufacturer but depends on importing IT from ICs, these countries will probably determine IT development activities including the process of IT policy-making (Mgaya, 1994; Shila, 1994; Machumu, 2000; Missoke, 2001). This situation implies that what appears on the surface level is that WTO objectives would mean to assist DCs like Tanzania, but the underlying reality indicates that WTO seems to be not fairly treating DCs regarding global trade (Handelman, 2000; Mwambande, 2001; Ubwani, 2001). This is because the "global trade giants" (that is - ICs), who control the WTO, still maintain the "colonial stand" of seeing and treating DCs as their marketplaces for their industrial products and at the same time places to get raw materials from for their industries (Machumu, 2000, 2001; Chege, 2001; Mwambande, 2001; Ubwani, 2001).

The other factor that still challenges decision and policy-makers in Tanzania is the impact of IT importation under open market conditions. This needs to be closely looked at and/or readdressed during the IT policy development process because it has been revealed that unsuitable technologies are imported in the country (Chege, 2001; Machumu, 2001; Ubwani, 2001). Institutions and also individuals have complained that outdated and obsolete technologies are finding their way into Tanzania without any control (Ubwani, 2001). These include unsuitable motor vehicles some with "very high" fuel consumption and without spare parts, and many types of computer hardware (COSTECH, 1999; Machumu, 2000a; Chege, 2001; Ubwani, 2001). In this case, there are loopholes under trade liberalisation whereby everyone is allowed to import technology in a free market economy. Ubwani (2001, p. 1) quotes COSTECH to describe the situation:

> *It was pity that institutions responsible for importation of technologies have done very little to stop outdated and obsolete technologies being dumped in Tanzania...It is very amazing that*

one of such institutions is the Center of Development of Transfer of Technology (CDTT), a unit within COSTECH, whose one of its main functions is to advise the government on the choice of imported technologies. CDTT is responsible for matters relating to the transfer, adaptation and development of technology including the assessment and choice of imported technology. The center has not even maintained a registry of imported technology either.

This implies two things: either there may be negligence within such institutions to allow such an importation, or possibly it is easy for outdated and obsolete technologies to find their way into the country. Although this seems to be uneasily observed implication, both probabilities reflect post-colonial effects within the context of the IT dependence on ICs.

Another challenge facing decision and policy-makers in Tanzania, like most other DCs, is how to handle the foreign aid packages for development (Shivji, 1987; Inganji, 1997; ECA, 1999c). These may include IT packages. However, if they are not managed properly or not given to the intended people, these packages may cause economic and/or social violence in the country (Kivamwo, 2001). Consequently, foreign aid packages imply a post-colonial legacy because they always come to Tanzania with special conditions which in turn lead to influence certain national development policies, plans and strategies of the country (Kivamwo, 2001; Ubwani, 2001). A good example is the Tanzania's national investment promotion policy co-ordinated by the Tanzania Investment Center (TIC) (Mfanga, 2001). The TIC has been giving top priority to foreign rather than local investors, because the former donates various equipment to the center. (Mfanga, 2001). As a result, the center has been changing some of its plans and strategies to satisfy foreign investors. This causes complaints from local investors (Mfanga, 2001). Such a situation is a reflection of the impact of foreign packages on the implementation of the investment policy that reflects a post-colonial legacy.

Another important factor influencing this policy process is that IT can be of great value in various social and economic sectors in Tanzania if used for decision-making (Kilemile, 1995). This is a challenge for decision-makers to think about how they may facilitate broader IT applications in the country including IT use for decision-making activities. Currently the use of IT is still minimal in Tanzania. It is largely used for routine data processing, probably because of a lack of IT policy that could ensure the effective use of IT in all sectors (Mkunga, 2001; eSecretariat, 2002). The broader choice of IT use in Tanzania will mainly depend on decision-makers' vision and consideration regarding how Tanzania can exploit IT using social and economic resources available to enhance the country's socio-economic development activities. The main challenge for decision or policy-makers, is to create the conditions within the existing policies, and most important to adopt IT policy, to cater for the majority of Tanzanians to benefit from IT opportunities.

DEVELOPING A MODEL FOR IT POLICY

Developing a policy is a complex task, a continuous process and always involves various people's efforts. Marcelle (1999, p. 5) argues that:

> *The key elements of policy-making in the ICT sector are the context or the environmental factors, and policy objective, tools, and outcomes...The lead actors in this system are policy-makers, whose actions directly or indirectly influence other agents in the system - producers and users of ICTs. These elements working together constitute the system of policy intervention.*

However, policy-makers may also be influenced by various people and the socio-economic activities they do - being done by institutions (public or private), communities, non-governmental organizations (NGOs), trade associations and professional bodies (Marcelle, 1999).

Being aware of this, the government of Tanzania has recently stated its intention to formulate an IT policy to ensure that the country copes with current IT advancements especially global computer technology (Machumu, 2000b, 2001). However, what has come forward after the government's statement is the proposal of an ICT policy, which is still a draft but already published on the Internet (eSecretariat, 2002). The ESecretariat (2002, p. 14) elaborates on why it is important to formulate an ICT in Tanzania:

> *There has been considerable research in examining the causes of the "digital divide" and indeed attempts to link development to deploying ICTs appropriately. Additionally there have been some rather severe conclusions that argue that Internet access may mean little to "poor Africans" since lack of education will prevent effective use of new technologies. However, much of this research has relied on anecdotal evidence. Policy simulations also reveal that feasible and appropriate policy reforms could sharply narrow the digital divide over the next decade for many countries in Africa, including Tanzania.*

In this case, the eSecretariat (2002, p. 14) argues that, following the view presented by the Development Research of the World Bank, Tanzania needs to formulate a policy which is technology independent, progressive while promoting cost-effective intervention and which takes into account the all-important component of human capital development.

In the process of developing a model regarding IT policy in a former colony state like Tanzania, policy-makers have to put into consideration the global economic structure in order to develop a policy that is suitable for that country (Mkwayu, 2000c). Describing this issue Tomlison (1997, p. 37) argues that

> *A 'modern world system' consists of a global capitalist market economy in which the 'core' countries of the developed industrial West (in this study ICs)...dominate the allocation of human and natural resources. The nations of the Third World (in this study DCs) are located, according to this model on the 'periphery', at a distance in terms of economic, technological, strategic and political power, from the centers of control. Thus, ...[the] Third World [does] not have the control of [its] economic (and even arguably, of their political) development in the way that the term 'national development' implies.*

It is likely that ICs determine not only the world economy, but also political practices taking place in DCs (Tomlison, 1997; Kivamwo, 2001). This is because ICs always facilitate dependency whereby formerly colonized countries (DCs) remain economically and especially technologically dependent on ICs (Tomlison, 1997). In such an environment, ICs determine political activities and there is no way DCs can avoid that because social practices are normally determined by economic power (Tomlison, 1997; Sundaram, 1999).

Regarding IT policy development process, Tanzania is located in the "periphery" economically and technologically and thus is directly impacted by existing global capitalist market economy (Shivji, 1987; Wangwe, 1987; Wagao, 1992; Swantz & Tripp, 1996). In this case, Kivamwo (2001) suggests, Tanzania is to focus on how to reduce dependence on ICs by formulating policies that can enhance socio-economic development activities in the country without depending much on donors from ICs). Thus, in order to reduce post-colonial effects persisting today, Tanzania needs to design plans which will lead to the importation and application of appropriate IT for use in decision-making, solving technical problems and also to be used to enhance efficiency in various sectors in the country (Mkwayu, 2000c;

Ubwani, 2001). These plans and strategies for achieving required socio-economic development would probably derive from a well designed IT policy (eSeretariat, 2002). It would be easier for policy-makers to establish a properly designed policy if they can understand how Tanzania is affected by the entire system of global capitalist market economy (Tomlison, 1997; COSTECH, 1999; Mkwayu, 2000c; eSecretariat, 2002).

However, as Tomlison (1997) argues, most policy-makers in DCs (including Tanzania) are still influenced by Western models (ICs), which seems to be their "yardstick" in their policy-making activities. This is because they were first influenced through their studies in ICs or had studied in their countries, but with emphasis on Western theories (Rodney, 1972). This reflects what Tomlison (1997) has termed as post-colonial intellectual's dependence on Western models. Thus, although it is important to use the knowledge of the past as the basis to build on in the process of creating new knowledge, policy-makers in Tanzania may not need to continue depending too much on IC's policies and/or policy-making styles as their models in the IT policy development process. They may formulate IT policy focusing on the particular preconditions within the Tanzanian context.

There are various factors that differentiate Tanzania and ICs that have to be considered in the process of IT policy formulation. These include environment, natural resources, human resources (IT skilled people and public awareness), people's capacity to exploit IT, social and cultural environment, IT infrastructure and existing policies which relate to IT use and development in the country (MSTHE, 1996; Mkwayu, 2000c; Mkinga, 2001; eSecretariat, 2002). Policy-makers may focus on the following: information needs of the rural and "uninformed" Tanzanians – who are the majority of the population but with limited access to information (COSTECH, 1999). Probably their main issues focus on improving their farm products, getting improved health care, better education opportunities, clean water, power supply, and a wide range of services and products such as banking and shops (MSTHE, 1996; Kiplang'at, 1998; Ng'ang'a, 1998; Njau, 2001b). On the other hand, policy-makers may focus on how IT use can improve various socio-economic activities in different sectors and also how IT opportunities can help urban inhabitants, especially the unemployed, in terms of reducing the information access charges (Nassor, 2000; Njau, 2000a; ECA, 1999a; Menda, 2001).

People have to be at the "center" of any social and economic planning, whether this is taking place in the private or in the public sector (Hugo, 1998; ECA, 1999a; Mudenda, 1999; Mkwayu, 2000c). This means IT and e-Commerce policy formulation process has to fully involve people from the beginning in order to be effectively implemented (Corbitt, 1999). Babyegeya (2000, p. 2) gives an example of people's involvement in developing the education sector in Tanzania:

> *After pursuing socialist policies that culminated in nationalization of schools, Tanzania is now decentralizing the management of public schools. This decentralization aims to promote community participation in decision-making and cost sharing to ensure sustained effective provision of education and maintenance of school resources. The reform also aims to reinforce planning and management capabilities at all levels of the school system.*

Policy-makers in Tanzania have to develop plans aiming to provide opportunities that will enable people of different beliefs to participate in this process. According to Babyegeya (2000), people's participation in the planning and policy formulation activities has been given less attention in Tanzania in previous years. Probably their role has been to implement the formulated policy. People need not only be recipients of the already formulated policy, but have to participate in the formulation process because they are the intended group and main implementers of the policy objectives. People's participation in the IT policy development process may create their desire to use IT. Such a situation will probably lead to broader IT use in the country (Hugo, 1998; Mkwayu, 2000c). Thus, the people-centered IT policy development process may reduce the revealed post-colonial impact during its implementation.

The government can help people to understand the importance of IT use for their socio-economic development. This means policy-makers may think of how the government can build the attitude of resource sharing among the people to enable them participate in the policy formulation and implementation (Hugo, 1998; Corbitt, 1999; ECA, 1999a). To create an environment which may attract people to change their information-seeking behavior and become aggressive in using information for their daily activities is the task which IT policy-makers in Tanzania have to consider most. The success of such a strategic-plan may probably create effective IT policy adoption and implementation leading to the growth of IT use. Babyegeya (2000) points out that Tanzania needs to introduce new approaches in designing policies – that is, a decentralized approach which may enable various people participate fully in the formulation-implementation processes.

Thus, because appropriate IT use enhances socio-economic development activities, and since the Tanzania government has shown willingness to adopt new ITs, there is a need for new organizations at the policy level that may bring change from the traditional planning and governance approaches into new approach of policy-making. This action may reduce the post-colonial influence currently persisting in Tanzania and may be expected to focus on how to integrate peoples' thinking in the course of using IT potential.

Figure 1: The Traditional Model of Policy-Making Design

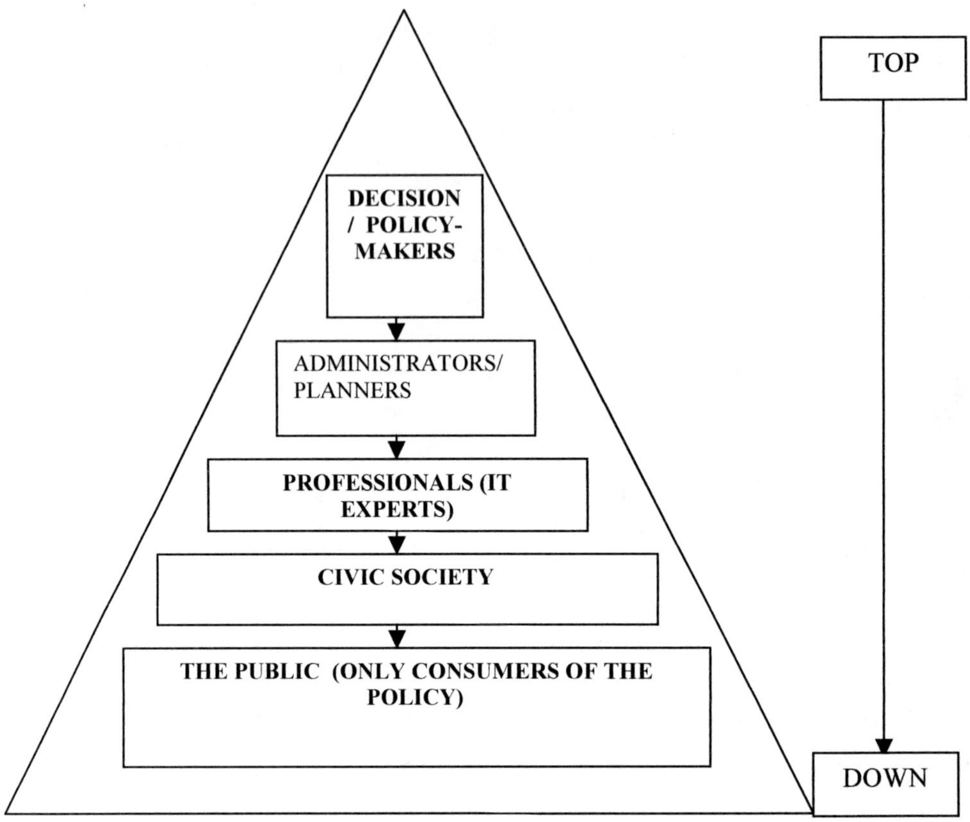

Source: Thomas (1998). "Where does Science fit in Public Policy."

Figure 1 indicates the existing model commonly used in policy-making design, while Figure 2 proposes the new approach to be considered by policy-makers in Tanzania.

The one-way direction in Figure 1 indicates the traditional five categories of actors involved in the policy formulation-implementation process whereby the last group (the public) is only the consumer (Hill, 1993; Career View, 1994; Hall & Jenkins, 1995; Parsons, 1995; Porter & Hicks, 1998; Thomas, 1998). In this top-down, one- direction policy formulation, only policy-makers initiate the policy; involve administrators in the formulation process; and then use the professionals to supervise the implementation process. The public is only the recipient of the ready-made policy although they are capable to participate in the formulation process. This has led to ineffective implementation of policies (Handelman, 2000; Mkwayu, 2000c).

Figure 2: The Proposed Policy Model for IT Policy Development Process in Tanzania

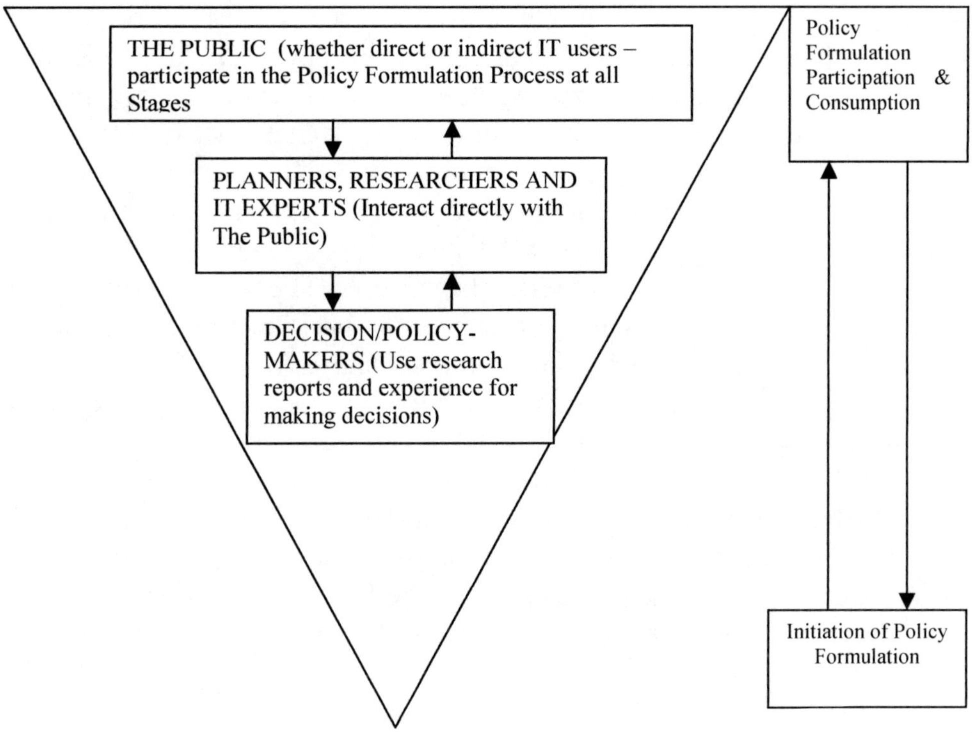

This study of Tanzania proposes a two-way direction approach, whereby the public is not only the consumer of the formulated policy, but can participate fully in all stages of the policy process—that is, formulation, adoption and implementation processes. This means, the policy-making activity has to involve people's thinking or perception regarding the central issue in that particular policy. Through researchers' and IT experts' survey reports, policy-makers get information and thus understand the public opinion including their conception and perception of that particular policy to be in the process. Policy-makers send a proposal to the public and wait for their reaction. It is easier to involve the public through institutions as each member of the public may be employed or involved in a certain institution in one way or another. However, this proposal does not mean that the Tanzanian government has to totally change from its current centralized control. Rather policy-makers have to consider the fact that decentralization in terms of involving the people in the policy formulation, adoption and implementation processes, probably makes the "journey" toward achieving full IT potential become easier. This means, the more leadership that encourages co-operation, better the relationship between decision-makers and the public in the IT policy development process.

This proposed approach aims to contribute to the process of formulating a suitable people-centered IT policy in Tanzania. The people-focused IT policy may ensure knowledge disseminate regarding effective use of IT in the country. This may enable Tanzania to continue being not only an IT consumer in terms of IT importation but also to participate in IT production through proper utilization of available resources. Such a situation may create a suitable environment leading this country to achieve full IT exploitation. Although it is also important for Tanzania to draw experience from other countries that have adopted IT policies, the knowledge gained from such an experience may only be used to assist the process but the design of the policy has to focus on particularities in the country. Thus, through such a new approach of policy adoption process, Tanzania may reduce the existing *"colonial hangover"* of fully dependent on Western Models and build confidence to design an approach regarding IT policy formulation.

This chapter has examined the post-colonial implications within the IT policy development process in Tanzania. It has also explored the mechanisms for designing an IT policy. The proposed policy model may assist policy-makers in their efforts to enable Tanzania adopt an effective IT policy.

REFERENCES

Adjibolosoo, S. (2000). A critical anatomy of performance effectiveness of the structural adjustment program in Tanzania: A human factor assessment. *The Balance*. ISSN: 1527-9303, (Spring), Trinity Western University. Retrieved from the World Wide Web: http://www.balanced- development.org/articles/issue2000/tanzania.htm.

Babyegeya, E. (2000). Education reforms in Tanzania: From nationalization to decentralization of schools. *International Studies in Educational Administration, 28*, 2-10.

Blommaert, J. (1996). Ideology and language in Tanzania: A brief survey. In Herbert, R. K. (ed.) *African Linguistics at Crossroads,* 501-510. Koln: Rudiger Koppe Verlag.

Career View (1994). Public policy. *Career View, 4*, September. The Career Advisory Committee, Victoria University of Wellington.

Chabal, P. (1997). Apocalypse now? A postcolonial journey into Africa: Angola and Mozambique: The weight of history. Inaugural Lecture delivered on

March 12, in King's College, London, ECA Papers online. Retrieved from the World Wide Web: URL: http://www.kcl.ac.uk/depsta/ humanities/ pobrst/pcpapers.htm.

Chege, W. (2001). Trade Ministers meet in Zanzibar to plan common WTO Stand. *The Guardian*, Dar es Salaam, July 24. Retrieved from the World Wide Web: URL: http://www.ippmedia.com.

Corbitt, B. (1999). Exploring the social construction of IT policy – Thailand and Singapore. *Prometheus, 17*(3), 309-321.

Corbitt, B. (2000). Developing intraorganizational electronic commerce strategy: An ethnographic study. *Journal of Information Technology, 15*, 119-130.

Corbitt, B. (2001). Why are we rushing so slowly towards a knowledge economy? *NZ INFOTECHNewspaper*, Issue No. 490, 6, Wellington, May 21.

COSTECH (1991). Project proposal on the establishment of a national information system for science and technology (NISST), prepared by COSTECH. Dar es Salaam: The Tanzania Commission for Science and Technology (COSTECH).

COSTECH (1996). *The Establishment of Science and Technology Policy in Tanzania.* Dar es Salaam: The Tanzania Commission for Science and Technology (COSTECH).

COSTECH (1999). *General information of the Tanzania Commission for Science and Technology (COSTECH).* Dar es Salaam: The Tanzania Commission for Science and Technology (COSTECH).

ECA (1995). *Statement Made by African Electronic Service Providers.* Statement Made at the Closing Session of the Addis Ababa Conference on Telematics for Development in Africa, Addis Ababa, Ethiopia, April 07, 1995. Retrieved from the World Wide Web: http://www.un.org. Depts/eca/ adif/pub.htm.

ECA (1996a). *Prospects for Information Technology in Africa.* A paper presented in the ninth session of the Conference of African Planners, Statisticians, Population and Information Specialists, Addis Ababa, Ethiopia, 11-16 March, 1996. Retrieved from the World Wide Web on [Date]: URL: http://www.un.org/Depts/eca/divis/disd/plan/pspi99.htm.

ECA (1996b). *Building Africa's Information Highway..* Ninth Session of the Conference of African Planners, Statisticians and Population, and Information Specialists, Addis Ababa, 11-16 March. Retrieved from the World Wide Web: http://www.un.org/Depts/eca/adif/pub.htm.

ECA (1999a). *Developing National Information and Communications Infrastructure (NICI), Policies, Plans and Strategies: The "How" and "Why."* A paper presented in the first meeting of the Committee on Development

Information (CODI), Addis Ababa, Ethiopia, June 28 – July 02. Retrieved from the World Wide Web: http://www.un.org/Depts/eca/adf/codipap2.htm.

ECA (1999b). *What Voluntary Business Associations should do to Promote Electronic Commerce in Africa*. A paper prepared for the African Development Forum-1999: The Challenge to Globalization and the Information Age, Addis Ababa, Ethiopia, October 24-28. Retrieved from the World Wide Web : http://www.un.org/Depts/eca/adf/pub.htm.

ECA (1999c). *Strengthening Africa's Information Infrastructure*. A paper prepared for African Development Forum - 1999: The Challenge to Globalization and the Information Age, Addis Ababa, Ethiopia, October 24-28. Retrieved from the World Wide Web: http://www.un.org/Depts/eca/adf/infrastructure.htm.

ECA (2000). *Policies and Strategies for Accelerating Africa's Information Infrastructure Development*. A paper prepared for African Development Forum-2000. Retrieved from the World Wide Web: http://www.bellanet.org/partners/aisi/adif99docs/infrastructure.htm.

Efraji, L. (2001, July). Making Tanzania major player in EAC trade. *Business Times Newspaper*, Dar es Salaam, July 13, 2001. Retrieved from the World Wide Web on [Date] : http://www.bcstimes. comeSecretariat (2002). *Proposal for Tanzania's ICT policy formulation – Final version*, Dar es Salaam, 25 January. Retrieved from the World Wide Web: URL: http://www.tzonline.org.

Esselaar, P. et al. (2001). *A country ICT survey for Tanzania: Final report*. A report prepared by Miller Esselaar and Associates for SIDA, Wilderness, South Africa, November. Stockholm: SIDA. Retrieved from the World Wide Web: http://www.tzonline.org/.

Gasper, P. (2001). *Global distance learning on-line, but unknown. The Guardian Newspaper*, dar es Salaam, March 2. Retrieved from the World Wide Web: http://www.ippmedia.com.

Goodman, S. et al. (1996). *Information Technology in Sub-Saharan Africa* A paper presented at the International Perspectives Conference, CACM. Arizona: University of Arizona.

Hall, C. M. & Jenkins (1995). *Tourism and Public Policy*. London: Routledge.

Hamelink, C. J. (2000). *The Ethics of Cyberspace.* London: Sage.

Handelman, H. (2000). *The Challenge of Third World Development,* 2nd ed. NJ: Prentice-Hall, Inc.

Harrasym, S. (ed.) (1990). *The Post-Colonial Critic: Interviews, Strategies, Dialogues.* London: Routledge.

Hill, M. (1993). *The Policy Process and Policy Analysis: A Reader*, 2nd ed. London: Prentice Hall.

Hill, M. (1997). *The Policy in the Modern State*, 3rd ed. Essex: Prentice-Hall, Inc.

Hugo, G. (1998). Putting people back into the planning process: The changing role of geographical information system. A chapter in Magarey, S. (ed.) *Social Justice: Politics, Technology and Culture for a Better World.* Kent Town: Wakefield Press.

Inganji, F. (1997). *Report of the Workshop on the Elaboration of an Information and Communications Policy and Plan for the United Republic of Tanzania, 12-15 May*; . Addis Ababa: ECA. Retrieved from the World Wide Web: http://www.bellanet.org/ partners/aisi/nic/tanzania/tanzapa1.html.

Kabalimu, J.M. (1994). *Treatment of verb derivatives in Swahili dictionaries*. M.A. Thesis, University of Dar es Salaam.

Kabalimu, J. M. (1996). *Development of an information support system for radio services in Tanzania*. M.Sc. thesis, Addis Ababa University.

Kilemile, J. (1995). *A Computer-Based Information Support System for Energy Resource Development in Tanzania*. M.Sc. Thesis, Addis Ababa University.

Kiplang'at, J. (1998). *An Analysis of the Opportunities of Information Technology in Improving Access, Transfer and Use of Agricultural Information in the Rural Areas of Kenya*, A paper presented in the Information for Sustainable Development in the 21st Century: Proceedings of the 13th Standing Conference of Eastern, Central and Southern Africa Librarians, Nairobi, July 27-31. Nairobi: Kenya Library Association.

Kivamwo, S. (2001). *PM warns against donor dependence. The Guardian*, Dar es Salaam, July10. Retrieved from the World Wide Web: http:// www.ippmedia.com.

Luninze, D. (2001). *Student benefits from global technology. Business Times*, Dar es Salaam, July 13, 2001. Retrieved from the World Wide Web: http:/ /www.bcstimes.com.

Lyimo, H. (2001a). U.S. firms say Tanzania's future in IT bright. *The Guardian*, Dar es Salaam, March 2. Retrieved from the World Wide Web: http:// www.ippmedia.com.

Lyimo, H. (2001b). Poverty Mindset cause of Tanzania's Underdevelopment. *The Guardian*, Dar es Salaam, August 2, 2001. Retrieved from the World Wide Web: http://www.ippmedia.com.

Lyimo, H. (2001c). Mkapa all out for more investment *The Guardian*, Dar es Salaam, September 11, 2001. Retrieved from the World Wide Web: http:/ /www.ippmedia.com.

Machumu, B. (2000a). E-touch smart card goes on stream next month. *Business Times*, Dar es Salaam, May 26, 2000. Retrieved from the World Wide Web : http://www.bcstimes.com.

Machumu, B. (2000b). Policy to Enhance IT use under way. *Business Times*, Dar es Salaam, June 16, 2000. Retrieved from the World Wide Web: http://www.bcstimes.com.

Machumu, B. (2001). Government Ponders Establishment of IT Policy. *Financial Times*, Dar es Salaam, April 25, 2001. Retrieved from the World Wide Web: http://www.bcstimes.com.

Marcelle, G.M. (1999). Getting gender into African ICT policy: A strategic view. Chapter 4 in Rathgeber, E.M. & Adera, E.O. (Eds.) *Gender and the Information Revolution in Africa.* IDRC: Resources: Books: Catalogue. Retrieved from the World Wide Web: http://www.idrc.ca/books/ focus/903/06-chp03.html.

Materu-Behitsa, M. (1994). *Information Support System for Education Planning (ISSEP) in Tanzania*. MSc. Thesis, Addis Ababa University.

Mdee, J (1990). Theories and methods of lexicography in the standard Swahili dictionary, Ph.D. Thesis, Karl-Marx University.

Mdoe, C. (2001). Computer use important in Tanzanian schools.. *Business Times*, Dar es Salaam, July 13, 2001. Retrieved from the World Wide Web: http://www.bcstimes.com.

Menda, A. (2001). Britain Steps up Anti-poverty Campaign. *Business Times*, Dar es Salaam, July 13, 2001. Retrieved from the World Wide Web: http://www.bcstimes.com.

Mfanga, M. (2001). Investors shun 75 percent of Tanzania's regions. *The EastAfrican*, 4 June, Dar es Salaam. Retrieved from the World Wide Web: http://www.nationaudio.com/News/EastAfrica/current/Business/index.html.

Mgaya, K. (1994). Development of information technology in Tanzania. Chapter 4 in Drew, E.P. & Foster, G. F. (Eds.) (1994). *Information Technology in Selected Coutries: Reports from Ireland, Ethiopia, Nigeria and Tanzania.* Tokyo: The United Nations University. Retrieved from the World Wide Web: http://www.unu.edu/unupress/unubooks/uu19ie/uu19ie0i.htm.

Mghenyi, H. (2000). Tanzania economy to improve.. *Business Times*, Dar es Salaam, July 07, 2000. Retrieved from the World Wide Web: http://www.bcstimes.com.

Michael, G. (2001). Skill upgradation vital for consulting engineers. *The Express*, Dar es Salaam, August 9, 2001. Retrieved from the World Wide Web: http://www.theexpress.com.

Mihayo, R. (2000, May). Merchant banking services come to Tanzania. *Business*

Times, Dar es Salaam, May 19, 2000. Retrieved from the World Wide Web: http://www.bcstimes.com.

Missoke, B. (2001a). Tanzania's position in e-com revolutions. *The Financial Times*, Dar es Salaam, March 21, 2001. Retrieved from the World Wide Web: http://www.ippmedia.com.

Missoke, B. (2001b). Postal services still link to rural population. *The Guardian*, Dar es Salaam, April 02, 2001. Retrieved from the World Wide Web: URL: http://www.ippmedia.com.

Mkinga, J. (2001). Most Tanzanians IT illiterate. A report on survey of the need for vocational training programme for ICT professionals in Tanzania. *The Guardian*, Dar es Salaam, January 23. Retrieved from the World Wide Web: http://www.ippmedia.com.

Mkwayu, B. (2000a). Demand for analogue technology is still felt. *Business Times*, Dar es Salaam, June 9. Retrieved from the World Wide Web: http://www.bcstimes.com.

Mkwayu, B. (2000b). Cats-net unveils vision for Internet. *Business Times*, Dar es Salaam, November 3. Retrieved from the World Wide Web: http://www.bsctimes.com.

Mkwayu, B. (2000c). Aggressive policies can double Tanzania's economic growth. *Business Times*, Dar es Salaam, November 10. Retrieved from the World Wide Web: http://www.bsctimes.com.

Mlolwa, R. N. & Sawe, D. (1988). Policy-makers and planners' view on information technology policy. A paper presented at a Regional Seminar on IT, held in Addis Ababa, Ethiopia, November 28 - December 2. Addis Ababa: ECA.

Mnyanyi, Z.V. (1999). Factors influencing the effective adoption of information and communication technology in Tanzania: A case study of the University of Dar es Salaam Academic Library and Documentation Centers. M.A. Thesis, University of Dar es Salaam.

Moore-Gilbert, B. (1997). *Postcolonial Theory.* London: Verso.

MSTHE (1996). *The National Science and Technology Policy for Tanzania.* Dar es Salaam: Ministry of Science, Technology and Higher Education (MSTHE), April.

Mudenda, G. (1999). Formulating technology policies in Africa: New directions. A chapter in M. Osita et al. (Eds) *Technology policy and practice in Africa.* Ottawa: IDRC. Retrieved from the World Wide Web: URL: http://www.idrc.ca/books/focus/790/chap08.html.

Mujuni, J. (2001a). Modern farming a must for a country. *The Express*, Dar es Salaam, May 17. Retrieved from the World Wide Web: http://www.theexpress.com.

Mujuni, J. (2001b). Brace for cheap Internet access. *Business Times*, Dar es Salaam, July 13. Retrieved from the World Wide Web: http://www.bcstimes.com.

Mwakalebela, L. (2000). Tanzania has no policy on intellectual property. *Business Times*, Dar es Salaam, July 07. Retrieved from the World Wide Web: http://www.bcstimes.com.

Nassor, M. (2000, May). Computer prices go down in Dar. *Business Times*, Dar es Salaam, June 30. Retrieved from the World Wide Web: http://www.bcstimes.com.

Ng'ang'a, J.M. (1998). The role of libraries and information centers in rural development. A paper presented in the Information for Sustainable Development in the 21th Century: Proceedings of the 13th Standing Conference of Eastern, Central and Southern Africa Librarians, Nairobi, July 27-31. Nairobi: Kenya Library Association.

Njau, A. (2000a). Seven Internet service providers get licences *Business Times*, Dar es Salaam, May 26, 2000. Retrieved from the World Wide Web: URL: http://www.bcstimes.com.

Njau, A. (2000b). Investment center underscores potential in agro-industry. *Business Times*, Dar es Salaam, September 22, 2000. Retrieved from the World Wide Web: http://www.bcstimes.com.

Njau, A. (2001). Tanzania plans for industrial park. *Business Times*, Dar es Salaam, July 13. Retrieved from the World Wide Web: http://www.bcstimes.com.

Nkhoma-Wamunza, A. (1997). *Information Technology Transfer, Policy Issues and Development in Tanzania: A Case Study*. Ph.D. Thesis, The University of North Carolina (at Chapel Hill).

Okuttah, M. (2001). Challenges of e-commerce in Kenyan small business. *Business Times*, Dar es Salaam, July 13. Retrieved from the World Wide Web: http://www.bcstimes.com.

Parsons, W. (1995). *Public Policy: An Introduction to the Theory and Practice of Policy Analysis.* Cheltenham: Edward Elgar Publishing, Ltd.

Planning Commission (2001a). *The Demographic Survey in Tanzania*. Dar es Salaam: Government Printers.

Planning Commission (2001b). *The Economic Survey in Tanzania*. Dar es Salaam: Government Printers.

Porter, R.W. & Hicks, I. (1998). *Knowledge Utilization and the Process of Policy Formulation: Towards a Framework for Africa*. A paper prepared under its subcontract with SARA Project as a component of the HRAA Project of the Africa Bureau, U.S Agency for International Development

(AFR/SD/HRD). Retrieved from the World Wide Web: http://sara.aed.org/publications/cross_cutting/knowledge_utilization/html/utilization.htm.

Purcell, T. (2002). Defining e-commerce according to goals. *NZ INFOTECH*, Issue No. *529*, 6, Wellington, March 18.

Rielly, C. (1998). *The Use of Information Technology to Promote Effective Democratic Governance.* A paper produced by Malian Offices of the President and Prime Minister, Africa Executive Office Network, Bamako, Mali. http://www.anais.org/Fr/documents/archives/reilly_en.htm.

Sabas, B. (2001a). Telephone drive for rural Tanzania starts. *The Financial Times*, May 24, Dar es Salaam. Retrieved from the World Wide Web: URL: http://www.ippmedia.com.

Sabas, B. (2001b). New "tele" network for TTCL released. The Financial Times, Dar es Salaam, July 18. Retrieved from the World Wide Web: http://www.ippmedia.com.

Sekimang'a, D. (1992). *A National Policy on Information Systems and Services for Tanzania: Formulation and Strategy for Implementation.* MSc Thesis, Addis Ababa University.

Shayo, J. (2000a). Information sector most underdeveloped *The Guardian*, Dar es Salaam, June 07. Retrieved from the World Wide Web: http://www.ippmedia.com.

Sheya, M. & Koda, G. (1987). *The State of Informatics in Tanzania: Policy Issues and Strategies.* Seminar on the Contribution of Informatics to Economic Development, Dar es Salaam, 10-12 August. Dar es Salaam: Tanzania National Scientific Research Council.

Shila, H. (1994). *Case Study Effectiveness of Informatics Policy Instruments in Africa: Tanzania.* A paper presented in the meeting of the Committee of Development Information (CODI), Addis Ababa, Ethiopia, April. Addis Ababa: ECA.

Shivji, I. (1987). The roots of agrarian crisis in Tanzania – A theoretical perspective. *Eastern Africa Social Science Review,* 3(1), 11-34.

Sundaram, N. M. (1999). The Impact of Imperialist Economic Power on Developing Countries. Center of Indian Trade Union (CITU). Retrieved from the World Wide Web : wysiwyg://87/http:// www.grocities.com/CapitolHill/2853/imperial.htm.

Tanzania Government (1972). *Legislation: The Press and the Law*, Article 18 (10 & 2), The Constitution of United Republic of Tanzania. Dar es Salaam: Tanzania Government.

Tanzania Government (1976a). *The Newspaper Act*. Act No. 3/1976. Dar es Salaam: Government Gazette.

Tanzania Government (1976b). *The Newspaper Printing Act*. Act No.9/1976. Dar es Salaam: Government Gazette.

Tanzania Government (2001a). *Tanzania Budget: July 2001–June 2002 Financial Year*. Presented on June 14, Dar es Salaam. Retrieved from the World Wide Web: http://www.ippmedia.com.

Tanzania Government (2001b). The United Republic of Tanzania National Website, Dar es Salaam. Retrieved from the World Wide Web: http://www.tanzania.go.tz/.

Thomas, C.R. (1998). Where does science fit in public policy. Statement by Ambassador Christopher R. Thomas at the American Association for the Advancement of Science, September 2, Washington, D.C. http://www.oas.org/en/pinfo/asg/090298.htm.

Tomlison, J. (1997). *Cultural Imperialism: A Critical Introduction*. London: Pinter Publishers Limited.

Ubwani, Z. (2001, July). Outdated Technology Dumped in Tanzania–COSTECH. *The Guardian*, Dar es Salaam, July 04. Retrieved from the World Wide Web: http://www.ippmedia.com.

UNESCAP (1999). Considerations for ICT Policy Formulation in Developing Countries. A report of the study conducted in 1999 by United Nations Economic and Social Commission for Asia and the Pacific (UNESCAP), Chapter VIII, Conclusion: From Passive Followers to Active Participants. Retrieved from the World Wide Web: http://www.unescap.org/stat/gc/box-ch8.htm.

Wagao, J. H. (1992). Adjustment policies in Tanzania, 1981-1989: The impact on growth, structure and human welfare. In Cornia, G.A., Hoeven, R. & Mkandawire, T. (Eds.) *Africa, a Recovery in the 1990s: From Stagnation and Adjustment to Human Development*. New York: St. Martin's Press.

Wangwe, S. (1987). Impact of IMF/World Bank philosophy: The case of Tanzania. In Havnevik, K.J. (Ed.) *The IMF and World Bank in Africa: Conditionality, impact and alternatives.* Uppsala: Scandinavian Institute of African Studies.

SECTION II:

E-COMMERCE AND ORGANIZATIONAL CULTURE

Chapter V

Gaining Knowledge from Post-Mortem Analyses to Eliminate Electronic Commerce Project Abandonment

Gary S.C Pan and Donal Flynn
University of Manchester Institute of Science and Technology, UK

ABSTRACT

This paper serves as a stimulus to investigators to examine the role project postmortem analyses plays in learning from abandoned electronic commerce (e-commerce) projects. While prior research has identified the importance of the review process, there has been very little research on project post-mortems on abandoned e-commerce projects. The case demonstrates six critical factors to conduct successful project reviews, highlights cultural impacts that might influence their effectiveness and offers several important managerial guidelines. Finally, when analyzing mistakes and their principal causes, there is one important lesson that we should learn. That is, all organizations make mistakes and there is the potential for learning from abandonment experiences.

INTRODUCTION

After a phase of intense Internet hype, the world of electronic commerce seemed to have imploded and fallen abruptly from grace. There are many abandonment stories with only few dot-com companies left struggling to survive. Barrons (May 18, 2000) reported that 25 percent of internet companies surveyed would run out of cash within 12 months, and that 74 percent had negative cash flows. But more importantly, did companies learn anything from their failed adventures or better put "abandonment" experiences? There are many resemblances between information systems (IS) project failure and IS project abandonment. "IS project failure may be the consequence of failing expectations of the implemented system and IS project abandonment is concerned with the anticipated failure of the project prior to its full implementation. Project abandonment can be said to have occurred when the management decides to discontinue temporarily or permanently a project under development" (Ewusi-Mensah & Przasnyski, 1991). The study of abandoned e-commerce projects is no longer a taboo, but is publicly debated from time to time and interest is bound to gather momentum in the near future. It should lead to improved management of future projects. Lessons can and should be learned from one project to another, from one organization to another.

The truth is if organizations want to avoid project abandonment, they need to start paying more attention to examine past mistakes and shortcomings in order to gain more knowledge, which would bring about future project success. Berghel (2001) stated that the key snag that caused the e-commerce meltdown is still with us - an over-reliance on technology in an aim to overcome the weakness of a bad business model. It shows that organizations just simply abandon their e-commerce projects without conducting any post-mortem analysis or learning from past oversights. Therefore, unless blunders are re-examined and learned, project abandonment would still occur with alarming regularity.

According to Collier et al. (1996), project reviews are activities carried out for the purpose of reviewing the events that occurred, evaluating not only what happened, but also why those events happened and determining the correct actions to take to improve the results of the next project. Boddie (1987) and Roman (1983) have suggested that project post-mortems might be the best precaution against future failures. Formal reviews must be conducted to provide a learning experience which is needed to avert the frequent abandonment decisions experienced industry wide on e-commerce development projects (Ewusi-Mensah, 1997).

It is therefore imperative for organizations to view failures as opportunities to learn rather than uneasy incidents to forget. It is a common fault for people to hide errors rather than report and evaluate them (Gaynor, 1996). Individuals are deterred from discussing with their management on what went wrong and why in the aftermath of the abandonment decision because of potential threat to their careers. Murray (2001) stated that the goal of the assessment should not be a blame-fixing mission but rather to identify causes of the difficulty and to determine areas of responsibility for the various components of the failure. In order to provide an environment that fosters openness and honesty, senior management must be prepared to take specific actions to reassure the project members that the reviewing process will be positive and blame-free. This is especially critical as maintaining social relationships typically matters more to most people than accurate diagnoses of isolated events. People can be reluctant to engage in activity that might lead to blame, criticism or recrimination (Argyris, 1977).

In order to transform failure into a smooth learning experience, Jacobs (1999) has developed a three-step reviewing process: 1) gather feedback from everyone involved about what went right and why went wrong, 2) organize the comments into a list of four categories: bad decisions, mistakes, unforeseen events, and good decisions, and 3) analyze project skills to assess and correct the weaknesses. In the same manner, Lowes (1999) suggested the running of a risk-management workshop as a first step to project implementation, which could also be usefully combined with a project team meeting in order to identify and manage project risks.

This article highlights issues critical to successful post-mortem analyses in abandoned e-commerce projects. What are the critical success factors? How should post-mortem exercises be carried out? What are some of the cultural impacts that might influence their effectiveness? Finally, what are some of the managerial implications for organizations? The contents of this paper are: research methodology, research context, results and discussions, and summary, limitations and conclusions.

RESEARCH METHODOLOGY

Research Strategy

As an employee of TechCo and a project team member, the author collected the data and was perceived as a participative researcher by the case company. Case study is adopted because one of the advantages of using case study methods is that they can "explain what goes on in organizations" (Avison et al., 1999). Case studies are deemed to be particularly good for answering the 'how' and 'why' questions (Yin, 1989). To justify the use of a single case study, Yin (1989) argues that single case study design is eminently justifiable in this particular situation because the case serves a revelatory purpose.

Data Collection

A period of three months of participatory research (Argyris & Schon, 1991) was spent where information was collected from the initial project study to the project post-mortem of the abandoned project at TechCo (a pseudonym) in Singapore. Primarily, semi-structured interviews and informal discussions were conducted with all the stakeholders. They were selected in order to cover a range of possible viewpoints and they included the information technology (IT) manager, the purchasing manager, project team members, users, suppliers and directors. Thirty-nine interviews were conducted, each lasting an average of one and a half hours. From these interviewees, information about the post-mortem analyses of the e-purchasing project was collated. Secondary data were also gathered to supplement the information obtained through interviews. The questions were open-ended and exploratory in nature. Observations on major stakeholders were also made during meetings, interviews and discussions.

We were able to collect data of all types, ranging from minutes of meetings, focused interviews with individuals, and materials from the company records. Researching one's own organization involves undertaking research in and on your own organization while a 'complete member' (Adler & Adler, 1987). One advantage of our research over any 'outside-researcher' was that we possessed valuable knowledge about the cultures and informal structures of the organization, though as 'insiders,' members found it harder to give us the kind of formal explanation for their behavior that they might have given to an 'outside researcher.' To support the use of a participatory research, Riemer (1977) argued that rather than neglecting 'at first hand' knowledge or expertise, researchers should turn familiar situations, timely events and special expertise into objects of study.

Analysis of Data

A common problem shared by all researchers is that of the vast amount of data generated and the problem of deciding what is important. Our analysis of the interview data consisted of three separate activities. Firstly, we compared the content of the interviewees' remarks that identify the key abandonment issues against the supplier's criticism and the director's commentary on the cancellation of the project. Secondly, we used other data such as minutes, memos, seminar notes and informal discussions to construct inferences regarding the project development process. Finally, we made inferences about the implications of conducting project post-mortem analyses, which might enhance learning process.

With the data collection and coding established, thematic analysis was introduced to provide an inductive study of these themes. Multiple source triangulations provide internal validity checks of the data. Stake (1995) defined triangulation as the protocols that are used to ensure accuracy and alternative explanations. Triangulation methodology (Denzin, 1978; Jick, 1979) was also used to gather different types of data that could be used to crosscheck for reliability. The external validity checks were done through participative discussions on the codified data and the analysis of the research.

RESEARCH CONTEXT

The study concerned the development of an e-purchasing system in a large Japanese corporation called TechCo. In 1998, the purchasing manager was desperately trying to reduce the purchasing expenses as the company's profit was eroding due to its rising purchasing costs (Internal Document, 1997). The purchasing manager had evaluated many options and opted for implementing a new e-purchasing system to help him in achieving his objective. The managing director endorsed the idea and assigned the purchasing manager as the project manager. A project team was immediately set up with the task of developing a system establishing the linkage between the purchasing department in TechCo and its material and parts suppliers by means of the Internet.

The Initial Reactions from the Internal Stakeholders

The users' scepticisms over the proposed system were due to some past unpleasant experiences, where numerous attempts made on system improvement failed to enhance their working condition. The users had identified manpower shortages in areas such as price negotiations but their manager had rejected all their requests for additional manpower. The project manager acknowledged their discontentment; nonetheless, he had discounted their influences in the project decision. He pointed out, *"I will ensure their full participation in adopting the new e-purchasing system. Besides, they have no say in the decision-making."* The IS manager and the IS programmers were neutral towards the project and refused to comment on potential rivalry among other stakeholders.

Suppliers' Suspicion Over the Project Motives and Their Offensive Strategy

No consultation was made with the suppliers prior to the development of the system. It was only after six months when the suppliers were informed of the new system. In June 1998, the project manager conducted the first suppliers' briefing session with almost 100 suppliers and other project members. He controlled the agenda and made one-way presentation with little room for discussions, questions, or disagreements. Most suppliers viewed the project objectives as vague and perceived the new system as a threat that could jeopardize their business positions in TechCo. In an interview with one of the suppliers, *"The new system will be connected with other virtual markets and new suppliers may be introduced to boost competition."* Having recognized the potential threats, the suppliers vowed to act coherently to hinder the development project. The suppliers requested for project deferment citing reasons such as incapability in meeting the technical requirement needed for the compatibility of the new system. The project manager was furious and rejected their request without consideration, and demanded their full compliance in meeting the requirements. With the software development nearly completed, the project manager was determined not to let the suppliers' action to affect his project. The key suppliers gathered to seek strategic solutions to resolve their conflicts and had devised a two-fold offensive strategy. First, they planned to convince the IS manager and seek his support in this battle. Second, they would appeal to the managing director and request for deferment or possibly, abandonment of the project. Without further delay, the suppliers immediately notified the IS manager of their anxiety towards the new system. The astonished IS manager was sympathetic and promised to provide assistance to them. After gaining the support of the IS manager, the suppliers approached the managing director regarding their concerns about the project. The managing director was ignorant of the clashes between his manager and the suppliers, and was taken aback to realize the gravity of the situation. Sensing the urgency of the matter, he immediately called for a project meeting.

The Confrontation

In the meeting, the stage was set for the clash between the project manager and the suppliers. Within minutes, discussions were turned into heated arguments as the project manager was heard yelling, *"They are trying to delay our project so as to safeguard their monopolistic positions in TechCo."* Several finger-pointing moments were witnessed throughout the three-hour meeting. Even though the managing director was anxious to reach a consensus on the matter, both parties seemed adamant on their grounds. After that meeting, the managing director was indecisive about the verdict of the project as his decision could draw widespread criticisms from both employees in the company and other suppliers in the industry. Therefore, he decided to seek opinions from other project stakeholders such as the IS manager, the users and the IS programmers. The IS programmers were first consulted, but were cautious and tactful in choosing their words and had refrained from taking sides with either party.

The Verdict on the Abandonment Decision

The IS manager showed sympathy towards the suppliers and spoke on their behalf, *"The suppliers were uninformed about the plan prior to the project development and had insufficient time to upgrade their own systems to meet the compatibility requirement."* With the IS manager clearly supporting the suppliers, the users' opinions were unexpectedly crucial at this stage. The user spoke, *"Several efforts have been made in the past but still failed to improve our system, which as a result, has caused distress among us. It is therefore, in our honest opinions to support the call to abandon the project."* After carefully considered the views from all the project stakeholders, the managing director decided to abandon the project (for the summary of the events that set the stage for project cancellation, see figure 1). In a subsequent interview, the managing director blamed the project manager for mishandling the situation. In his opinion, after knowing the suppliers' suspicion, the project manager ought to have clarified their doubts and offered them with valid explanations. Even if his efforts were to fail, he must report the matter to the top management without delay and not keep the matter in the dark.

Figure 1: Summary of the Events that Set the Stage for Project Cancellation

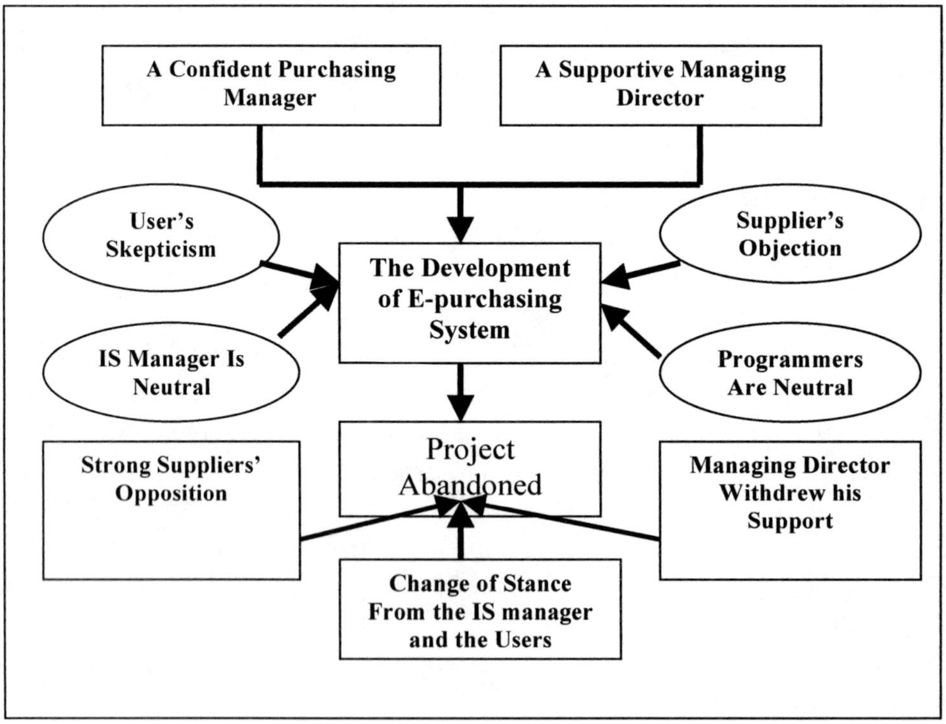

The Project Post-Mortem

The company has a policy of conducting project reviews at the end of every project. The objective of the review is to re-evaluate the project development and implementation process. The purchasing manager, who was also the project manager conducted the post-mortem session. During the session, half of the project team members including the directors failed to turn up. The main reason for the low turnout was that the programmers were already involved in other overdue projects. One of the programmers explained during the interview, *"Every one of us is involved in at least three other concurrent projects. Where do we find time to attend the project review session?"*

Even though project post-mortems have been carried out over the years, such sessions are actually insignificant to most of the project members. One of the informants who have attended several project post-mortems explained, *"The senior managers and directors have never attended the meeting and they never seem to be interested. All they want to see is the end result from the project. They are not too keen to promote learning from mistakes or successes. They are purely result-oriented."* Another close informant added, "*Besides, we are not rewarded for being participative and sharing our experiences during such meetings. Our performances are measured against our project outcome and not the post-mortem exercise. That is the reason why few people attend such sessions.*"

The purchasing manager was still brooding over the project being abandoned at a time when the development was almost completed. Instead of trying to identify any wrongdoings for the project, he was seen blaming the suppliers throughout the session. On top of that, he was also pointing his fingers at the programmers for their delay during the development stage, which had provided the suppliers with ample time to stop the project before it was launched. He commented during the meeting, *"Part of our failure was due to some delays from our programmers. If they had followed the project schedule closely, the software development would have been completed before any outsiders could intervene."* His blunt accusation had clearly angered the IT manager who was seen leaving the meeting after the comment. It was observed however that most of the members who attended the review session had remained quiet throughout the session. One of the attendees commented, *"What can we say? If we made any negative comments, the purchasing manager would offer several excuses for it. It is better to keep quiet than to risk offending him."*

In a later interview, the IT manager offered his perspective on why the project was cancelled, *"There were basically three problems. Firstly, the purchasing manager should have communicated the benefits to the suppliers and allayed their fears instead of clashing with them. Second, the purchasing manager failed to market the project effectively to the top management. Even though initial approval was obtained, the purchasing manager ignored maintaining and further strengthening of his relationships with the directors. There was no periodic update from him regarding the progress of the project during the development. He could have marketed his project more aggressively to the directors. If he had portrayed the project as one that would bring about drastic improvement to the company's bottom-line, then the directors might not relent to the supplier's pressure and abandon the project so easily. Lastly, there was no proper documentation for minutes and memos in project meetings. Often, there seemed to be communication breakdown between my programmers and the purchasing department."*

Even though there seemed to be many problems, the IT manager did not bring up those issues during the post-mortem session. He explained, *"In our environment, we have to be cautious with our criticism. If I bring up those issues, the purchasing manager is going to be unhappy with me. I do not wish to have any enemies in this company."* In a separate interview, the directors had denied that they caved in to the suppliers' pressures. One of the directors commented, *"The purchasing manager had mishandled the whole situation. We should maintain close relationships with our suppliers as we view them as our partners. We ought to explain and assure them that the objective of the new system is to enhance the whole purchasing efficiency, which might benefit them as well. The project was cancelled because it would never have worked without the support of the suppliers."*

RESULTS AND DISCUSSIONS

Critical Success Factors for a Post-Mortem Analysis

The following discussions seek to describe the role project post-mortem analyses plays in learning from abandoned e-commerce projects. The factors critical to successful post-mortem analyses as emerged from the case are summarized in Figure 2.

Open and Forgiving Corporate Culture. It is important for organizations to nurture an open and forgiving corporate culture. Efforts must be made to reinforce the good intentions of learning from failures, so that project members are willing to share their experiences. The impact of the decision on individual careers should be minimized whenever possible so as not to create an atmosphere in which individuals would not be willing to discuss with management what went wrong and why in the aftermath of the decision (Ewusi-Mensah, 1997).

Figure 2: Critical Success Factors for a Project Postmortem Analysis

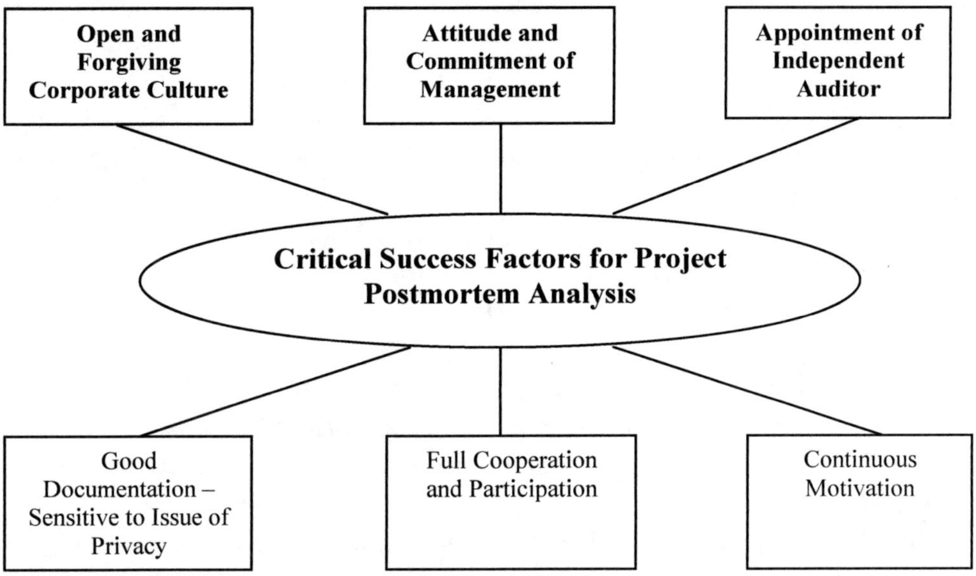

Attitude and Commitment of Senior Management. The senior management must be committed to the post-mortem exercise (Harris, 1994). The importance of the exercise must be emphasized and made known to every member of the project group in order to guarantee full participation from them. In the case, if the senior management had recognized the importance of learning from past mistakes, they would have been more committed and placed more emphasis in such sessions. This would create more interests and encourage active participation among the members. It is only through such avenue that the post-mortem analyses would become beneficial. The senior management should also establish a culture of trust throughout the organization—for example, if it deals with project grievances and maintains open communication—there is less likely to have resistance from the members. However, if senior management remains aloof with group antagonisms perpetuated at work, effective implementation would then be hindered.

Appointment of Independent Auditor. An independent auditor should be appointed with an objective to protect the interests of the organization as a whole. It could either be an internal or an external auditor who does not have a stake in the project being audited and is with vast relevant project management experience. The appointee should act as a facilitator to encourage participation among the members. To insure that auditors' recommendation would avoid any accusation from the project team members, the appointee should report directly to the top management. It was a mistake to assign the purchasing manager to conduct the post-mortem meeting in the case. Being a leading character in the project, his opinions might have already been swayed by his emotions. It would be difficult for him to offer an objective opinion in the project reviews when facing an outcome of project failure.

Good Documentation Throughout the Project and During Post-Mortem Process. Minutes, memos and activities conducted during the project development must be well documented (Busby, 1999). This is to ensure that any mistakes made during the project can be easily traced and clearly identified during the project review process. At the same time, findings concluded after the post-mortem exercise are extremely valuable to the organization for learning and might be utilized as guidelines for future software development projects. However, organizations have to be sensitive about the issue of privacy because people tend to avoid admitting their own mistakes and are only willing to reveal the truth when their identities remain anonymous.

Full Cooperation and Participation Among Project Manager and Team Members. People tend to hide mistakes rather than report and evaluate them. But there are some who chose to keep mom because of risks to their own careers. The prospective whistle blower needs to face the reality that the critical audit report may contradict the best judgment and vested interests of the powerful players in the project group (Keil & Robey, 2001). Overcoming the fear is critical and is a challenge for all project teams in their attempts to learn from past experiences and improve future project management. In the case, project members were seen keeping quiet throughout the session and hardly provided or shared any experiences gained from the project. The purchasing manager, when conducting the review session should have encouraged more participation from the team members and assured them that such learning session would not inflict any ill feelings within the group.

Continuous Motivation is Needed Throughout the Process. The post-mortem exercise acts as an internal group relationship process, which regulates and strengthens internal group interactions. By examining the mistakes together, it helps to create an environment in which team members share positive, friendly feelings as well as a sense of loyalty and responsibility towards each other (Swanson, 1998). Value is placed on open communication, supportiveness, commitment to the team and positive interpersonal relations. Thus relationship process may prove to be a particularly important contributor to the cause of building better systems.

Cultural Factors that Influence the Success of Post-Mortem Analysis

This section highlights how some of the traits of Japanese culture might influence the success of post-mortem analyses in a Japanese corporation: the end of lifetime employment and group membership. Japanese management approaches have often been scrutinized on the cause-and-effect on their success in the market place (Mestre et al., 1997). Cultural influence can function as a positive factor that draws out the best of their workers' potential and values, or it can act as a negative factor. To reinforce its importance, Glass (1991) stressed that the key to Japanese effectiveness is the combined brainpower of all its employees and the fostering of intense exchange and communication.

The End of Lifetime Employment

Traditionally, Japanese society can generally be described as stable and homogeneous. Companies prefer long-term, stable and close relationships with employees, customers and suppliers. Successful Japanese corporations would provide their professional, technical and managerial employees with jobs for life as the management has deep commitments to employees and personnel issues. Furthermore, Japanese legislation has made it illegal to sack their employees, so as to make these companies responsible for their social and economic aspects of life. On top of everything else, the emphasis on company loyalty has also inhibited typical Japanese workers from leaving his or her company (Herbig & Jacobs, 1997).

In spite of this, the business environment has changed rapidly in recent years. Economic slowdown has, however, altered the long-standing policy of lifelong employment to meet new demands of cost cutting for survival. There are four ways Japanese companies have adopted to reduce their wage bills: moving production to countries with lower minimum wage, employing more temporary employees, transferring employees to work for suppliers and forcing senior employees into early retirement. The demise of lifetime employment has seriously weakened the ties employees have with these corporations. Existing practices have replaced the traditional practices that emphasized on harmony, stability, continuity and consensus. Employees are feeling insecure about their jobs, as many companies have resorted to retrenchment solution in this economic crisis. In the case of TechCo, we cannot deny that cultural factors might have played a major role in influencing the members' behaviors during their post-mortem session. The fear of losing their jobs could have forced project members to refrain from sharing their experiences, let alone admitting their own mistakes. Even though it is important to establish a culture of trust throughout the organization when dealing with project grievances, however, we should highlight that it is difficult to establish trust in such situations, due to likely resistance from the members. Therefore, by taking the risk of such cultural influences into account, we stress that the senior management plays a key role in building a trusting relationship within the organization, which may prove to be a particularly important contributor in conducting a successful post-mortem analysis.

Group Membership

Central to the Japanese is the concept of "groupism" (Hayashi, 1990). In Japanese corporations, it is important to maintain harmonious relationships in the group to which one belongs. Various social events are held regularly to strengthen group bonding among its employees. Group harmony and collectivism are key Japanese values in their culture (Hodgetts & Luthans, 1997). Furthermore, employees are expected to work beyond their official working hours to demonstrate their sense of belonging to the company. Harmony is considered as one of the most important requirements in order for the maximization of organizational outcomes. If an employee has a different opinion from the rest, it is better for him to remain silent (Kubo et al., 2001). All employees are perceived as interchangeable and, as such, are almost considered as non-entities since there is no difference between one individual and another (Mestre et al., 1997). The more institutionalized the form of socialization is, the greater are job satisfaction and commitment generated and the lower is the intention to quit (Jones, 1986). The challenge for Japanese organizations is therefore to make every individual a productive team member, emphasizing the importance of the two components of Japanese business success: membership and productivity. In order to reinforce the process of identity with the group, dormitories, collective meals, team banners and names, assigned meeting locations, are all ways to help bring people together (Mestre et al., 1997). Japanese believes that when a team tackles a task, it is more likely to get done effectively and efficiently. They have made a tradeoff: in exchange for occasional moments of greatness from individual superstars they have substituted the steady progress of a cohesive, and of a unified group (Rehfeld, 1994). Collective needs are more important than individual needs in a Japanese corporation. Japanese has a very people-oriented way of viewing their employees. Many chief executives of major Japanese companies frequently describe the firm as a 'family' (Hatvany & Pucik, 1981). This culture of collectivism might help to explain why TechCo's project members had remained silent during their post-mortem session, as they might be afraid to speak up for fear of offending the purchasing manager or their colleagues. Furthermore, they might also be preventing any potential conflicts arising from the situation in order to maintain cohesiveness within the group. Their concepts of 'unity' and 'teamwork' have certainly proved to hinder their learning process. Even though, we are aware of such existing cultural impacts that might be influencing employees' behaviors, one has to bear in mind that corporate culture is supported by traditions that have been developed since company's foundation, and have grown in succession. Therefore, making fundamental changes are difficult.

Implications for Practitioners

Some managerial guidelines are recommended for managers to adopt when conducting their project reviews. While individuals play an important role in the project development process, much of what causes abandonment is in the nature of organizations, not people. The organizational context into which a post-mortem analysis is introduced has a crucial bearing on its acceptability and subsequent effectiveness. Organizations may face with resistance to learn from past mistakes. Resistance should not be seen merely as a problem to be solved. In fact, resistance is a good clue as to what is going wrong and what can be done about it. The main reasons for individuals to resist project reviews are feelings of embarrassment from failure or facing the unknown to their job security, disturbance of social relationship among project group and lack of understanding of the review purposes. There are many steps, however, that organizations can take to create an environment in which managers and project team members are encouraged to learn from the post-mortem results that can avoid or diminish future project abandonment. However, without any incentives, it is naïve to expect that all managers and members will be motivated to learn (Bowen & Clark, 1994). One suggestion is to link project members' performance evaluation against their initiatives and commitment towards learning from post-mortem analyses. In that way, project members would be more committed and participative in post-mortem analyses.

Organizations should create a tracking system that gives senior management a full account of all on-going information systems projects and their current stages. Clear guidelines should be established to mark the point at which projects move from one stage to another. After every stage, project managers should review their progress to see whether there are any serious problems they will face in continuing pursuit the project (Gaynor, 1996). Managers must be made aware that there are many advantages in pursuing such a staged and incremental approach to reviewing projects so as to ensure that managers fully utilize such tracking system.

Finally, reviews should be held during project development and post-mortems (Jacobs, 1999; Schmidt et al., 2001). The exact timing and frequency would depend on the scale of the project and should differ among individual companies. Organizations ought to be focused on whether the progress made is moving towards meeting the project goal. The review should also uncover any potential project obstacles (Chikofsky, 1990). Any deterioration in the project conditions should trigger re-evaluation to see if the troubled project should be abandoned to avoid any escalation of commitment.

CONCLUSIONS

In this paper, we have used a case study of the short-lived e-purchasing project experience as a vehicle for exploring issues critical to successful project post-mortems, which might help organizations in their learning process and prevent future project cancellations. Through the interviews with the stakeholders, we gathered qualitative data about the project post-mortem practices in the company. Our findings revealed six factors that were critical to whether or not a project post-mortem would be successfully carried out. We found that creating a healthy climate for successful project post-mortem is essential for reducing project abandonment. Post-mortems should not be for the purpose of seeking scapegoats and assigning blame, but to help first the project in distress and those who follow after. Our objective is to encourage one to broaden the experience by laying hold of the experiences of others, reluctant though they were to, discuss them at times and so learn with them the lessons that they had to learn the "hard way." Experience is undoubtedly the key to success. If one is to learn from the past, one must listen. It is most difficult to get people to listen, let alone learn. It is therefore our sincere hope that the recommended factors and managerial guidelines can help organizations to re-examine their project post-mortem processes and at the same time, create more awareness on the importance of learning from past experiences.

Given that abandonment is a common and costly problem among IS projects (Ewusi-Mensah, 1997), there can be no question about the importance of understanding the nature of abandonment and hence try to avoid it if necessary. As there are very few empirical studies on e-commerce project abandonment, this study represents a contribution to knowledge in this field as it complements the existing studies by demonstrating the importance of learning from past experiences, which could enhance future project management practices. One particular feature that distinguishes this study clearly from previous research is that we have developed a learning perspective by providing prescriptions to avoid future projects from being cancelled. Managerially, the result could provide managers with better knowledge in managing project development process. Moreover, the factors and cultural influences that we discussed could be of great value in terms of guiding management in making decision throughout their development process, especially with regard to managing relationships with stakeholders.

Finally, even though we are convinced that the findings of this study will prove useful to both academics and practitioners, we believe there are many avenues for further research into IS project abandonment. The study breaks new ground in providing systematic evidence that could help explain the need to understand the process of learning from past project experiences. Another direction for future research could be to investigate and understand the dominant factors and their relative influence in the learning process to stamp out project abandonment.

ACKNOWLEDGMENTS

The authors are most grateful to Professor Kweku Ewusi-Mensah for his constructive feedback on earlier versions of this chapter.

REFERENCES

Adler, P. & Adler, P. (1987). *Membership Roles in Field Research.* Thousand Oaks, CA: Sage.

Argyris, C. (1977). Double loop learning in organizations. *Harvard Business Review*, September, 115-125.

Argyris, C. & Schon, D. (1991). *Participatory Action Research and Action Science Compared: A Commentary*. (pp. 85-97) Newbury Park, CA: Sage.

Avison, D., Lau F., Myers, M. & Nielsen, P. (1999). Action research. *Communications of the ACM, 42*(1), 94-97.

Berghel, H. (2001). The Y2K e-commerce tumble. *Communications of the ACM*, 44(8), 15-17.

Boddie, J. (1987). The project post-mortem. *Computerworld*, December.

Bowen, H. & Clark, K. (1994). Development projects: The engine of renewal. *Harvard Business Review*, September, *72*(5).

Busby, J. (1999). An assessment of post-project reviews. *Project Management*, September, *30*(3).

Chikofsky, E. (1990). Changing your endgame strategy. *IEEE Software*, *7*(6).

Collier, B., Demarco, T., & Fearey, P. (1996). A defined process for project postmortem review. *IEEE Software*, July, *13*(4), 65.

Denzin, N.K. (1978). *The Research Act: A Theoretical Introduction to Sociological Methods*. NY: McGraw-Hill.

Ewusi-Mensah, K. (1997). Critical issues in abandoned information systems development projects. *Communications of the ACM*, September, *40*(9), 74-80.

Ewusi-Mensah, K. & Przasnyski, Z. (1991). On information systems project abandonment: An exploratory study of organizational practices. *MIS Quarterly*, March, 67-85.

Gaynor, G. (1996). Monitoring projects - It's more than reading reports. *Research Technology Management*, March, *39*(2).

Glass, N. (1991). *ProActive Management – How to Improve Your Management Performance*. (pp. 197-201) East Brunswick, NJ: Cassell.

Harris, G. (1994). Keeping the boss informed – Three ways. *Research Technology Management*, July, *37*(4).

Hatvany, N. & Pucik, V. (1981). An integrated management system: Lessons from the Japanese experience. *Academy of Management Review*, 6(3), 469-480.

Hayashi, S. (1990). *Culture and Management in Japan.* NY: University of Tokyo Press.

Herbig, P. & Jacobs, L. (1997). A historical perspective on Japanese innovation. *Management Decision*, 35(10), 760-778.

Hodgetts, R. & Luthans, F. (1997). *International Management*. 3rd Edition, NY: McGraw-Hill.

Jacobs, P. (1999). Recovering from project failure. *InfoWorld*, 21(39).

Jick, T. (1979). Mixing qualitative and quantitative methods: Triangulation in action. *Administrative Science Quarterly*, December, 24, 602-11.

Jones, G. (1986). Socialization tactics, self-efficacy and newcomers — Adjustments to organizations. *Academy of Management Journal*, *29*(2), 262-279.

Kanfman, C. (1975). Tokyo: One city where crime doesn't pay. *The Citizen Crime Commission of Philadelphia*, Philadelphia.

Keil, M. & Robey, D. (2001). Blowing the whistle on troubled software projects. *Communications of the ACM, 44*(4), 87-93.

Kubo, I. et al. (2001). Behind the scenes of knowledge sharing in a Japanese bank. *Human Resource Development International*, *4*(4), 465-485.

Lowes, J. (1999). Information systems: How to run a simple risk management workshop. *Management Accounting: Magazine for Chartered Management Accountants*, *77*(7).

Mestre, M., Stainer, A. & Stainer, L. (1997) Employee orientation – The Japanese approach. *Employee Relations*, *19*(5), 443-456.

Murray, J. (2001). Recognizing the responsibility of a failed information technology projects as a shared failure. *Information Systems Management*, Spring, *18*(2).

Rehfeld, J. (1994). *Alchemy of a Leader – Combining Western and Japanese*

Management Skills to Transform Your Company. (pp. 386-387) NY: John Wiley.

Riemer, J. (1977). Varieties of opportunistic research. *Urban Life*, *5*(4), 467-477.

Roman, D. (1983). A proposed project termination audit model. *IEEE Transactions Engineering Management*, August, 123-127.

Schmidt, R., Lyytinen, K., et al. (2001). Identifying software project risks: An international delphi study. *Journal of Management Information Systems*, Spring, *17*(4), 6-36.

Stake, R. (1995). *The Art of Case Study Research.* Sage Publication, London.

Swanson, D. (1998). IT project review. *Management Accounting Magazine for Chartered Management Accountants*, July, *76*(7).

Yin, R. (1989). *Case Study Research: Design and Methods (Rev. eds.).* Beverly Hills, CA: Sage.

Chapter VI

Analysis of Cultural Conflict in the Development of Web-Enabled Information Systems

Pradipta K. Sarkar and Jacob L. Cybulski
Deakin University, Australia

ABSTRACT

Web-enabled applications are used increasingly to facilitate business transactions between and within organisations. Designing a successful web-based information system requires considerable insight into collaborating organisations, their technological needs, having the substantial management and development experience, and a thorough knowledge and understanding of the cultural issues arising from the diverse base of stakeholders involved in the development, implementation, and the usage of the system. Cultural differences in particular, often ignored in information systems development, if not addressed appropriately, may lead to impaired communication, misunderstood requirements, flawed decisions, and ultimately conflict among various stakeholder groups. In this paper, we propose a method of identifying cultural issues early in the development process and we do so by focussing on stakeholder concerns, commonly perceived as a barrier to effective development process, but which we find a useful instrument in studying cultural divergence and in some cases also conflict.

INTRODUCTION

The advent of the World Wide Web (WWW) and the emergence of Internet commerce have given rise to the web as a medium of information exchange. In recent years, the phenomenon has affected the realm of transaction processing systems, as organizations are moving from designing web pages for marketing purposes, to web-based applications that support business-to-business (WEB) and business-to-consumer (B2C) interactions, integrated with databases and other back-end systems (Isakowitz, Bieber, et al., 1998). Furthermore, web-enabled applications are increasingly being used to facilitate transactions even between various business units within a single enterprise. Examples of some of the more popular web-enabled applications in use today include airline reservation systems, internet banking, student enrollment systems in universities, and Human Resource (HR) and payroll systems.

The prime motive behind the adoption of web-enabled applications are productivity gains due to reduced processing time, decrease in the usage of paper-based documentation and conventional modes of communication (such as letters, fax, or telephone), and improved quality of services to clients. Indeed, web-based solutions are commonly referred to as *customer-centric* (Li, 2000), which means that they provide user interfaces that do not necessitate high level of computer proficiency. Thus, organizations implement such systems to streamline routine transactions and gain strategic benefits in the process (Nambisan & Wang, 1999), though the latter are to be expected in the long-term.

Notwithstanding the benefits of web technology adoption, the web has ample share of challenges for initiators and developers. Many of these challenges are associated with the unique nature of web-enabled applications. Research in the area of web-enabled information systems has revealed several differences with traditional applications. These differences exist with regards to system development methodology, stakeholder involvement, tasks, and technology (Nazareth, 1998). According to Fraternali (1999), web applications are commonly developed using an evolutionary prototyping approach, whereby the simplified version of the application is deployed as a *pilot* first, in order to gather user feedback. Thus, web-enabled applications typically undergo continuous refinement and evolution (Ginige, 1998; Nazareth, 1998; Siau, 1998; Standing, 2001). Prototype-based development also leads web-enabled information systems to have much shorter development life cycles, but which, unlike traditional applications, are regrettably developed in a rather adhoc fashion (Carstensen & Vogelsang, 2001).

However, the principal difference between the two kinds of applications lies in the broad and diverse group of stakeholders associated with web-based information systems (Gordijn, Akkermans, et al., 2000; Russo, 2000; Earl & Khan,

2001; Carter, 2002; Hasselbring, 2002; Standing, 2002; Stevens & Timbrell, 2002). Stakeholders, or organizational members participating in a common business process (Freeman, 1984), vary in their computer competency, business knowledge, language and culture. This diversity is capable of causing conflict between different stakeholder groups with regards to the establishment of system requirements (Pouloudi & Whitley, 1997; Stevens & Timbrell, 2002). Since, web-based systems transcend organizational, departmental, and even national boundaries, the issue of culture poses a significant challenge to the web systems' initiators and developers (Miles & Snow, 1992; Kumar & van Dissel, 1996; Pouloudi & Whitley, 1996; Li & Williams, 1999).

In this paper, we propose a method of identifying cultural issues that could lead to situations of conflict in the development of web-enabled applications. We focus on conflict that results from differences in organizational and departmental culture. Discussion of conflict in general and from the perspective of cultural differences is the subject of the next section.

THE CONFLICT OF CULTURES

Organizational conflict and its pervasive nature can be observed in any organization (Schermerhorn Jr., Hunt, et al., 1997). Conflict of such nature may occur at personal, group, and organizational levels, and its manifestation could take the form of intra-personal conflict, inter-personal conflict, intra-group conflict, inter-group conflict, intra-organizational conflict, and inter-organizational conflict. Business stakeholders may disagree on matters such as the setting of a group, organizational goals and values, allocation of resources, distribution of rewards, policies, procedures, and task assignments (Putnam & Poole, 1987). In extreme situations, unless it is detected early and dealt with promptly, intra-organizational conflict could lead to express struggle between stakeholders who have incompatible goals, who share scarce resources and compete for few rewards, and who are the source of mutual interference (Hocker & Wilmot, 1985). Some practitioners, nevertheless, consider conflict as an intrinsic part of organizational life and, if properly managed, an instrument of growth and desired change (Deutsch, 1973; Robbins, 1974; Renwick, 1975).

Conflicts commonly develop over an extended period of time, and they follow a number of easily recognizable stages (Pondy, 1967), i.e. latent accumulation of *conflict antecedents*, feeling or perception of early signs of conflict, manifestation of conflicting behavior, and the conflict aftermath upon its suppression or resolution. Since conflict antecedents are directly responsible for the development of manifest conflict, the focus of our study is directed towards gaining better understanding of these conflict-conducive conditions, of which there exist three main types, i.e., socio-political, structural and technological (Kumar & van Dissel, 1996; Li & Williams, 1999).

Socio-political antecedents frequently relate to the issues of mutual trust among participant firms in the sharing of sensitive business information and the control of information resources in the inter-organizational network. Opportunistic behavior, poaching, shirking, and overt sponsor dominance are capable of triggering significant conflict (Sherer, 1995; Kumar & van Dissel, 1996; Li & Williams, 1999).

Structural antecedents on the other hand are related to the differences in organizational structure (organizational differentiation) and business processes (structural differentiation) of the respective stakeholders. As most organizations are resistant to fundamental changes in their structure and operating procedures, this is definitely a source of conflict. Furthermore, if the inter-organizational network extends beyond national boundaries, the differences between national regulations and customary business practices could also cause conflict (Kumar & van Dissel, 1996).

Sometimes inter-organizational conflict transpires through the use of technology employed in support of building relationships, inter-organizational communication and business transactions. Typically such technological antecedents are only a reflection of structural or socio-political inadequacies and incompatibilities of interacting organizations. In some cases, however, the technological solutions can become the main cause of inter-organizational conflict. Technological antecedents are usually associated with mismatched IT infrastructures of the participant firms, the adoption of new and untested technologies by sponsors, or the overreliance on the business process improvement due to the technological change. However, regardless of the nature of the conflict antecedents, it is the process of system *requirements determination* that provides an opportunity to identify and minimize the effect of potential conflicts, including those sourced in cultural factors, at the earliest stage of developing technological infrastructure for the collaborating or competing originations. Conflict, power and control have already been recognized as playing an important role in requirements engineering and have been previously studied in the context of organizational and multicultural project settings (Easterbrook, 1994; Bubenko, 1995; Thanasankit, 2002).

Researchers in Information Systems persistently declare cultural antecedents of conflict as posing one of the greatest challenges to the effective development and deployment of inter-organizational systems (Kumar & van Dissel, 1996; Li & Williams, 1999), of which web-enabled applications, being at the focus of our research, are simply the sub-class. Issues related to organizational culture are commonly concealed, subtle, irrational, and developing over long periods of time, thus such issues are hard to detect, communicate and subsequently track. At the same time, in view of the prior research in organizational management and conflict, it is possible to distinguish two major classes of cultural antecedents of conflict (Schermerhorn Jr., Hunt et al., 1997; Wood, Wallace et al., 1998), which are related to:

- *Organizational* differentiation, which occurs when the stakeholders follow different time horizons for their projects, have different goals and perspectives, and use distinct language and terminology;
- *Structural* differentiation, which may exists due to the difference in stakeholders' rules, procedures, and policies.

Thus, our proposed method of detecting cultural antecedents of conflict is aimed at identifying situations, in particular in web development, where organizational and structural differentiations exist and as such which may lead to the development of acute and possibly recurring manifestation of conflict.

DETECTION OF CULTURAL ANTECEDENTS OF CONFLICT

The presented framework for conflict detection, analysis and representation has been proposed by the authors (Sarkar & Cybulski, 2002b) to combine a number of analytic methods currently employed in other information systems development areas, namely viewpoint, stakeholder and domain analysis.

In requirements engineering, the methods of identifying system inconsistencies, and thus avoiding the potential risks and conflicts, include *stakeholder analysis* (Smith, 2000) and *viewpoint analysis* (Finkelstein, Nuseibeh, et al., 1994; Leite, 1996; Sommerville & Kotonya, 1996). Stakeholder analysis focuses on determining system stakeholders, their interests, influences, their similarities and differences, and their impact on the project. Viewpoints, on the other hand, represent the organizational and developmental knowledge as perceived by individual stakeholders. Such knowledge commonly provides a reference model for the requirements of the newly constructed systems. Comparison of viewpoints leads to discovery of inconsistencies in the stakeholders' understanding of the web-enabled processes or in their respective policies.

Sommerville and Kotonya (1996) further extend the viewpoint approach by introducing the notion of stakeholder *concerns*. In general, stakeholder concerns impose constraints on system requirements and themselves are treated as obligatory requirements for all systems in a given application domain. Compliance with organizational stakeholder concerns is critical to developing systems, which are less likely to cause or support inter-organizational conflict (Easterbrook, 1994). In web-based e-commerce systems, stakeholder concerns are usually related to the systems' accessibility, scalability, reliability, performance, security, and attractiveness of the web presentation (Abolhassani, 2000; Li, 2000). We define a "concern" as an issue voiced by a particular stakeholder with regards to some aspect of the proposed information system, which impacts the stakeholder's involvement in this system and which when addressed will determine selection of the system requirements (Sarkar & Cybulski, 2002c). If analyzed systematically, concerns could help uncovering cultural antecedents of conflict. As dealing with organizational and cultural conflict in software development is often a recurring event, developers' experience in identifying and resolving the earliest stages of cultural antecedents of conflict should be captured, recorded and preserved for future use and reuse.

Past research indicates that stakeholders' knowledge, their characteristics, needs and concerns, as well as their requirements for systems in the domain, can be effectively reused between multiple projects within a single application domain (Prieto-Diaz, 1990; Arango, 1994; Cybulski, Neal, et al., 1998). Software engineering practice also suggests that reuse of various software life-cycle work-products could lead to higher quality of software and more cost-effective systems, as compared with the systems produced entirely from scratch (Basili, Dieter, et al., 1987; Tracz, 1987; Prieto-Diaz, 1990). Reuse of requirements is especially relevant to web application development, where in the absence of a stable community of easily accessible stakeholders, system requirements are commonly inferred by developers rather than elicited from users in a systematic process (Gordijn, Akkermans et al., 2000). In this context, we have proposed and evaluated a method of identifying and analyzing developers' experience in dealing with stakeholder concerns. These concerns include those regarding to differences in organizational cultures, of which concerns could be gathered and consolidated across an entire application domain, then packaged in a form suitable for discussion, training and dissemination, and subsequently reused from one web project to another (Sarkar & Cybulski, 2002a).

An effective form of packaging experience related to solving frequently occurring problem in a certain domain, in our case identification of antecedent cultural conflict in web systems, is known as *patterns* (Buschman, Meunier, et al., 1996; Rising, 1999). Patterns are known to be particularly effective in sharing and reusing expert knowledge in such applications as architectural design (Alexander, 1979), education (Anthony, 1996), design of organizational processes (Coplien, 1995), software development (Gamma, Helm et al., 1995; Buschman, Meunier, et al., 1996; Fowler, 1997) and multimedia construction (Rossi, Schwabe, et al., 1997; Cybulski & Linden, 1998).

Patterns are fashioned to facilitate effective problem solving, i.e. identification of a problem in some specific context, understanding the reasons for the problem to occur and persist, selection of the problem solution, and predicting the consequences of applying a particular problem solution. Our conflict patterns are thus formulated according to the most commonly used pattern schema, which consists of the following components (Gamma, Helm et al., 1995, 3, 6-8):

- *Name* of the pattern;
- A statement of the *problem*, which calls for the application of a pattern or set of patterns to resolve it;
- *Context*, a description of the situation in view of which the problem has arisen;
- A set of *forces*, preventing effective application of certain classes of solutions to the problem at hand;
- The *solution(s)*, which describe(s) how the forces could be resolved in order to come up with the best solution;
- The *consequences* of applying the pattern in terms of the expected results and trade-offs;
- *Known uses,* or real-life situations where the patterns have been successfully applied in some form.

Viewpoints, concerns and patterns are an integral part of our approach to detecting cultural conflict antecedents. The model describing our approach is shown in Figure 1. The model shows two stakeholders, namely A and B, represented by stick figures. The stakeholders are two enterprises or two organizational that interact via a web medium. The two stakeholders are assumed to be culturally different in light of their viewpoints about work processes and "the way they do things." The number of stakeholders may vary depending upon their direct participation in a workflow.

As the participating stakeholders may have differing viewpoints on the workflow they jointly participate in, there might exist, in view of the assumptions made about cultural differences, antecedents of conflict. To counter such development, we capture the stakeholder viewpoints by identifying the stakeholder concerns, and subsequently comparing these concerns against the patterns collected in an experience base, depicted by the cylinder labelled "Domain Concerns" in Figure 1. If the match should occur, we use the patterns to guide web systems developers in the analysis of conflict antecedents, possible renegotiation of workflow requirements, and adopting a proven solution that is likely to reduce the stakeholders' concerns about the adverse effects of cultural differences.

Figure 1: The Model of Conflict Detection in the B2B Systems Development

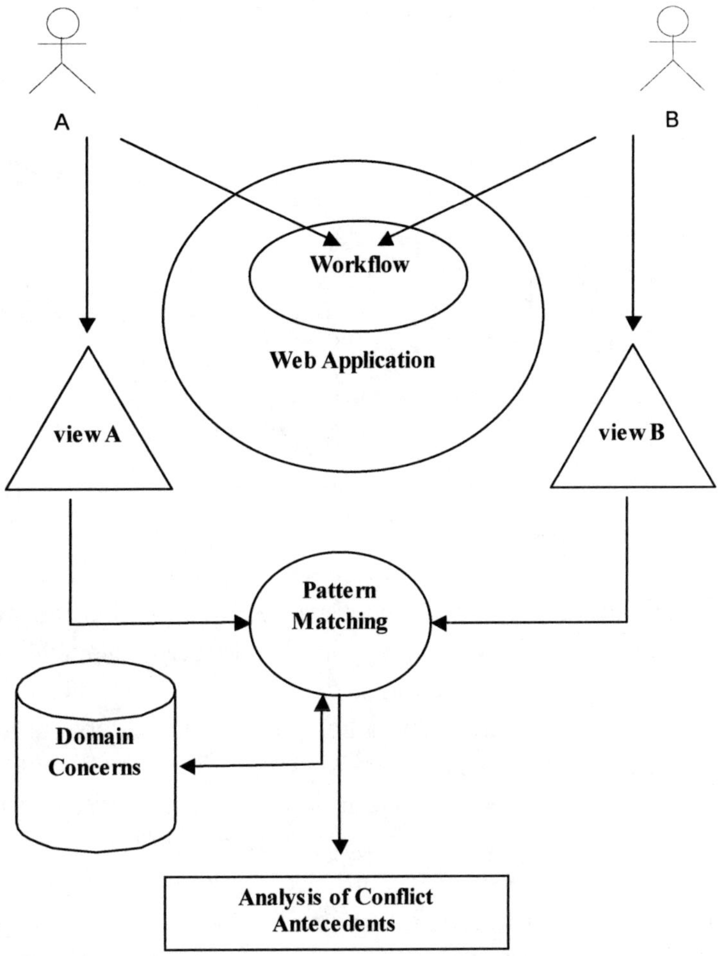

ANALYSIS OF STAKEHOLDER CONCERNS

We undertook our study of cultural antecedents prevailing in web development projects, by conducting in-depth qualitative interviews of stakeholders in the web-enabled Human Resource (HR) domain in Melbourne, Australia. Our choice of a domain was influenced by *elite* interviews with two e-business consultants (Marshall & Rossman, 1989). The consultants suggested the domain of web-based HR and payroll systems as of particular interest to the research, due to the recent adoption of web technology in outsourced and in-house HR and payroll services in Australia, the significant scale of the deployed systems, and the fact that cultural

Figure 2: Method of Gathering Concerns

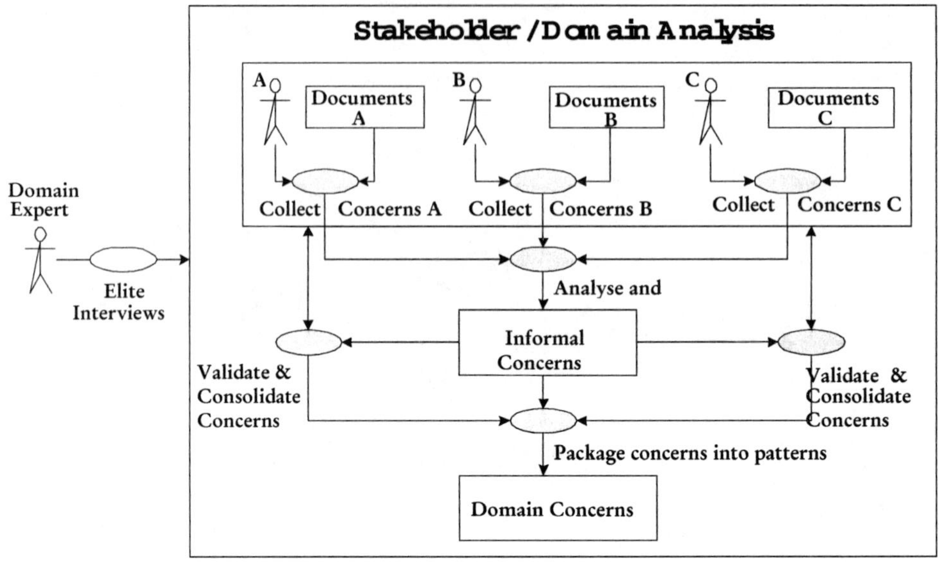

issues are present in such systems. Based on their suggestions, we proceeded to collect comprehensive data reflecting stakeholders concerns (Marshall & Rossman, 1989; Creswell, 1994), by conducting in-depth interviews with HR departments implementing web-based systems, web-based payroll providers, solutions developers, and application service providers (ASPs). This was supplemented by audiovisual materials, such as demonstration software and presentations.

The method we employed in this regard comprises of four steps, namely, the collection of concerns, analysis and recording of concerns, validation and consolidation, and packaging concerns into patterns. Figure 2 illustrates all of the conducted activities and provides a methodological framework for our study. It shows the stakeholders (shown as stick figures), activities (ellipses), and the output of each activity (rectangular boxes). **Description of the methodological steps follows.**

- **Collection of Concerns**
  This step involved the collection of comprehensive data reflecting the experience of web-based HR/payroll *initiators*[1] and developers in incorporating the concerns of the most significant stakeholders, and the resultant system requirements that emerged (Marshall & Rossman, 1989; Creswell, 1994). The multi-case studies enabled us to gather rich data that could be used in establishing domain knowledge of concerns (Yin, 1994).

- **Analysis and Recording of Concerns**
  In this stage, the collected concerns were looked upon as domain artefacts and their similarities and differences were subjected to analysis, in accordance with the principles of domain analysis. This allowed the determination of domain features (Arango & Prieto-Diaz, 1987; Kang, Cohen, et al., 1990; Prieto-Diaz, 1990; Arango, 1994; Kang, Kim et al., 1998). The data was analyzed qualitatively in order to spot regularities (Miles & Huberman, 1994).
- **Validation and Consolidation**
  In order to represent the collected data as patterns that depicted cultural antecedents, it was imperative to consolidated and validate the stakeholder concerns. This was done through a series of structured follow-up interviews with the participants. In these interviews, the interviewees were presented with concerns collected across the entire domain to ascertain the relevance of these concerns to their particular organization, as well as to classify each concern statement as a pattern component, i.e., its problem, force, solution or consequence. Interviewees were also asked to provide some insight into their particular decisions associated with the concern's relevance and its classification. The rich insight information was used to derive the context of each pattern. The consolidation and the relevance ranking were also helpful in shedding some light on the similarities and variation between the stakeholder concerns.[2]
- **Packaging Concerns into Patterns**
  Finally, a series of structured interviews helped packaging the identified concerns into patterns as per the classification of their features. Such packaging allowed systematic representation, sharing and reuse of experience in dealing with stakeholder concerns among the domain developers. The packaging of concerns was the final step in the method.

DISCUSSION OF FINDINGS

Our findings revealed that cultural issues although recognized were not of outmost concern to providers of commercial payroll services. These organizations catered to small and medium-sized enterprises (SMEs). The commercial payroll provider acted as a *hub* in the web venture, and thus, the work culture of various clients did not have an overbearing impact on it. In fact, technological antecedents were more of a concern, as stated by a prominent member of the web team of one of the providers:

"...most of our clients are small businesses. So, they may not be at a stage where they could claim to be PC-ready or Internet-ready. So, we are more inclined to support them from a technical point of view."

On the contrary, the HR departments of organizations, which had deployed web-enabled applications to facilitate their interactions with other units, reported the prominence of cultural issues in the setting of system requirements. Furthermore, these organizations were all tertiary-level educational institutions consisting of various faculties and departments that differed greatly in their culture and outlook. The role of the HR departments was to provide support to these units, and in doing so, needed to comply and work alongside the peculiarities of the diverse cultures and modus operandi. Thus, cultural antecedents had to be dealt with in the establishment of requirements for the web-based systems. The importance of cultural issues was reiterated by one of the interviewees, a web system administrator in the HR department:

"The various departments have their own ways of doing things, which might have not much in common with each other. Besides, some of the people from these departments could be high up in the power structure (of the institute) and have their own little cliques. So, we had to be very careful when we approached them with our plans to involve them in the usage of the web system."

We also discovered that some of these concerns called for additional features to be included or restricted some of the requirement specifications. For example, supervisors could reject timesheets or leave applications submitted by employees without providing any explanations on the web, even though this was not initially intended by HR. The reason, according to the developer, was:

"Most of the users are academics. We cannot expect them adhere to strictly enforced business rules embedded into the application. Moreover, if there was a problem with an employee document, they would rather sort it out internally without using the web system. So, we decided not to enforce the entry of rejection comments on the web."

Yet, another participant stated:

> *"They (the academic departments) were initially not keen on using the web system, because they thought this would change the way they have been working for years. This is why we had to take steps to clarify and explain the benefits of the web system to them, and the fact that this would not necessarily mean a radical change in their culture."*

The initiators were also aware of the importance of informal communication mechanisms and nuances prevalent in the individual departments, which they took into account while embedding business rules into the applications. An instance of such a scenario related to the internal agreement that was made between a supervisor and an employee, when the latter was applying for leave for duration longer than for which he was eligible. In the words of the systems manager, responsible for overseeing the development and maintenance of the web system:

> *"Like I said, this (the application for leave) involves communication between the employees and supervisors within the departments. Usually, the employee would have spoken to the manager about this leave involving the extra days. So, these applications are already verbally approved even before they make it to the system. So, we have not actually hard-coded this (business rule permitting leave only for the period allocated) into system, as this would take away the flexibility (desired by the various user groups in view of their group cultures)."*

Our case studies also revealed the manifestation of conflict between two entities owing to different cultural perspectives. The issue was associated with a security requirement involving the use of digital signatures, and was enforced upon the system by the developers in line with their culture of technological innovativeness. According to the chief developer:

> *"I think we are not at all behind in terms of the web-enabled HR system that we've developed. In fact, most applications in the domain don't have digital certificates for authorization. So, we are using leading edge technologies."*

A conflicting viewpoint on the issue of digital signature was held by the HR manager, who headed the division's web initiative:

"While it is certainly true that digital signatures are far more secure than ordinary usernames and passwords, but the administrative burden of maintaining digital certificate technology, at the level of technology that was around at that time, far exceeded any benefits gained from the increased security. The burden of administration fell onto us (HR), but we were inadequately resourced to do this."

The end-users of the system were likewise, not keen on digital signatures either. From the feedback obtained as part of the incremental approach to the evolution of the web system, it was revealed that supervisors also considered the implementation of this technology as burden as it was time consuming to install and required additional training for effective usage of the technology.

Moreover, in the words of the HR manager:

"This digital signature initiative was railroaded by the developers, it was not an HR requirement... nor was it a requirement by finance for their part in the workflow (for which they use their own digital certificates). Since, the IT division (developers) knew how to use the technology (in line with their culture of going for cutting-edge stuff)... everyone else should use this... this was their justification. This impeded our progress in the roll-over and further evolution of the web system."

Ultimately, the feature was dropped as a consequence of the conflict, as stated, in disappointment, by the chief developer:

"We set the features... we put in digital signatures so that authorized personnel could sign on very securely. HR will then say, 'what's that?' to which we give our explanation. So, sometimes, when it's a new technology, it's our suggestion. But when it comes to the nature of transactions—what will be implemented and in what order—it is their specifications."

This was undoubtedly a conflict that manifested out of a cultural factor, though it took the form of a dispute over the adoption of a certain technology. Hence, the method enabled us to conduct in-depth studies into the various web-enabled HR applications and identify cultural antecedents of conflict as reflected by the concerns of the relevant stakeholders.

REPRESENTATION OF CONCERNS AS PATTERNS

Based on the elaboration of our empirical findings in the preceding section and in line with the steps in our method, we arrived at data that was cast into patterns. In this section, for the sake of brevity, we discuss two patterns that represent cultural antecedents of conflict in a particular business setting. These include the *No*

Table 1: A Sample Pattern 1

Pattern Name	***No Comments Please***
Problem	What happens if supervisors are concerned about spending too much time and effort while approving employee applications online?
Context	The main workflows of a web-enabled HR system include the submission and approval of timesheets and leave applications by employees and supervisors, respectively. Ideally, web developers would embed business rules into the workflows to ensure that, in the event of a timesheet or leave application rejection, supervisors explain the reasons behind their decision, i.e., include comments. This is aimed at reducing hiccups in HR work processes due to grievances by anxious employees.
Forces	1. Supervisors may not be willing to spend too much time carrying out online administrative tasks, especially if they are not entirely computer or Internet proficient. 2. In many cases, employees and supervisors prefer to communicate informally within their work units with regards to matters of pay and leave. 3. Unhappy supervisors will express aversion to online administrative tasks. 4. Complaints will be lodged by anxious employees whose applications have been turned down without proper comments.
Solution	**The system shall allow supervisors to make decision to online employee application without including comments**
Consequences	1. A separate set of access codes will ensure a simple yet secure level of supervisory workflow. 2. It relieves the burden of the initiator's dedication of vast resources in maintenance. 3. Such a simple level of security may not be adequate for more mainstream financial transactions, such as purchase orders and large fund transfers.
Known Uses	Internet banking sites grant access to personal customers on the basis of account numbers and passwords.

Table 2: A Sample Pattern 2

Pattern Name	***Simple but Secure***
Problem	What happens if supervisors and/or initiators are concerned with the use of digital signatures as a security feature?
Context	Digital signatures are used to enforce security on open system, such as application on the web. These technological artefacts ensure, in the context of web-based HR solutions, that the approval of timesheets and leave applications are done by authorized personnel only.
Forces	1. The maintenance of digital certificates necessitates the allocation of vast resources. 2. The nature of administrative workflow tasks related to pay and leave approvals are very moderately sensitive. 3. The installation and usage of digital signatures requires considerable time and training on the part of supervisors. 4. Unhappy supervisors will express aversion to online administrative tasks.
Solution	**The system shall designate a separate set of access codes for supervisors.**
Consequences	1. This requirements specification will ensure that supervisors use the web system 2. It also alleviates supervisor concerns about the disruption of their divisional work practices. 3. No online explanation for employees with regards to the rejection of their application.
Known Uses	Many websites allow registration or online booking without the inclusion of comments.

Comments Please, and the *Simple but Secure* patterns, presented in Table 1 and Table 3, respectively.

The substance of the patterns was derived from the responses of the interview participants to the various concerns of cultural conflict, which have been discussed in our findings. It should be noted that the findings were obtained empirically from the data generated and qualitatively analyzed according to the method illustrated in Figure 2. Note that the *problem* statements of the patterns were actually requirement specifications about which stakeholders expressed concerns, while *forces* reflected the actual concerns identified. The *solution* component presents system requirements that were actually adopted in the organizations studied to alleviate

Figure 3: Classification of Domain Concerns

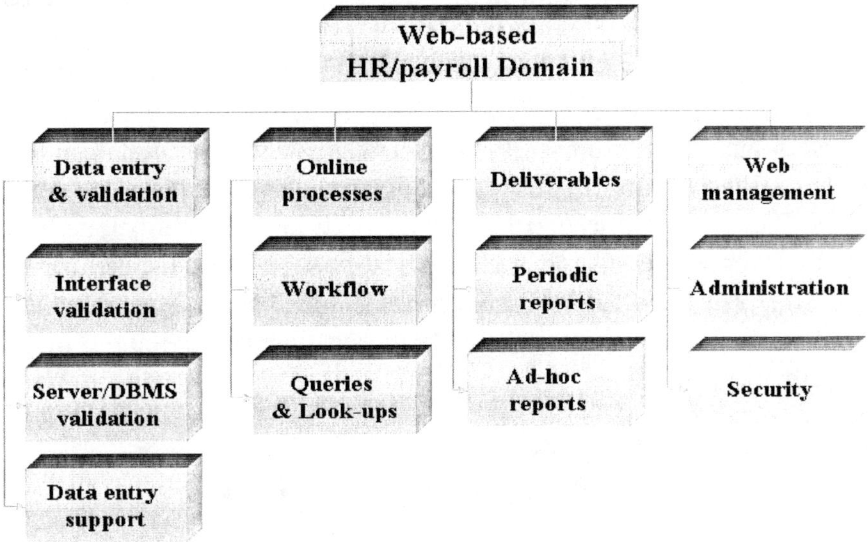

stakeholder concerns, while *consequences* indicate effects of the requirement artefact. However, the *Known Uses* section was not generated empirically, but came about through the authors' experience with applications in various domains.

The majority of patterns related to the cultural antecedents of conflict describe divergent views of two communities of stakeholders, each having different sets of concerns and priorities. For example, the *No Comments Please* pattern (see Table 1) captures the beliefs of both employees and supervisors (see forces) regarding their business rules and preferences. On the other hand, *Simple but Secure* pattern (see Table 3) seems to describe opinions of supervisors alone, yet it is dealing with the cultural issues of two stakeholder groups, i.e., supervisors and developers. The presented patterns illustrate the main point in this paper that the experience captured and packaged in patterns need to be written with a specific user in mind – in our case, the information systems developers, who are to avoid embedding conflicts from the social sphere of organizational interaction into the technological dimension of the inter- or intra-organizational system. The patterns serve numerous purposes, i.e., that of an organizational experience base (capture and codify experience), a communication and learning tool (dissemination of experience among developers), and finally that of a problem-solving tool (identification and elimination of cultural antecedents of organizational conflict). To be effective in its multiple classes of uses, the collected patterns need to be well-written to facilitate their easy understanding by development staff, organized into a well-maintained repository to ensure their accuracy and timeliness, and thoroughly indexed to allow efficient access to patterns and their components.

In our work, we have created a repository of 27 patterns for the HR / payroll domain. The patterns have been collected and classified according to the features that emerged during our study of the applications in the domain. The major stakeholders in the chosen domains validated our patterns to ensure their correctness, their sufficient generality and their applicability and reusability for effective dealing with stakeholder concerns. The classification scheme is illustrated in Figure 3. Although many of the patterns focused on the technical aspects of developing and running HR services, many of the collected patterns addressed the cultural aspects of the system in place.

SUMMARY AND CONCLUSIONS

Cultural conflict poses a serious challenge to the development of all e-Business systems in general. The difficulty in dealing with such a conflict is two-fold. In the first instance, the ineffectiveness in identifying conflict antecedents accounts for the intractability of conflict. Secondly, the inability to determine and reconcile the incompatible perspectives and concerns of stakeholders interacting across the electronic networks that span organizational and departmental boundaries.

As there exist few practical solutions to dealing with this situation, we thus proposed a method of predicting the possibility of conflict due to cultural antecedents. Our method focuses on recording and collecting the experience of developers and project initiators in dealing with conflict antecedents across a particular application domain. The generalization, formalization, and packaging of such experience could enhance its reusability in new projects in the same domain (Basili, Dieter, et al., 1987; Biggerstaff & Perlis, 1989; Arango, Schoen, et al., 1993; Cybulski, 1996; Mannion, Keepence, et al., 1999; Rising, 1999). In our research, stakeholders' concerns form the basis of reusable experience. They are captured from multiple domain sources in the form of patterns and they represent possible stakeholder viewpoints that may occur in some future projects. The cultural antecedent patterns are used to guide web system developers in determining inconsistencies of stakeholder viewpoints and their concerns over requirements for a proposed system. They provide typical solutions to alleviate such inconsistencies, reduce stakeholder concerns, and minimize the possibility of cultural manifestations of conflict, owing to organizational and structural differentiation of stakeholders, developing later in the system implementation or its operation.

We conducted a study of six HR and payroll systems provided by outsourced payroll companies and HR departments of organizations. To arrive at a collection of useful patterns, we had to devise a novel pattern mining procedure, based on a series of exploratory, consolidating and validating in-depth interviews and qualitative data analysis. In the process, we have discovered our method to be effective in collecting and packaging stakeholder concerns. Using a feature-based domain analysis, we have also discovered the similarities and variations in the stakeholder concerns, which enabled us to construct the classification of domain concerns. Such classification is useful in dealing with new domain concerns by instantiating them into high-level or low-level patterns.

Moreover, our studies revealed that cultural antecedents of conflict prevailed in a number of web-based system development projects initiated by HR departments. However, it was the identification of the stakeholder concerns that can lead to the reuse of relevant solutions. Thus, if the problems and the contexts pertaining to a new application in the domain match with that of the corresponding patterns that we have gathered, we will have an idea of what stakeholder concerns may be present implicitly, as well as how the solutions of the patterns can be adapted and applied in the new situation. Since patterns represent system developmental experience in a manner that is aimed at its reuse, such patterns should help identify antecedent conflicts and formulate a solution to minimize the manifestation of conflict, despite the complex nature of conflict ensuing from cultural differences. Our study of the web-based HR/payroll domain revealed concerns that were generic not only to the applications in the domain, but also to other web systems, such as web-based purchasing and procurement solutions.

The consideration of concerns and consequent reduction in conflict caused by organizational cultures is likely to support or ease the resistance to the adoption of new technology in organizations. This is especially important in light of cross-organizational workflow systems and virtual work groups, where there are diverse groups of stakeholders with varying viewpoints, owing to intra- and inter-organizational politics and various cliques are prevalent. In view of this diversity of the stakeholder base associated with web-enabled applications, a multitude of concerns exist and could potentially inhibit the optimal performance of workflow systems that support collaboration between the various stakeholder groups (Allen, Colligan, et al., 1999; Sarkar & Cybulski, 2002b) Therefore, the consideration of stakeholder concerns contributes to the understanding and appreciation of the cultural issues that prevail in web-information systems.

ENDNOTES

1 Initiators are organizations or organizational units that propose the e-business system to their trading partners or clients (Riggins & Mukhopadhyay, 1999).

2 Variations are those features, which are not shared by all applications.

REFERENCES

Abolhassani, M. (2000). *Reviewing the Requirements of Traditional E-Commerce.* CollectR.

Alexander, C. (1979). *A Timeless Way of Building.* NY: Oxford University Press.

Allen, D., & Colligan, D., et al. (1999). Trust, Power, and interorganizational information systems: The case of the electronic trading community translease. Copenhagen, Denmark: ECIS.

Anthony, D.L.G. (1996). *Patterns for Classroom Education. Pattern Languages of Program Design.* Kerth, N.L. Reading, MA: Addison-Wesley Publishing Company. 2: 391-406.

Arango, G. (1994). *Domain Analysis Methods. Software Reusability.* Schafer, W., Prieto-Diaz, R. & Matsumoto, M. London, Ellis Horwood: 17-49.

Arango, G. & Prieto-Diaz, R. (1987). Domain analysis concepts and research directions. *IEEE Computer Society*: 9-34.

Arango, G., Schoen, E., et al. (1993). Design as evolution and reuse. Advances in software reuse: Selected papers from the *Second International Workshop on Software Reusability*. Prieto-Diaz, R. & Frakes, W.B. Los Alamitos, CA: IEEE Computer Society Press: 9-18.

Basili, V.R. & Dieter, R. et al. (1987). Software reuse: A framework for research. *The 10th Minnowbrook Workshop on Software Performance Evaluation,* Blue Mountain Lake, NY.

Biggerstaff, T.J. & Perlis, A.J. (Eds.) (1989). *Software Reusability.* Reading, MA: Addison-Wesley.

Bubenko, J.A., Jr. (1995). Challenges in requirements engineering. *The 2nd IEEE International Symposium on Requirements Engineering,* Stockholm, Sweden.

Buschman, F., & Meunier, R., et al. (1996). *Pattern-Oriented Software Architecture: A System of Patterns.* John Wiley & Sons.

Carstensen, P.H. & Vogelsang, L. (2001). Design of web-based information systems - New challenges for systems development? *ECIS*, Bled, Slovenia.

Carter, J. (2002). *Developing E-Commerce Systems*. Prentice-Hall.

Coplien, J.O. (1995). A generative development-process pattern language. *Pat-*

tern Languages of Program Design. Coplien, J.O & Schmidt, D. Addison-Wesley: 204.

Creswell, J.W. (1994). A qualitative procedure. *Research Design: Qualitative & Quantitative Approaches.* SAGE Publications.

Cybulski, J.L. (1996). Reusing requirements specifications: review of methods and techniques. *1st Australian Requirements Engineering Workshop,* Monash University, Melbourne, Australia.

Cybulski, J.L. & Linden, T. (1998). *Composing Multimedia Artefacts for Reuse. Pattern Languages of Program Design.* N. Harris, F.B. & R. H., Addison-Wesley Longman (1999). 4: 461-488.

Cybulski, J.L., Neal, R.D.B., et al. (1998). Reuse of early life-cycle artefacts: Work products, methods and tools. *Annals of Software Engineering 5*: 227-251.

Deutsch, M. (1973). *The Resolution of Conflict.* New Haven, Yale University Press.

Earl, M. & Khan, B. (2001). E-commerce is changing the face of IT. *MIT Sloan Management Review, 43*(1): 64-72.

Easterbrook, S. (1994). Resolving requirements conflicts with computer-supported negotiation in requirements engineering. *Requirements Engineering: Social and Technical Issues*. Jirotka, M. & Goguen, J. London, Academic Press: 41-65.

Finkelstein, A., & Nuseibeh, B., et al. (1994). A framework for expressing the relationships between multiple views in requirements specification. *IEEE Transactions on Software Engineering 20*(10): 760 - 773.

Fowler, M. (1997). *Analysis Patterns.* MA, Addison-Wesley.

Fraternali, P. (1999). Tools and approaches for developing data-intensive web applications: A survey. *ACM Computing Surveys, 31*(3): 227-263.

Freeman, R.E. (1984). *Strategic Management: A Stakeholder Approach.* Boston, Pitman.

Gamma, E. & Helm, R., et al. (1995). *Design Patterns: Elements of Reusable object-Oriented Software.* Reading, MA, Addison-Wesley.

Ginige, A. (1998). Web engineering: Methodologies for developing large and maintainable web-based information systems. *IEEE International Conference on Networking India and the World,* Ahmedabad, India.

Gordijn, J. & Akkermans, H., et al. (2000). Value based requirements creation for electronic commerce applications. *The 33rd Hawaii International Conference on Systems Sciences,* Hawaii.

Hasselbring, W. (2002). Web data integration for e-commerce applications. *IEEE Multimedia 9*(1): 16-25.

Hocker, J.L. & Wilmot, W.W. (1985). *Interpersonal Conflict,* Brown, W.C. Dubuque, IA.

Isakowitz, T. & Bieber, M., et al. (1998). Web information systems. *Communications of the ACM, 41*(7): 78-80.

Kang, K.C. & Cohen, J.A. et al. (1990). *Feature-Oriented Domain Analysis (FODA) Feasibility Study*. Pittsburgh, PA, Software Engineering Institute, Carnegie Mellon University.

Kang, K. C. & Kim, S., et al. (1998). FORM: A feature-oriented reuse method with domain-specific reference architectures. *Annals of Software Engineering:* 143-168.

Kumar, K. & van Dissel, H. (1996). Sustainable collaboration: Managing conflict and cooperation in interorganizational systems. *MIS Quarterly 20*(3): 279-300.

Leite, J.C.S.P. (1996). Viewpoints on viewpoints. *The 2nd International Software Architecture Workshop (ISAW-2) and the International Workshop on Multiple Perspectives in Software Development (Viewpoints '96) on SIGSOFT '96 Workshops.*

Li, F. & Williams, H. (1999). New collaboration between firms: The role of interorganizational systems. *The 32nd Hawaii International Conference on System Sciences,* Hawaii.

Li, X. (2000). Perspectives in engineering web-enabled electronic commerce systems. *Pacific Asia Conference in Information Systems (PACIS)*, Hong Kong.

Mannion, M. & Keepence, B. et al. (1999). Reusing single system requirements from application family requirements. *Proceedings of 21st IEEE International Conference on Software Engineering (ICSE-21)*, Los Angeles, CA.

Marshall, C. & Rossman, G.B. (1989). *Designing Qualitative Research,* SAGE.

Miles, M.B. & Huberman, A.M. (1994). *Qualitative Data Analysis: An Expanded Sourcebook,* SAGE.

Miles, R. E. & Snow, C.C. (1992). Causes of failure in network organizations. *California Management Review:* 53-72.

Nambisan, S. & Wang, Y.M. (1999). Roadblocks to Web technology adoption? *Communications of the ACM, 42*(1): 98-101.

Nazareth, D.L (1998). Designing effective Websites: Lending structure to a chaotic process. *Fourth Americas Conference on Information Systems,* Baltimore, MD.

Pondy, L.R. (1967). Organizational conflict: Concepts and models. *Administrative Science Quarterly, 12*: 269-320.

Pouloudi, A. & Whitley, E.A. (1996). Discussing the role of information systems in the manifestation of organizational and inter-organizational conflict. *The Systemist, 18*: 217-238.

Pouloudi, A. & Whitley, E.A. (1997). Stakeholder identification in interorganizational systems: Gaining insights for drug use management systems. *European Journal of Information Systems, 15*(2): 85-96.

Prieto-Diaz, R. (1990). Domain analysis: An introduction. *Software Engineering Notes 15*(2): 47-54.

Putnam, L. & Poole, M (1987). *Conflict and Negotiation. Handbook of Organizational Communication: An Interdisciplinary Perspective.* Porter, L: 549-599.

Renwick, P.A. (1975). Impact of topic and source of disagreement on conflict management. *Organization Behavior and Human Performance, 14*: 416-425.

Riggins, F.J. & Mukhopadhyay, T. (1999). Overcoming adoption and implementation risks of EDI. *International Journal of Electronic Commerce.*

Rising, L. (1999). Patterns: A way to reuse expertise. *IEEE Communications Magazine, 37*(4).

Robbins, S.P. (1974). *Managing Organizational Conflict: A Nontraditional Approach.* Englewood Cliffs, NJ: Prentice-Hall.

Rossi, G. & Schwabe, D. et al. (1997). Design reuse in hypermedia application development. *Eighth ACM Conference on Hypertext Technology (HyperText '97)*, Southampton, Inglaterra: ACM Press.

Russo, N.L. (2000). *Developing Applications for the Web: Exploring Differences Between Traditional and World Wide Web Application Development. Managing Web-Enabled Technologies in Organizations: A Global Perspective.* M. Khosrowpour, Hershey, PA: Idea Group, 23-35.

Sarkar, P.K. & Cybulski, J.L. (2002a). Alignment of stakeholder concerns with system requirements. *The Austral-Asian Workshop on Requirements Engineering (AWRE)*, Melbourne.

Sarkar, P.K. & Cybulski, J.L. (2002b). Analysis of stakeholder concerns with a view to avoid organisational conflict in B2B systems. *The 15th International Conference in Electronic Commerce*, Bled, Slovenia.

Sarkar, P.K. & Cybulski, J.L. (2002c). Consideration of stakeholder concerns in the development of Web-enabled systems. (forthcoming) *Proceedings of the IADIS International Conference WWW/Internet,* Lisbon, Portugal.

Schermerhorn Jr., J.R., Hunt, J.G., et al. (1997). Conflict and negotiation. *Organization Behavior,* John Wiley & Sons: 377 - 398.

Sherer, S.A. (1995). Risk in interorganizational information systems. *The First Americas Conference on Information Systems.*

Siau, K. (1998). Method engineering for Web information systems development: Challenges and issues. *Fourth Americas Conference on Information Systems*, Baltimore, MD.

Smith, L.W. (2000). Project clarity through stakeholder analysis. CROSSTALK: *The Journal of Defense Software Engineering*: 4-9.

Sommerville, I. & Kotonya, G. (1996). Requirements engineering with viewpoints. *BCS/IEE Software Engineering Journal, 1*(11): 2-26.

Standing, C. (2001). The Requirements of Methodologies for Developing Web Applications. *ECIS*, Bled, Slovenia.

Standing, C. (2002). Methodologies for developing Web applications. *Information and SoftwareTechnology, 44*(3): 151-159.

Stevens, K.J. & Timbrell, G.T. (2002). The implications of e-commerce for software project risk: A preliminary investigation. *IFIP*, Copenhagen.

Thanasankit, T. (2002). Requirements engineering - Exploring the influence of high power distance on social status in Thailand. *European Journal of Information Systems, 11*(2): 128-141.

Tracz, W. (1987). *Software Reuse: Motivators and Inhibitors.* COMPCON S'87.

Wood, J., & Wallace, J., et al. (1998). Conflict and negotiation. *Organization Behavior: An Asia-Pacific Perspective.* Brisbane, Jacaranda Wiley Ltd.: 578-605.

Yin, R.K. (1994). *Case Study Research: Design and Methodology.* Thousand Oaks, Sage.

Chapter VII

Stakeholder Relationships and Electronic Commerce: A Comparison of Singapore and Australia

Chia Yao Lee and Wei-Chang Kong
The University of Melbourne, Australia

ABSTRACT

This chapter investigates the characteristics and features that set Business-to-Consumer (B2C) and Business-to-Business (B2B) e-commerce apart. A Differentiation Framework was developed to better describe 1) Stakeholder Characteristics, 2) Transaction Characteristics, and 3) Stakeholder Relationship Characteristics, as the criteria for differentiation. Data was collected from organizations operating in various industries in Australia and Singapore to provide a descriptive insight into early stage B2C and B2B e-commerce implementation for the Asia Pacific region. This study found that e-commerce reduces face-to-face interaction between stakeholders, hence e-commerce organizations will need to put in additional effort in addressing stakeholder relationship issues. It was also found that stakeholder relationship is a useful unit of analysis for future e-commerce research.

INTRODUCTION[1]

E-commerce is often associated with the buying and selling of consumer products over the Internet. While this narrow definition of e-commerce is correct, many other commerce and business activities also fall under the term "e-commerce." The stakeholders who create commerce, either actively or passively construct and determine the nature of the commercial relationship. The aim of this chapter is to suggest the e-commerce Differentiation Framework, which uses the nature and activities of stakeholders to distinguish between the two major types of e-commerce, namely *Business-to-Business* (B2B) e-commerce and *Business-to-Consumer* (B2C) e-commerce. This framework will use examples of e-commerce in Small and Medium Enterprises (SMEs) in Singapore and Australia. The study was carried out in these two countries over a period of four months in 1999.

E-commerce has captured the attention of businesses large and small, government officials, academics, and the greater public, due to its rapid growth in recent years and the amount of money it commands. According to a recent forecast by the GartnerGroup, the global market for B2B e-commerce alone is expected to rise from US $145 billion in 1999 to US $7.29 trillion in 2004 (GartnerGroup, 2000). While not being overwhelmed by such forecasts and statistics (OECD, 1999), e-commerce is a phenomenon that promises to impact business operations, government policies, consumer buying behavior, and many other elements of the modern society.

The definition of e-commerce is still indeterminate (Clarke, 1998; DCITA, 1999, USDC, 1999). For the purpose of this chapter, e-commerce includes commerce and business activities that are performed over electronic networks (both fixed and mobile networks), including upstream and downstream supply chain activities, and consumer purchases that are initiated through electronic means. The different types of e-commerce activities are essentially determined by the stakeholders involved. A review of existing literature in e-commerce (Kalakota & Whinston, 1996; Lawrence et al., 1998; Rangan & Bell, 1998; Riggins & Rhee, 1998; Whinston et al., 1997) identified the two major types of e-commerce as Business-to-Business e-commerce, and Business-to-Consumer e-commerce. Creating a framework for distinguishing the two types of e-commerce activities aids in identifying and understanding the stakeholders involved, the roles they play, the nature of e-commerce relationships, and the potential benefits to different stakeholders. It is hoped that the outcome of this study will enable businesses to formulate strategies to align their business operations more closely with e-commerce strategies, thus improving the management of resources like raw materials, labor, capital and entrepreneurship.

This study draws on e-commerce examples in Singapore and Australia as these two countries are considered early adopters of technological innovations in the region.

LITERATURE REVIEW AND RESEARCH FRAMEWORK

On the surface, the two identified categories of e-commerce (B2B and B2C) appear to share the similarity of using electronic networks to enable commerce activities. However, a more detailed analysis will highlight where the similarities end, and what the distinguishing features are. This chapter thus proposes the e-commerce Differentiation Framework for distinguishing and categorizing the two major categories of e-commerce. Figure 1 illustrates how the e-commerce Differentiation Framework is used for differentiating B2C and B2B e-commerce relationships. The three criteria for differentiation are stakeholder characteristics, transaction characteristics, and stakeholder relationship characteristics.

Stakeholder Characteristics

In this section, we intend to give an insight into stakeholder characteristics like the number of stakeholders, location and dispersion of stakeholders, and the business nature of stakeholders.

Figure 1: The E-Commerce Differentiation Framework

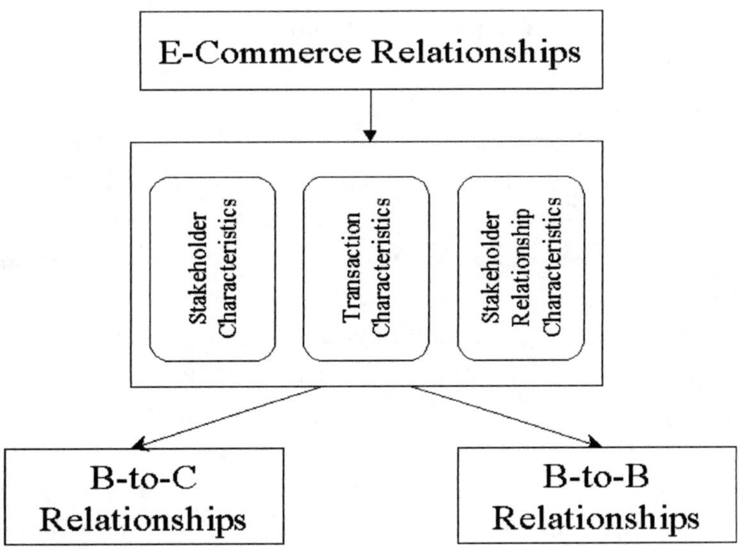

In B2C e-commerce, the primary participants are members of the public who form the customer base, and the retailers, who sell the products via an electronic storefront. Buyers in B2C e-commerce purchase products for their own consumption. B2C sellers may target buyers in the local geographical proximity, or those distributed across time, geographical and national boundaries. Sellers in B2C e-commerce are retailers, distributors, resellers, or even the product manufacturer itself. Examples of manufacturers who sell products direct to consumers via an electronic storefront are Dell.com[2] (Rangan & Bell, 1998), and Toyota Australia[3]. These organizations bypass their traditional distribution channels by selling direct to the public. The manufacturers themselves are progressively getting more involved in promoting and marketing the products. Consumers tend to buy direct from manufacturers' electronic storefront when they are able to enjoy reduced price, good customer service, or simply have faith in the product/brand.

On the other hand, many B2C businesses consist of resellers and distributors selling consumer goods and services to consumers electronically. These B2C businesses may have an existing brick and mortar storefront, or may exist electronically only. Examples of B2C retailers that maintain both brick and mortar and virtual storefronts are NTUC-Fair Price[4] in Singapore and the Dymocks Booksellers[5] book retailer in Australia. B2C e-commerce pioneers like Amazon.com and CDNow are virtual retailers which do not maintain a brick and mortar storefront, although Gateway.com moved from an Internet-only operation to become a clicks and mortar operation.

Very often, B2C e-commerce retailers band up together and operate from an electronic shopping mall. In this way, they increase their exposure to the public, as well as benefit from cross-promotion and providing one-stop shopping to customers; the very same idea which has led to the boom of shopping complexes and malls in the 20th century. Examples of electronic shopping malls are Telstra's "The Arcade[6]" in Australia, and the Yellow Pages Electronic Mall[7] in Singapore. Many of these shopping malls provide additional services like transaction processing facilities, albeit accepting the reticence of many customers to use credit cards online.

In contrast, B2B e-commerce usually involves trading partners that are located in the same geographical region. Members of the supply chain may use B2B e-commerce technologies like Electronic Data Interchange (EDI) and Extranets to link up their inventory management systems or accounting systems. More often than not, B2B e-commerce participants are existing trading partners that utilize inter-organizational systems to trade. As such, B2B e-commerce involves electronically linking manufacturers, suppliers, distributors, retailers, service providers and financial institutions. In more recent years, electronic marketplaces for B2B purposes have been developed to provide a trade and exchange facility for the respective industries. In Australia, the Pharmaceutical Extranet Gateway[8] (PEG) provides a marketplace for hospitals, clinics, pharmacies, and of course, the pharmaceutical suppliers, to trade. Other similar B2B electronic marketplaces are the Covisint[9] for the automotive industry, and Elemica[10] for laboratory products, both of which are highly successful B2B electronic marketplaces in North America.

Transaction Characteristics

This study also intends to gain an insight into transaction characteristics like transaction volume, frequency, monetary value, and the item being exchanged between stakeholders in e-commerce. Starting with the B2C scenario, transactions are expected to be low-volume or once-only events. Unless buyers use the electronic storefront to purchase day-to-day products like groceries, they are unlikely to use B2C e-commerce to purchase consistently, or at regular intervals. The dollar value of each B2C transaction is expected to be lower than that of B2B transactions.

Typically, B2C e-commerce activities consist of the sales and purchase of consumer goods like toys, compact discs, and stationery products. Digital products (Torlina et al., 1999; Whinston et al., 1997) like computer software, and electronic magazine subscription make up the rest of B2C e-commerce. Innovative B2C e-commerce in recent years includes the distribution of sample goods to consumers for evaluation prior to the actual purchase. For example, a sample audio track of the latest music album can be downloaded (Wang & Chong, 1999), or an evaluation copy of the software can be downloaded and used for a limited period of time. Other B2C e-commerce activities include consumers obtaining product specifications, and participating in online share trading, confirming payment, tracking product delivery, obtaining after-sales service, and B2C electronic auctioning (e.g., eBay Australia[11], and Yellow Pages Auction[12]), although electronic auctioning is also rife in the B2B e-commerce arena (Kambil & van Heck, 1998).

In contrast, B2B e-commerce usually involves the exchange of information among trading partners. Distributors may access a supplier's Extranet to check production levels, inventories, and delivery details. As such, the B2B transactions are of greater volume, and occur at fixed and close intervals. For convenience, cost-effectiveness, and to save time, many businesses use B2B e-commerce to present and bid for tenders. Incidentally, the monetary value of all B2B e-commerce transactions is significantly higher than that of B2C e-commerce. In addition, many B2B transactions are automated and require minimal human intervention. Instead of engaging store managers and sales personnel to check the inventories and manually key in purchase orders, many B2B e-commerce systems are integrated with point-of-sale (POS) systems, enabling inventory information to be updated automatically, and orders for new stock generated when inventories drop below the stipulated level. The development and advances in B2B e-commerce have catalyzed and enabled many supply chain initiatives like Just-In-Time (JIT) manufacturing, Vendor Managed Inventory (VMI), and Quick Response (QR) retailing. B2B e-commerce is also used extensively in the banking sector. Increasingly, organizations are using B2B e-commerce to purchase digital products like computer software, and to obtain commercial services (e.g., mySAP.com[13] B2B portal).

Stakeholder Relationship Characteristics

Stakeholder relationship characteristics refer to the nature and characteristics of relationships between sellers and buyers in e-commerce. Although existing work in e-commerce (Bensaou, 1997; Kalakota & Whinston, 1996; Kambil & van Heck, 1998; Kumar & van Dissel, 1996; Lee et al., 1999; Mukhopadhyay et al., 1995; Whinston et al., 1997) highlights the characteristics of stakeholder relationships, few actually use stakeholder relationships to distinguish B2B and B2C e-commerce. Elements in stakeholder relationship characteristics are: formation, structure, nature, complexity of relationships, uncertainty, trust, inter-stakeholder reliance, duration, and industry-wide relationships.

In B2C e-commerce, the electronic storefront has to attract potential customers, encourage customers to purchase, and if possible, encourage customers to make future purchases. The relationship is formed when customers decide to make a purchase. Since customers are the end-users of the product, the relationship between the buyer and seller is more intimate and personal than in the B2B scenario. The retailer has to gather information like personal preference, liking, financial capability, delivery, and payment methods from the customer. Essentially, the retailer has to build-up trust and confidence with customers by giving them assurance of product quality and satisfaction. The intimate and personal information that retailers obtain allows them to provide customized, one-to-one service to customers, using a strategy known as micro-marketing. The uncertainty level in B2C relationships is higher than that in B2B. This is especially true in terms of product quality uncertainty because consumers who are purchasing physical goods electronically may not have the opportunity to visit a showroom or salesperson for product inspection or trial. Uncertainty in product availability and payment is also a big issue in B2C e-commerce. Trust in B2C has dissipated because of a lack of trust resulting from accelerated fraud on payment systems across the world.

The duration of many B2C relationships is short to medium-term. In fact, a B2C relationship may be a once-only event since buyers are not obliged to return to the same seller if they are not satisfied the first time. The inter-stakeholder reliance in B2C e-commerce is also expected to be lower than that in B2B e-commerce. An individual customer does not represent a huge portion of income to a retailer, and an individual retailer is not the sole supplier of the product to the customer. Benefits arising from using B2C e-commerce usually flow to individual consumers, or the individual retailer.

On the other hand, stakeholder relationships in B2B transactions have several distinguishing features. According to an industry contact[14], "Business-to-Business e-commerce is about using electronic means to maintain and manage existing trading relationships." Many B2B e-commerce relationships are expected to be based on existing trading relationships. As a higher volume of products is transacted in B2B e-commerce, B2B relationships require a higher level of trust between the transacting parties. Buyers and sellers need to have prior agreements and contracts to agree and guarantee product quality, shipment schedule, payment, and future transactions. B2B e-commerce thus becomes the platform on which these pre-agreed terms of trade are carried out. Regarding the structure of B2B relationships, four structures (as shown in the following) suggested by Clarke (1998) will be investigated.

- 1-to-1 relationships (inter-organizational systems)
- 1-to-1-to-1 relationships (cascading systems)
- 1-to-n relationships (hub and spoke systems)
- m-to-n relationships (networking systems)

As for the nature of B2B relationships, they are expected to be more impersonal than is the case for B2C. The transacting parties in B2B e-commerce are businesses. Security in B2B e-commerce becomes a major issue when organizations give trading partners access to their internal information system. Personal preference and liking have less influence on B2B transactions because B2B transactions are bound by agreements, company policies, and legislation. Consequently, the complexity of the B2B relationship is high, and such B2B relationships are expected to last for medium to long-term. Businesses will find it costly and inconvenient to form and terminate B2B relationships quickly, hence increasing the barriers to entry and exit to B2B relationships.

B2B e-commerce enforces the rules and policies in inter-organizational relationships, hence it enhances the level of trust between trading partners and reduces uncertainties and risks. B2B e-commerce also levels the playing field for businesses of different sizes. Big players cannot bully smaller players using tactics like delaying payment or shipment. Trading partners can use B2B e-commerce to track and change transaction processes, thus, late delivery and payment may result in instantaneous penalties. Suppliers are encouraged to deliver promptly to get prompt payments. Customers are pressured to pay promptly as B2B e-commerce supports and enhances debt tracking. With B2B e-commerce, trading partners have the ability to foresee shortfalls in supplies, and then source from alternative suppliers. Incidentally, B2B e-commerce tightens the coordination and level of integration among trading partners, enabling them to operate with less inventories, leading to more efficient production runs, and increasing the flexibility and responsiveness of the supply chain. The inter-stakeholder reliance in the B2B environment is expected to be much greater than that in B2C.

Stakeholder relationship in B2B e-commerce promises to have an impact on industry-wide practices as well, with benefits expected to be distributed among various stakeholders. In B2C e-commerce, businesses compete for customers, leading to increased customer satisfaction. The flow of benefit is greater from seller to buyer than vice versa. However, in the case of B2B e-commerce, a win-win scenario is more obvious. According to a study by the Automotive Industry Action Group (AIAG, 1999) in USA, if EDI is implemented across the automotive supply chain, a cost savings of US$1 billion could be realized industry-wide. eSteel[15] is another example of a B2B e-commerce initiative which provides industry-wide benefits. Small and medium enterprises stand to enjoy reduced telecommunication costs, while the major players stand to enjoy reduced transaction processing costs.

Table 1: Summary of the Differentiation Criteria and Elements Within Each Criterion that was Brought Up Earlier

Criteria	**Elements**
Stakeholder Characteristics	Number of stakeholders Location and dispersion of stakeholders Business nature of stakeholders
Transaction Characteristics	Volume of transaction Frequency of transaction Monetary value of transaction Products involved in transaction
Stakeholder Relationship Characteristics	Formation of relationship Structure of relationship Nature of relationship (intimacy) Complexity of relationship Uncertainty and trust in relationship Inter-stakeholder reliance Duration of relationship Industry-wide relationships

RESEARCH METHODOLOGY

To verify the stakeholder relationship issues identified above, the researchers conducted a series of open-ended in-depth interviews with fifteen SMEs in Australia and ten in Singapore (Kong, 1999). These firms were chosen from responders to two surveys, one in Australia and one in Singapore, which were based on lists supplied by the Association of SMEs in Singapore and a number of industry associations in Australia. To gain a broader understanding of the stakeholder relationships in both countries, the researchers chose to interview a selected number of SMEs chosen randomly from responders until a cross-section of business types/industry types had been covered. In searching for meanings in people's actions, and in seeking to identify practices within the SMEs as they relate to their stakeholders, this research hopes to describe and analyze the forms of e-commerce used in SMEs in Singapore and Australia. As part of this study, accounts of the decision-making process and the interactions between a consistent set of actors or players, each with its own agenda and operating mechanism, are used to frame the data that emerged from the study.

An informal, semi-structured, interview technique was used following the techniques developed and used by Kitwood (1980) and Wilson and Arnold (1986). Fetterman (1989: p. 48) notes that "formal or structured interviews have an explicit agenda, while informal interviews have a specific but implicit research agenda and informal interviews can be used to discover the categories of meaning in a culture and are useful in discovering what people think and how one person's perceptions compare with another's." A sample of questions asked are included the Table 2.

Non-directive questioning which is open-ended and acts as a stimulant for the subject's thoughts, was often used to make the subject feel at ease so that he/she would be able to give considered views and opinions rather than just giving yes or no answers. The questions themselves emerged from an understanding of the constituent nature of the stakeholder relationships (Corbitt, 1997) garnered from existing literature and other research.

Table 2: Example of Questions Asked in Interviews

1. Can you describe the nature of the relationships you have with suppliers?
2. Can you describe the nature of the relationships you have with your customers?
3. Of the relationships you have described, which are the most significant for the business? Why is this so?
4. Do these stakeholder relationships change? If yes, how?
5. What issues are important to you in the formation and continuation of these relationships with stakeholders?

The data collected were analyzed using development of a matrix reporting text about relevant issues on stakeholder relationships in e-commerce using a hermeneutic approach (Lee, 1994) combining literature with emergent themes from text in an iterative form. The results are summarized in tabular form to highlight differences that emerge. To evaluate the validity of the research process and the

Table 3: Schematics for Qualitative Research in Information Systems

• The principle of the hermeneutic circle:	Interview data was transcribed. Analysis of that data initially sought to understand the obvious. Repeated iterations of searching for themes and ideas created some understanding of what happened with e-commerce adoption and why.
• The principle of contextualization:	Interviews were conducted in Singapore and in Australia. The researchers are a mixture of Singaporean and Australian.
• The principle of interaction:	With the use of open-ended questions in the interviews, the researchers were able to extend the interviews explanations and extend the depth of understanding about the processes and human agency being described. In this way the researcher was able to ensure understanding of the way the mangers interviewed were constructing their interpretation. The researchers stretched the interviewees when statements suggesting judgements or opinions were expressed.
• The principle of abstraction and generalization:	Interpretation of the data was based in sustained application of EC literature. The theoretical frameworks in that literature enabled the researchers to facilitate some generalization and theorizing from the data. The findings generated in the study were then applied to existing conceptualizations of e-commerce adoption.
• The principle of dialogical reasoning:	In the analysis of divergence from existing e-commerce frameworks, deviation of practice from theory was accepted as an integral part of this study adding to knowledge and suggesting modification of existing theories and structures within the Information Systems.
• The principle of multiple interpretations:	Using three researchers to interpret the data enabled emergence of different interpretations. However, the study accepts that the natural bias of the researchers is embedded in the interpretations offered accepting that any other researcher will construct interpretations that may be different.
• The principle of suspicion:	There is no doubt that the interview data and the interpretations derived from that data by the three researchers are infused with bias. Each person involved is informed by sets of values and beliefs that are expressed in this type of research. The researchers recognize this but as the research is set within a critical perspective, such bias is accepted as real meaning. To ensure that the bias of the researchers was not imposed in the construction of the stories, all transcribed data was returned to them to check that meaning generated was the same as the meaning written.

integrity of the data, this research adopts the schematics for qualitative research in Information Systems in Klein and Myers (1999) and Corbitt and Thanasankit (2000). (See Table 3.)

RESEARCH RESULTS AND ANALYSIS

The preliminary analysis reported below attempts to search for cultural differences as they impact on the adoption of e-commerce in the stakeholder/organization relationship. Preliminary analysis of raw data confirmed many characteristics of Stakeholder Relationships that distinguish B2B and B2C e-commerce as suggested in Table 1 earlier. Table 4 summarizes the data collected in this research, matching them with elements of stakeholder relationships from Table 1. Qualitative judgements are made based on the nature of language used by respondents in their interviews. Each element of Stakeholder Relationship characteristic is qualitatively compared based on the differentiation of word usage. Table 4 shows there is little difference between existing practices in B2B and B2C e-commerce in Singapore and Australia at the stakeholder level. However, the data clearly distinguishes the two types of e-commerce.

B2C E-Commerce in Singapore and Australia

In both countries, *B2C* e-commerce implementations take on a more "market-like" structure. Many buyers and sellers operate in the same market. The public makes up the buyers, while small and medium-sized suppliers and distributors make up the sellers. The products being exchanged in B2C e-commerce are mainly consumer goods. There is a small fraction of digital products being exchanged. B2C e-commerce transactions do not occur at fixed intervals. More often than not, the timing and regularity of purchases are dictated by consumer buying behavior, which is influenced by trend and fashion, as well as special occasions.

As for the formation of stakeholder relationships in B2C e-commerce, there is no prior agreement or contact prior to the B2C transaction. Consumers may have a history of purchasing from the same supplier, but the buyer-seller relationships last for only the duration of each transaction. New relationships are formed for each transaction. In the observed cases, customer loyalty programs, like airline frequent flyer program, are not used to encourage long-term stakeholder relationships. The relationship between buyer and seller in B2C is more intimate and personal, as personal preference and liking are often used by the retailer to provide customized service. Nevertheless, the relationships remain simple, since the buyer and seller do not enter into purchasing contracts, apart from abiding to legislative obligations to deliver goods (by the seller) and pay up (by the buyer). The buyer-seller reliance

Table 4: Summary of Research Results in Singapore and Australia, Matched Against Stakeholder Relationship Differentiation Criteria and Elements

	B2C e-commerce in Australia	**B2C e-commerce in Singapore**	**B2B e-commerce in Australia**	**B2B e-commerce in Singapore**
Number of Stakeholders	Large	Large	Small	Small
Number of Sellers	Varied	Varied	Usually small	Usually small
Number of Buyers	High	High	Low	Low
Location & Dispersion of Stakeholders	Widespread	Very localized	Widespread	Localized
Business nature of stakeholders	Retailer-to-Consumer	Retailer /Distributor-to-consumer	Manufacturer/ Supplier-to-Retailer/Distributor	Manufacturer/ Supplier-to-Retailer
Volume of Transaction	Low	Usually low	High	High
Frequency of Transaction	Irregular, seasonal, or once-only	Irregular and often seasonal	High and regular. High levels of consistency	High and regular. High levels of consistency
Monetary Value of Transaction	Low	Low	Medium-high	Medium-high
Products (Transaction content)	Consumer goods. Limited amount of digital products	Limited amounts of consumer goods and digital products	Mostly information exchange. Increasing adoption of information exchange and extended EDI applications	Very high information exchange. Localized product exchange processes and extended application of EDI for import/export
Formation of Relationships	Always new. Multiple movements into and out of the relationship by customers	Always new. Multiple movements into and out of the relationship by customers	Quite often new relationships are formed and stabilized	Based on existing trading relationships and other social contacts

Table 4: Summary of Research Results in Singapore and Australia, Matched Against Stakeholder Relationship Differentiation Criteria and Elements (continued)

Structure of Relationships	One seller-to-many buyers	Usually one seller-to-many buyers, but electronic malls feature many sellers-to-many buyers	One seller-to-one buyer, one seller-to-few sellers, few sellers-to-few buyers (within the supply chain)	One seller-to-one buyer, one seller-to-few buyers
Nature of Relationships (Intimacy)	Highly intimate and personal	Highly intimate and personal	Impersonal, formalized.	Impersonal, based on existing trading relationships where prior personal contact is significant
Complexity of Relationships	Simple	Simple	Complex	Highly Complex
Uncertainty	High	High	Low	Low
Trust	Low	Very low	High	High
Inter-stakeholder Reliance	Low and variable	Low and variable	High and sustained	High and sustained
Duration of Relationships	Short	Short	Extended	Extended
Industry-wide Relationships	Low	Low	Highly inter-related and inter-dependent	Highly inter-related and inter-dependent

is low, since many consumer goods in this study do not command high monetary value, nor require constant after-sales interactions. Software purchases are exceptions to this circumstance.

B2B E-Commerce in Singapore and Australia

Observation of ***B2B*** e-commerce in Singapore and Australia confirmed that the number of stakeholders is small. The relationship is usually one-to-one. B2B e-commerce activities are primarily made up of information sharing and exchange, with extended implementation of EDI. As such, the transaction volume is high, and transactions occur at regular intervals. B2B relationships also have a sense of consistency, like the daily exchange of inventory data among upstream and downstream supply chain members.

The complexity of stakeholder relationships is high. Information exchange and the transaction of physical goods between organizations are bound by strict company policies, like budgetary restrictions, confirmation of purchases, guarantee of on-time delivery, and conditions for future transactions. As such, the formation of B2B relationships occurs in a face-to-face manner, instead of online contract negotiation and formation. The relationships are based on existing trading relationships, although the formation of B2B relationships in a few Australian cases are initiated electronically, i.e., buyers found the sellers online. B2B relationships last longer than the duration of a single transaction. This is due to the high cost of setting up and terminating B2B relationships. Although information of commercial importance is exchanged between stakeholders in B2B e-commerce, none of the information includes personal details of individuals. There is a high level of inter-stakeholder reliance as each trading partner commands a significant amount of income or spending. A tightly knit relationship it is, but a personal relationship, it is not.

A particular B2B e-commerce case in Singapore involves an import-export business. The level of trust between buyer and seller is high. The stakeholder relationships are closely bound by contracts in connection with shipment of products, payment, currency exchange, custom clearance, and product quality. The customers of this business are located all over the world, hence e-commerce allows this organization to accept orders on a 24 ´ 7 ´ 365 basis, and maintain a global point of presence without having to set up branches overseas, confirming arguments from existing literature (CTRC, 1997).

Comparison of E-Commerce in Singapore and Australia

Comparing the observations across countries, observations from Singaporean e-commerce cases (both B2B and B2C) highlight that all the stakeholders are located within a close geographical proximity, apart from the import-export business mentioned above. Singaporean businesses do not have huge incentives to use e-commerce if they already have an efficient traditional distribution channel. In the Singaporean B2C cases, the added advantage of expanding into new markets exists only in the sense of selling to targeted-groups who are not accessible through traditional distribution chain, or for marketing the product overseas. This confirms the ideas of micro-marketing, and exploitation of niche markets.

In the Australian cases, the buyers and sellers (in B2C and B2B) are located within the same city, or in different states and territories within the same national boundary. E-commerce implementation (both B2C and B2B) in Australia allows local businesses to serve remote population centers. Local businesses can become nation-wide businesses easily with e-commerce.

In all cases, it was found that the readiness of the market is a major determinant of e-commerce implementation. In B2C e-commerce, consumers' readiness to use e-commerce determines whether or not traditional businesses will set up an electronic storefront. Some participants of this study reported that the need to achieve a competitive edge encourages them to venture into the e-commerce frontier. Pressure by trading partners to implement e-commerce is a major factor why many SMEs choose to implement B2B e-commerce. As B2B e-commerce becomes more pervasive, issues like expanding into new markets may then become factors in implementing e-commerce. This is already the case in a few Australian B2B practices.

DISCUSSION AND FUTURE RESEARCH

Preliminary results from this study suggests that although the two major types of e-commerce can be distinguished using the e-commerce Differentiation Framework, more empirical data will be needed to verify and improve the proposed framework. New criteria may be required to describe and distinguish these two types of e-commerce, since the boundary between the two major types of e-commerce is often blur and ambiguous.

The study contributes to existing literature in e-commerce by identifying and emphasizing stakeholder relationships in e-commerce, and how they can be used to differentiate B2C and B2B e-commerce types. Clear understanding of the distinction of the two types of e-commerce may assist organizations to formulate the appropriate business strategies when venturing into the dot com territory. In addition, this study allows strategies for integrating both types of e-commerce [e.g., a retailer which integrates its virtual storefront with its backend Enterprise Resource Planning (ERP) system] to be developed. E-commerce reduces face-to-face interaction between stakeholders, hence e-commerce organizations will need to pay additional attention to stakeholder relationship issues in order to satisfy trading partners and customers better.

The current state of e-commerce in Singapore and Australia places emphasis on the B2C and B2B e-commerce types. Other e-commerce models that are expected to draw attention in the near future are Business-to-Government and Consumer-to-Consumer e-commerce. As more governments begin to realize the benefits of e-commerce and come under new pressures to increase efficiency, e-commerce will turn out as a viable cost-reduction tool. The B2B e-commerce model can be adapted to suit the Business-to-Government case easily, or rather, governments can operate in a more business-like manner and adopt the B2B e-commerce model. The Victorian State Government in Australia has already implemented online purchasing and project tendering[16]. The Internet is expected to encourage the growth of Consumer-to-Consumer e-commerce. Consumer-to-Consumer e-commerce exists today in the form of subscribing to mailing lists that cater for the sale of second hand products and niche market products. However, trading post-type websites will give individuals more freedom and convenience to exchange information to enable the buying and selling of goods and services among individuals. Apart from finding answers to the initial research questions, this study also raises several issues like:

- How does cultural background affect e-commerce adoption?
- What is the role of governments in promoting e-commerce?
- How does e-commerce impact intra and inter-industry competition?

Based on this study, we found that "to" (as in B-to-C) can better emphasize the relationships between stakeholders than "2" (as in B2C). Lessons learned from stakeholder relationship analysis in B2C and B2B e-commerce will enable future researchers to develop substantive hypotheses that will frame research which engages more companies. This study is but a first step towards developing a more rigorous method of using stakeholder relationship issues to differentiate e-commerce types. Data collected from this study have indicated that future studies would benefit by using stakeholder relationship as the unit of analysis.

ENDNOTES

1 An earlier version of this chapter was presented as a paper to The Pacific Asia Conference on Information Systems at University of Science and Technology in Hong Kong, June 2000.

2 Dell.com, URL: http://www.dell.com

3 Toyota Australia, URL: http://www.toyota.com.au

4 NTUC-Fair Price, URL: http://www.ntuc-fairprice.org.sg

5 Dymocks Booksellers, URL: http://www.dymocks.com.au

6 Telstra eCommerce The Arcade, URL: http://192.148.138.172/thearcade default.asp

7 Singapore Yellow Pages Electronic Mall, URL: http://www.yellowpages.com.sg

8 Pharmaceutical Extranet Gateway, URL: http://www.pecc.org.au

9 Covisint, URL: http://www.covisint.com

[10] Elemica, URL: http://www.elemica.com
[11] eBay Australia, URL: http://www.ebay.com.au
[12] Yellow Pages Online Bidding, URL: http://www.ebid.com.sg/ypa
[13] mySAP.com, URL: http://www.mysap.com
[14] Personal communication with a supply chain manager of a major electronics component company in Australia.
[15] eSteel, URL: http://www.esteel.com
[16] http://www.vgpb.vic.gov.au

REFERENCES

Bensaou, M. (1997). Interorganizational cooperation: The role of information technology: An empirical comparison of U.S. and Japanese supplier relations. *Information Systems Research* 8(2), 1997, 107 – 124.

Clarke, R. (1998). *E-Commerce Definitions*. Xamax Consultancy Pty. Ltd., Canberra, ACT, Australia, 1998, Retrieved from the World Wide Web: http://www.anu.edu.au/people/Roger.Clarke/ EC/ECDefns.html

Corbitt, B.J. (1997). Implementing policy for homeless kids in schools: Reassessing the micro and macro levels in the policy debate in Australia. *Journal of Education Policy 12*(2), 165–176.

Corbitt, B.J. & Thanasankit, T. (2000). *Using and Validating Critical Ethnographies in Information Systems Research – Finding the 'Hidden' in Thai Requirements Engineering Processes.* Working paper, Department of Information Systems, The University of Melbourne.

CTRC (1997) *E-commerce: The New Business Platform for the Internet*, Computer Technology Research Corp., Charleston, USA, 5 – 53.

DCITA (1999). *Australia's E-Commerce Report Card*, Department of Communications Information Technology and the Arts, Canberra, ACT, Australia, Retrieved from the World Wide Web: http://www.dcita.gov.aunsapi-graphics/?MIval=dca_ftp&path=%2fpub%2fecommerce%2freport%2edoc

Fetterman, D.M. (1989). *Ethnography: Step by Step.* Sage Publications, USA.

GartnerGroup. (2000). *GartnerGroup Forecasts Worldwide Business-to-Business E-Commerce to Reach &7.29 Trillion in 2004.* Press Release, Stamford, Connecticut, USA, 2000. Retrieved from the World Wide Web: http://gartnerweb.com/public/static/aboutgg/pressrel/pr012600c.html

Kalakota, R. & Whinston, A. B. (1996). *Frontiers of E-Commerce.* Reading, MA: Addison-Wesley.

Kambil, A. & van Heck, E. (1998). Reengineering the dutch flower auctions: A framework for analyzing exchange organizations. *Information Systems Research*. *9*(1), 1998, 1-19.

Kitwood, T. (1980). *Disclosures to a Stranger: Adolescent Values in an Advanced Industrial Society.* London: Routledge and Kegan Paul

Klein, H.K. & Myers, M.D. (1999). A set of principles for conducting and evaluating interpretive field studies in information systems. *MIS Quarterly* 23(1), 67 – 89.

Kong, W. (1999). *Issues Affecting the Implementation of Electronic Commerce in SMEs in Singapore.* Honors thesis, Department of Information Systems, University of Melbourne, Australia.

Kumar, K. & van Dissel, H. G. (1996). Sustainable collaboration: Managing conflict and cooperation in interorganizational systems. *MIS Quarterly 20*(3), 279 – 300.

Lawrence, E., Corbitt, B., Tidwell, A., Fisher, J. & Lawrence, J. R. (1998). *Internet Commerce: Digital Models for Business*. Milton, QLD, Australia: John Wiley & Sons.

Lee, A.S. (1994). Electronic mail as a medium for rich communication: An empirical investigation using hermeneutic interpretation. *MIS Quarterly*, *18*(2), 143 – 161.

Lee, C. Y., Seddon, P. & Corbitt, B. (1999). Evaluating the business value of Internet-based business-to-business e-Commerce. *Proceedings of the 10th Australasian Conference on Information Systems*, Wellington, New Zealand, 508 – 519.

Mukhopadhyay, T., Kekre, S. & Kalathur, S. (1995). Business value of information technology: A study of electronic data interchange. *MIS Quarterly, 19*(2), 137 – 156.

OECD (1999). *The Economic and Social Impact of E-Commerce: Preliminary Findings and Research Agenda.* Paris: OECD.

Rangan, V. K. & Bell, M. (1998). Dell Online. *Harvard Business School Case 598-116.*

Riggins, F. J. & Rhee H. S. (1998). Toward A unified view of e-commerce, *Communications of the ACM.* 41(10), 88 – 95.

Torlina, L., Seddon, P. & Corbitt, B. (1999). Attributable characteristics of goods and services in e-Commerce. *Proceedings of the Twelfth International Bled E-Commerce Conference*, Bled, Slovenia, 94 – 105.

USDC. (1999). *The Emerging Digital Economy II*, U.S. Department of Commerce, Washington, D.C., U.S.A., Retrieved from the World Wide Web: http://www.ecommerce.gov

Wang, P. S. & Chong, C. (1999). Applying the hypercube model of E-commerce strategies to the case of MP3. *Personal Communication*.

Whinston, A. B., Stahl, D. O. & Choi, S. (1997). *The Economics of E-Commerce*, Macmillan Technical Publishing, Indianapolis, U.S.A.

Wilson, P. & Arnold, J. (1986). *Street Kids: Australia's Alienated Young*, Collins Dove, Blackburn, VIC, Australia.

SECTION III:

BUSINESS TO CONSUMER E-COMMERCE AND CULTURAL VALUES

Chapter VIII

Trust in B2C E-Commerce: The New Zealand Mäori Internet Shopper

Konrad Janusz Peszynski
Deakin University, Australia

ABSTRACT

This chapter identifies relevant factors of Mäori trust in terms of encouraging online shopping of B2C e-commerce by Mäori in New Zealand. The concepts of trust, risk and reputation are used to explore the uptake of Internet shopping in a B2C context by Mäori, a minority—but significant—racial group, in New Zealand. Reputation and adoption of e-commerce in Mäori culture emanates from family and tribe, typically by word of mouth. This chapter suggests that specific cultures like the Mäori have different elements in their trust of e-commerce, which needs to be addressed to encourage broader use.

INTRODUCTION

This chapter aims to report what issues of trust apply to the Mäori Internet shopper. Mäori arrived in New Zealand from the Pacific about a thousand years ago, and have since become a minority in New Zealand (Belich, 1996). Although it is difficult in defining an ethnic group, the definition of Mäori includes "all those who identify themselves as belonging to the New Zealand Mäori ethnic group, either alone or in combination with any other ethnic group" (Statistics New Zealand, 1998, p. 94). Their culture, language and values have become secondary to those of the dominant European culture (Liu, Wilson, McClure & Higgins, 1999).

This chapter will also help the reader to understand trust and Internet shopping from a Maori New Zealander's perspective. As a result, this chapter will reveal the key trust issues for Mäori that either hinder or assist them to purchase via the Internet.

BACKGROUND

The following subsections review the current literature in regards to the nature of e-commerce and business-to-consumer e-commerce before developing a picture of the Internet customer.

The Nature of Electronic Commerce

There is currently little consensus as to what exactly constitutes e-commerce (Jones, Wilikens, Morris & Masera, 2000; Riggens & Rhee, 1998). For example, Zwass (1996) loosely defines e-commerce as "the sharing of business information, maintaining business relationships, and conducting business transactions by means of telecommunications networks." Applegate, Holsapple, Kalakota, Radermacher and Whinston (1996) view e-commerce as more than simply buying and selling goods electronically, pointing out that e-commerce involves using network communications technology to engage in a wide range of activities up and down the value-added chain both within and outside the organization. However, Wilkins, Swatman, and Castleman (2000) suggest that the sheer number of definitions is in itself problematic and reflects the variety of research and thought being described as *e-commerce*.

Four types of information technology are converging to create the discipline of e-commerce (Kalakota & Whinston, 1996). These include electronic messaging in the form of fax and e-mail; sharing a corporate digital library to promote collaborative work; electronic document interchange using EDI and electronic funds transfer; and electronic publishing to promote marketing, advertising, sales and customer support (Riggins & Rhee, 1998; Ah-Wong, Gandhi, Patel, Shah, Tran & Targett, 2001). This supports the notion that e-commerce not only includes buying and selling goods and services, but also includes the background processes within that organization.

Because the definition of e-commerce is broad, a focus is needed. Therefore, I believe that e-commerce focuses on the trading and transactional relationship between an organization's web site and an end user (Dedhia, 2001; Lawrence, Corbitt, Fisher, Lawrence, & Tidwell, 2000; Riggins & Rhee, 1998). This is also known as business-to-consumer (B2C) e-commerce. The relationship begins when a consumer logs onto the organization's web site to purchase a good or service. Once the consumer has selected the product, they move into a trading and transactional relationship with the organization, paying for that product via credit card, check' or mail order. The good or service is then delivered to the consumer, concluding the trading relationship.

The Nature of Business-to-Consumer Electronic Commerce

Business-to-consumer (B2C) e-commerce focuses on direct transactions between businesses and end consumers (Dedhia, 2001; Lawrence et al., 2000; Riggins & Rhee, 1998; Schneider & Perry, 2000; Ah-Wong et al., 2001). In other words, B2C e-commerce is the trading and transactional relationship between an organization's web site and an end user (Dedhia, 2001; Lawrence et al., 2000; Riggins & Rhee, 1998). Consumers are able to purchase goods and services such as books, computer products, music, at any time convenient to the consumer.

Some of the key differences between B2C e-commerce and the other common form of e-commerce, Business-to-Business (B2B) e-commerce, include the volume of money traded, and the transactional relationship of the parties involved (Ah-Wong et al., 2001). B2C e-commerce involves smaller amounts of money in each exchange, while a greater volume of money is exchanged in the B2B environment due to the volume of goods and services being transacted. Transactional relationships tend to be intimate for business-to-consumer e-commerce as the objective is to satisfy customer preferences and shopping habits, but in the B2B setting, relationships are formal and impersonal (Ah-Wong et al., 2001; Riggins & Rhee, 1998; Lawrence et al., 2000).

E-commerce creates lower purchasing costs, reduced and more accurate inventory, lower cycle times, improved customer service and lower sales and marketing costs (Bolin, 1998). Another important factor leading to the growth in e-commerce, especially in the realm of B2C, e-commerce is the Internet customer.

The Internet Customer

One of the key benefits of B2C e-commerce is convenience. That is, day and night trading, 365 days of the year (Dedhia, 2001; Chen, Ingraham & Jenkins,

2001; Lohse & Spiller, 1998). Shopping via the Internet is easy for working people, who do not have time to shop, as there is no need to visit a physical store, wait for a salesperson and stand in line to purchase the goods. Further benefits include quality of service, personalized products and services, rapid response to needs and new products and services (Dedhia, 2001).

Despite all the benefits of B2C e-commerce, would-be consumers are still concerned about purchasing over the Internet. While B2C e-commerce increases, so do trust concerns (Gray & Debreceny, 1998; Cheung & Lee, 2001). Consumers have a vast array of unanswered questions. In studies by Ernst and Young (1999), and Gray and Debreceny (1998), the main questions asked by would-be consumers were:

- Is this company real?
- Is this a trustworthy company?
- If I send credit card or bank information, is it safe?
- If I place an order, will I receive what I asked for?
- Will any problems I have be resolved quickly?

There is a common theme to these questions, with a majority of them referring to the trust and risk in the trading relationship between the web site and the consumer.

Issues Affecting Internet Shopping

Before the Internet, face-to-face communication typically formed the basis for long-lasting and profitable ventures, instilling confidence in both parties (Sklar, 2001). Recent studies show that face-to-face interaction promotes the greatest trust, followed by telephone, then text chat, and, lastly, by e-mail (Daft & Lengel, 1986; Sklar, 2001). But changes brought about by the Internet have even broader implications. With the advent of Internet technology, every company becomes a global company, with which comes the opportunity to buy and sell. This brings with it many issues that are stopping would-be consumers to shop online.

Trust

The notion of trust has been examined under various contexts (Cheung & Lee, 2001; Stewart, 1999; Choudhuri & Holbrook, 2001; Steinauer, Wakid & Rasberry, 1997; Hoffman, Novak & Peralta, 1999). Facets of trust include trust in bargaining (Schurr & Ozanne, 1985); distribution channels (Dwyer, Schurr & Oh, 1987); industrial buyer-seller relationships (Doney & Cannon, 1997); partner cooperation in strategic alliances (Das, 1998); and the use of market research (Moore, Deshpande & Zaltman, 1993). According to Lewicki and Bunker (1995), three theoretical perspectives exist. The first is the view of personality theorists, who conceptualize trust as a belief, expectancy or feeling that is deeply rooted in the personality of the individual. The second is the view of sociologists and economists, who see trust as a phenomenon within and between organizations and as the trust individuals put into those organizations. The third view is that of social psychologists, who characterize trust in terms of expectation and willingness of the trusting party to engage in a transaction (Lewicki & Bunker, 1995).

Trust in the context of this chapter is identified using the definition offered by McKnight, Cummings, and Chervany (1998), "an individual's beliefs about the extent to which a target is likely to behave in a way that is benevolent, competent, honest, or predictable in a situation" (p. 459). The consumer needs to believe that the Web merchant is trustworthy before they purchase online.

Hoffman et al. (1999) analyzed consumer responses to two biannual surveys carried out by the Nielsen Media Research/CommerceNet Internet Demographics Study (as cited in Hoffman et al., 1999) and the Georgia Tech Graphics, Visualization and Usability Centre's GVU 7th WWW User Survey (as cited in Hoffman et al., 1999). Both studies were done in 1997 and combined had 14,014 responses from Web users.

The combined surveys found that 86 percent of commercial Web sites provided no information regarding how any demographic information collected will be used, or even if information is being collected (Hoffman et al., 1999). Interestingly, it was found that over 72 percent of Web users *would* give Web sites demographic information if the sites would provide a statement of any kind informing users how the information collected would be used (Hoffman et al., 1999).

In the 'bricks-and-mortar' environment, it has been found that the most important source of a consumer's trust in the merchant organization is the salesperson (Jarvenpaa, Tractinsky, Saarinen & Vitale, 1999). Factors contributing to trust in the salesperson include the salesperson's expertise, likeability, similarity to the customer, and prior interactions with that salesperson (Doney & Cannon, 1997; Geyskens, Steenkamp & Kular, 1998).

Factors that can increase the trust of an Internet consumer include assurance services such as those provided by MasterCard and TRUSTe (Cashell & Aldhizer III, 1999; Nöteberg, Christiaanse & Wallage, 1999). These services permit a web site to display their Web trust seal (a graphic) provided their "practices... [comply] with the WebTrust principles and criteria for business-to-consumer e-commerce" (Cashell & Aldhizer III, 1999, p. 51). Web sites that show a seal are more likely to be purchased from than sites that carry no seal at all (Nöteberg et al., 1999). It made no difference as to which seal was displayed on the Website, just as long as a seal was visible.

A consumer's willingness to buy from an Internet seller is dependent on the their attitude towards the store, which is affected by the seller's ability to create consumer trust. Jarvenpaa et al. (1999) proposed a model for the consequences of trust in an Internet store, seen in Figure 1 . According to Jarvenpaa et al. (1999), the model suggests, that consumers' evaluation of a store's reputation and size affect their trust in a store.

Higher trust will directly improve attitudes towards a store (Jarvenpaa et al., 1999). Besides helping to shape attitudes, perceived risk might also have an independent, direct influence on the willingness to buy. According to the model, a consumer may be willing to buy from an Internet store that is perceived as low risk, even if the consumer's attitudes towards that merchant are not highly positive. Conversely, a consumer may not be willing to buy from a merchant perceived as being high risk, even in the presence of positive attitudes towards that merchant.

Risk

Risk is defined as the consumer's perceptions of the uncertainty and adverse consequences of engaging in an activity (Dowling & Staelin, 1994; Jarvenpaa et al., 1999; Jarvenpaa, Tractinsky & Vitale, 2000; Camp, 2000; Bhatnagar, Misra & Rao, 2000). There is little assurance that the customer will get what he or she sees on the computer screen, in the quantity ordered.

It has been suggested that two types of risk are predominately associated with Internet shopping (Fram & Grady, 1997; Jarvenpaa et al., 1999, 2000; Lynch, Kent & Srinivasan, 2001): product category risk and financial risk. Product

Figure 1: The Internet Consumer Trust Model (Jarvenpaa, Tractinsky, Saarinen and Vitale, 1999)

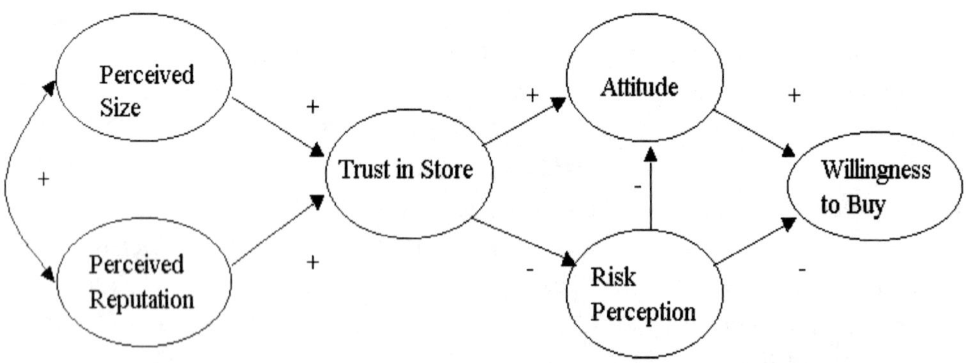

Note: The (+) symbol denotes a positive relationship and (-) denotes a negative relationship between variables.

category risk is associated with the product itself and is the consumers' belief that the product will function according to their expectations. Financial risk refers to the risk associated with the Internet as a purchasing medium. Consumers are apprehensive about putting their credit card information over the Internet because it puts the consumer at risk of losing money via credit card fraud (Jarvenpaa et al., 1999, 2000; Fram & Grady, 1997).

Reputation

The reputation and size of the web merchant has also been suggested as factors that contribute to consumer trust in a seller organization (Anderson & Weitz, 1989; Doney & Cannon, 1997; Ganesan, 1994). Reputation is the extent to which buyers believe that the selling organization is honest and concerned about its customers (Doney & Cannon, 1997).

One of the popular methods used by organizations to promote their reputation is by publishing customer testimonials on their sites (Quelch & Klein, 1996; Lohse & Spiller, 1998; McKnight et al., 1998). Testimonials have been found to help people decide who to trust, encourage trustworthy behavior and deter participation by those who are unskilled or dishonest, especially when the parties have not interacted before (Lohse & Spiller, 1998; McKnight et al., 1998).

Reputation requires a long-term investment of resources, effort and attention to customer relationships' (Jarvenpaa et al., 1999). The better the seller's reputation, the more resources the seller has presumably committed to build that reputation. The perception of a large organization implies that the merchant has significant resources invested in the business and has much to lose by acting in an untrustworthy way (Stewart, 1999; Jarvenpaa et al., 2000).

New Zealand and the Internet

Quantitative studies have been completed on the demographics of New Zealand people on the Internet (UMR Insight, Ltd, 1999; Ministry of Economic Development, 2001). It was found that in 2000, 50 percent of New Zealanders surveyed declared they had access to the Internet either at home or at work (Ministry of Economic Development, 2001). The type of New Zealander on the Internet tended to be either on a high income (NZD$50,000 or more) or was 18 to 30 years old. Fifty-four percent of males surveyed were more likely to have access to the Internet than females (43 percent) (UMR Insight, Ltd, 1999).

Eleven percent of those surveyed had made a purchase over the Internet using a credit card (Ministry of Economic Development, 2001). The frequency of purchasing via the Internet was higher in Wellington (eighteen percent) amongst the 'white-collar' occupational group (seventeen percent) and those in the top income group (eighteen percent). Twelve percent of males surveyed were more likely to have made a purchase than females (four percent). In 2000, 21 percent of those surveyed felt comfortable when shopping over the Internet and 21 percent felt uncomfortable using a credit card (Ministry of Economic Development, 2001).

In May 2001, the Labour Market Policy Group, of the Department of Labour gathered information in regards to the gap between those people who have good access to information and communications technology (ICT), and the skills and motivations to make effective use of it, and those who do not (Labour Market Policy Group, 2001). This has been commonly referred to as the digital divide in New Zealand. One of the key stakeholders identified in this report were the New Zealand Mäori.

According to the report, four dimensions were identified that created the digital divide in New Zealand, lack of access to ICT; lack of ICT education and training; negative attitudes towards and lack of motivation to use ICT; and lack of relevant content (Labour Market Policy Group, 2001). Perhaps the most significant dimension is that of lack of access to ICT. Lack of access to ICT is identified as an inability to afford hardware, software or ongoing Internet access; and a lack of adequate telecommunications infrastructure, which is a major hindrance for those located in rural areas (Labour Market Policy Group, 2001).

Mäori and Internet Shopping

It is only recently that studies have been carried out on Mäori and their presence on the Internet (Smith, 1997; Smith & Sullivan, 1996; Kovacic, 2001). However, no studies examining the relationship between Mäori, trust and Internet shopping were found. There has been no mention of the word 'trust' in the literature, but many articles discuss the notion of Mäori beliefs and values with *respect* being the common term (Patterson, 1992).

Jarvenpaa et al. (1999, 2000), Dawar, Parker, and Price (1996) and Lynch et al. (2001) found that trust varies across nationalities and cultures. One commonly referenced definition of culture is that by Hofstede (1991), who defines culture as "the collective programming of the mind that distinguishes the members of one category of people from those of another" (p. 5). Hofstede (1980) identified four constructs that have been the foundation of much cultural research: power distance, uncertainty avoidance, individualism and masculinity. Hofstede (1980) found the individualism construct to have the strongest variation across cultures. Javenpaa et al. (1999, 2000) claim that consumers coming from an individualistic culture may have greater trust and be more willing to base their trust in a Website than consumers from a collectivistic culture. As a result, only the individualism construct will be investigated here. According to Hofstede (1980), those in an individualistic society:

- Take care of him or herself and his or her immediate family
- Have an "I" consciousness
- Have a self-orientation
- Have greater economic development.

Those in a collectivistic society:

- Born into extended families or clans, which protect them in exchange for loyalty
- Have an emphasis on belonging to an organization
- Have a "We" consciousness
- Have less economic development (Hofstede, 1980).

A Mäori concept of community is based on collective strength, which includes sharing, nurturing, supporting and empowering of interdependent groups. The Mäori see community as a form of relatedness, in which people are interdependent (Gregory, 2001). An important method of communication for Mäori is through the *whanau* (family) structure (Light, 1999). That is, the connections are about relationships to people and to place. Patterson (2000) backs this up by claiming, "in Mäori eyes, a person without family is scarcely a person at all, and the *mana* of any member of a family extends to all members" (p. 232). *Mana* is a (supernatural) power that can be present in a person, place, object, or spirit. It is commonly understood as prestige, power, or authority; but really such status is derived from possessing *mane*. The power of *mane* is undifferentiated and dangerous if uncontrolled (Patterson, 2000; Perrett & Patterson, 1991; Harple, 1996).

Individualism tends to promote a trusting stance in an individualistic society (Jarvenpaa et al., 1999). As a result, one gets better outcomes assuming that others are reliable. Individualists are more likely to trust others until they are given some reason not to trust. By contrast, those high in collectivism are more likely to base their trust on relationships with first-hand knowledge. Members of collectivist cultures are less likely to trust someone who is not part of their in-group (Yamagishi & Yamagishi, 1994; Thanasankit, 1999).

One other issue is that Mäori view their personal information as *taonga*, that is, their property or treasure (Te Puni Kokiri, 1994). Mäori do not feel comfortable letting people have their information. Although a person's details may seem small, they are precious as they relate to the individual concerned. Questions normally asked when personal information is required include:

- Why do you want this information?
- How will my personal information be used?
- Who will have access to my personal information?

Note that these Maori questions parallel those in general e-commerce transactions. The question of how the information collected could be used, could be a strong deterrent for Mäori to shop online as it is their information, or *taonga*, that will be collected and possibly misused or passed onto a third party.

There are some benefits of displaying Mäori information on the Internet (Smith, 1997). One such benefit is the ability to preserve and disseminate Mäori information, such as tribal (*iwi*) information. However, there are still many factors that hinder Mäori from displaying their information on the Internet. Particularly, Mäori see risks to their culture in making information too freely available on the Internet (Smith, 1997). Smith (1997) outlines issues such as:

- Threats to cultural values
- Loss of control of information when it is digitized
- Intellectual and cultural property ownership issues
- Accuracy and authority
- Commercialization of information
- Access issues

Access issues here refer to the digital divide, outlined in an earlier section. A face-to-face survey carried out by ACNielson and Netwatch in 2000 interviewed 12,000 New Zealanders. Of this 12,000, 1,156 classified themselves as Mäori and of those 1,156; 133 individuals stated they had Internet access at home (Hawkins, 2001). Either Mäori do not have easy access to computers and the Internet as compared to New Zealand Europeans, or there are an insufficient number of computer literate Mäori due to economic deficiencies (Statistics New Zealand, 1998), referenced earlier as the "digital divide."

According to the Labour Market Policy Group (2001), it was found that a proportion of stakeholders in the report had a strong wish not to use ICT. Some of these reasons relate to culture. For example, Mäori prefer *kanohi-ki-te-kanohi* (person-to-person contact), something the Internet does not offer and would be very difficult to implement. Similarly, in regards to the content of web sites, the perception of groups such as the Mäori, is that the Internet is largely for (young) white males (Labour Market Policy Group, 2001).

Mäori appear to be under-represented in terms of Internet shopping; this can be attributed to the lack of access to such information and communication technologies. The digital divide is prevalent in New Zealand, but this is not necessarily the only reason as to why there is a lack of uptake in Internet shopping for Mäori. Cultural values, traditions and beliefs also play a role, and as we have seen, the issue of cultural and personal information property (*taonga*) is a good example of this. However, Mäori are being encouraged to use the Internet and as a result are making an attempt to shop online.

SOLUTIONS AND RECOMMENDATIONS

This chapter discusses the possibility of a model proposed by Peszynski and Thanasankit (2002). The framework model, depicted in Figure 2 below, is an adaptation of the model created by Jarvenpaa et al. (1999, 2000). The difference is the extra step leading to reputation.

It is believed that as Mäori are part of a collectivist society, they are more likely to base their trust on relationships with immediate family members (*whanau*) and tribal (*iwi*) elders. The repetition of ones (good) reputation will normally lead Mäori to increase their personal trust towards purchasing products and services online (Peszynski & Thanasankit, 2002). For example, through the creation of the extra parameter (word of mouth), if a would-be Mäori Internet shopper heard many good recommendations about a specific web site, the perceived reputation of the web site would increase. This leads to an increase in the trust in that web site. As stated before, Mäori are less likely to trust someone who is not part of their in-group (Yamagishi & Yamagishi, 1994; Thanasankit, 1999). It is therefore proposed that through positive word of mouth about a web site from someone that person knows and trusts, typically someone from their in-group or society, the better the reputation of that web site will be. The better the seller's reputation, the more likely the would-be consumer would trust that web site.

In conjunction with reputation and following trust, is risk. Jarvenpaa et al. (1999) found that when risk is present, trust is needed to make transactions possible. It is therefore proposed that when trust in the web site is reduced, risk

Figure 2: Suggested Model

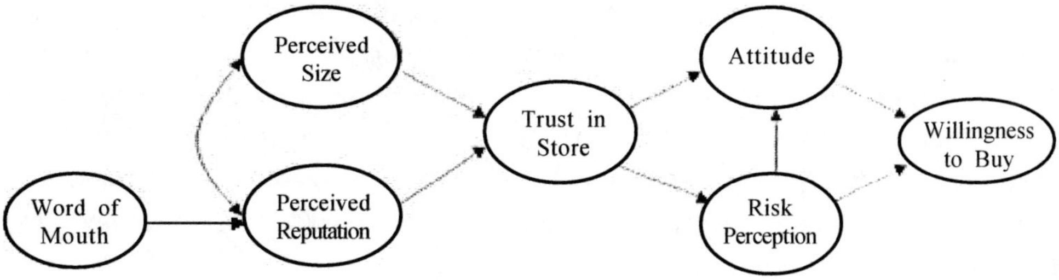

(product category or financial category) is reduced, which leads to a reduction in a willingness to buy from that web site. Finally, when there is a high reputation for an organization's web site and high trust in the web site, then the risk associated with the trading and transactional relationship between the organization and the consumer decreases, leading to an increase in a willingness to buy.

Issues of Trust Apparent to the Mäori Internet Shopper

It was found that the incidence of Internet shopping was higher in Wellington among a white-collar occupational group (UMR Insight Ltd., 1999). As a result, the study by Peszynski and Thanasankit (2002) involved eight interviews. Five interviewees were female and the remaining three were male. All were full-time professionals in either the private or public sector in Wellington.

Face-to-face, one-on-one, interviews were used to obtain participants views and opinions. This method was selected as, according to Daft and Lengel's (1986) information richness theory, it is the "richest medium because it provides immediate feedback so that interpretation can be checked. It also provides multiple cues via body language and tone of voice" (p. 560). It was also found, by Light (1999), that the preferred medium for Mäori is face-to-face since it creates a trusting relationship between the interviewer and interviewee.

To obtain reliable results, steps were taken during the interview to help reduce the distance between the interviewer and the interviewee. OPRA Limited (1998) claim that the interviewer can increase the respect and interest with the Mäori interviewee by "facing the interviewee when sitting and maintaining good eye contact by way of spontaneous glances to express interest" (p. 18). Questions were modelled around guidelines by OPRA Limited (1998). What helped define a 'good' question was one that was "open ended; single focused; and start with 'what', 'how' or 'could'" (p. 19).

The process consisted of three stages. The first stage was to obtain general impressions of what the Mäori Internet shopper looks for as signs of trust in a Website. This also helped get the interviewee into the right context for the remainder of the interview. In the second stage, the interviewee read a one-page summary of trust and Internet shopping, and this was followed by the third stage, where more questions were asked to find out, by means of an interview schedule, what that literature means to them as a Mäori Internet shopper.

As the data collection method was face-to-face, one-on-one interviews, the information was collected via written notes made by the researcher, and, with the permission of each participant, an audio tape recorder was used, from which, a transcription of the interview was made. Notes were also made during the interview, including reflective ones.

The hermeneutic cycle was employed for the data analysis component of the Peszynski and Thanasankit (2002) study. Hermeneutics is primarily concerned with the meaning of text. Myers (1997), Klein and Myers (1999) and Gadamer (1976) claim that the hermeneutic cycle helps us in the understanding of the text as a whole and the interpretation of its part, in which descriptions are guided by anticipated explanations. That is, the researchers read the complete transcript of each interview before analyzing the answer given by interviewees to each question. This also enabled the researchers to generate a variety of categories that tentatively fit the information given in the interviews (Marshall & Rossman, 1989). The eight-step guideline proposed by Tesch (1990, pp. 142-145) allowed the researchers to group similar categories together into a theme based on the transcripts of the interviews. These themes were then abbreviated into codes and these codes were placed next to the appropriate segments of text. Categories that were related were then grouped together. The hermeneutic cycle was repeated until all apparent themes emerged from each transcription.

For Mäori, the security of systems used by online organizations creates a fear in regards to the confidentiality of their personal information (Peszynski & Thanasankit, 2002). This, in turn, raises issues about information being accessible to other people or even the possibility of the web site being hacked. Fears are increased when financial details are being transmitted via the Internet. When answering the question of what issues of trust are apparent to the Mäori Internet shopper, we initially look at whether or not the trustworthiness of a site enters their mind, particularly in regards to the protection of personal information. The respondents had the same concern as can be seen in the following example:

P6: Absolutely. Particularly over the Internet, where you know people can hack in and get your personal details and things like that... What worries me more about Internet shopping is that you're giving over financial details and access to your bank accounts and things like that, which I'm not keen on doing.

As shown in the above comment, the security of the systems used by the online organization create a doubt in the minds of those interviewed, as there is a fear of personal information, being accessible to other people or even the possibility of the web site being hacked. Fears are increased when financial details are being transmitted via the Internet.

One concept that developed early in the interview process was that of levels of trust. Specifically trust in terms of personal information:

P1: Level 1 trust, which is name, e-mail address, it's pretty easily given away, I mean, as soon as you start using the net, people get that information anyway. Level 2 trust is when you start giving things like your actual street address and you know, people could track you down if they wanted, and then the financial stuff with credit cards, that's when you start thinking, oh is this a secure site? Have they got high-tech security built around their web-server and network?

Using the response taken from one participant and applying it to the remaining participants, a model was developed (Figure 3).

When reviewing the interview transcripts, it was found that there are some differences between the literature and the Mäori respondents. For example, Mäori are responsible for more than just their personal information. When the respondent is performing a transaction via the Internet on behalf of their tribe, they are providing "historical information." That is, information about their tribe (*iwi*), sub-tribes (*hapu*), family (*whanau*), and cultural knowledge and information. *Taonga* stands out here, as it is the protection of such private and personal information.

The reoccurring theme about trust and Internet shopping is that of the reputation of the organization and their web site. This issue was also raised in the literature, however, Mäori place heavy emphasis on the reputation of a web site.

P2: ...now the reputation of, I think I'm still people based. The reputation of a web site doesn't come from the web site itself. It still comes from the people around me. So like if I know people order stuff off the net, say books, I'll go and ask them [off] which sites [do] they order?

The ability to increase the reputation of the web site, is not through customer testimonials, as they "could've been trumped up" (P3), but through word of mouth:

Figure 3: Levels of Trust as Proposed by Interviewees

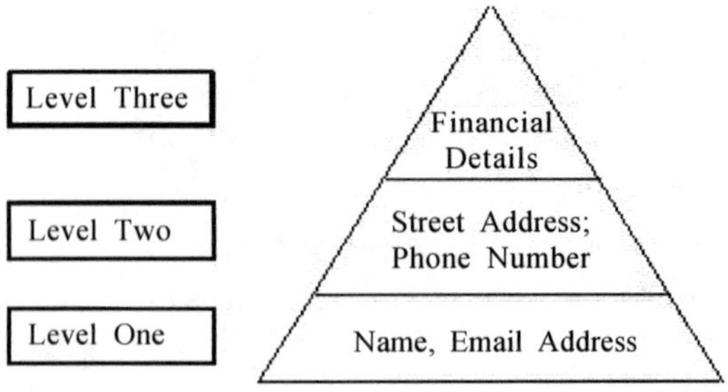

P8: I tend to go with the supplier or service provider if it's been recommended to me by somebody else…it would have to be someone else I know.

However, no matter how trustworthy the site may look, and how good the reputation is, there is still that doubt that "nothing is infallible, especially on the net" (P4). It is up to the organization to provide policies and honor those policies.

Trust in Internet Shopping

Interviewees were asked what helps them classify the web site as being trustworthy. Responses include:

P2: What I do like though, is being able to contact a person, even if it's by e-mail, but just so I know I have a person to contact, rather than just some nebulous being.

P4: Purely getting what you think you've bought [pause] in the time specified…Usability…definitely affects my shopping habits.

P6: First that it's a reputable product, and that there's a guarantee that if you don't like it, you can send it back…And contact details—I'll try them out and see if I get a reply. I'll e-mail them and see if I get a response, or contact telephone number and ring that and see the kind of service I get there, because I find it hard to get past the need to speak to someone, whether it be on the phone or face-to-face.

P8: For me, it's all of those things, that's what would make me trust them more…If I were shopping for a Mäori item, then I would like to see what contribution that they actually make to the Mäori society.

Themes repeated in the majority of interviews include reputation, the ability to contact someone and the guarantee that the goods you order are actually the goods you receive in the delivery period as promised by the seller. There is also a sense of collectivism in the comment made by Participant Eight. They want to see a contribution to Mäori society for any Mäori product they purchase.

The use of assurance services, such as Web seals (Cashell & Aldhizer III, 1999; Nöteberg et al., 1999), was noted as helping increase the trust of a consumer. Interviewees claimed to recognize few groups and organizations supporting the web seals. However, when interviewees were asked about the benefits of webseals, the majority of respondents gave similar responses such as these:

P3: ...this bit about increasing the trust and these assurance services, apart from MasterCard, I don't recognize these groups. So unless it was a recognized group, to me, that would hold no weight with me...if it were certified by someone that I know, that would probably help.

P4: I don't really look for them. Perhaps I just don't understand them. I don't understand the organizations that are supporting them.

As can be seen in the above quotations, those that were interviewed claimed to pay little attention to these web-seals. Bringing this into a New Zealand context, a further question in the interview process was developed, asking participants if the creation of a New Zealand web-seal would affect the respondent's trust in a web site:

P3: That would be good, because I think...I don't know what things to look for until these problems are highlighted...there might be occasions where we find what they're saying is misrepresented, and until these problems start popping up, I won't know what solutions to look for...there's going to be a lot of cowboys in there, and we're going to need some protection at some stage.

It was suggested that the creation of a web-seal for New Zealand web sites would make a difference in terms of increasing the sense of trust in that web site. However, it depends who creates that web-seal:

P4: Only if that organization has substance and credibility to it...I don't know how you would achieve substance or credibility...I think the consumer watchdog, like the Commerce Commission, whose jurisdiction covers fair trading...people who can guarantee or underwrite security, you know, you can guarantee performance, and keep them to their policies, so you are going to get what you ordered, and when you pay for it, your payment details are not threatened.

P6: Yeah, to have someone like the Commerce Commission checking, giving their seal of approval and that anyone that has that sign over the Internet, that they should actually be registered. I think that's really important. It's like a protection for New Zealand citizens, for us, we need that.

As seen in the above responses, an institute such as the Commerce Commission is seen as being a reputable source that those interviewed would trust. The idea would be to have all New Zealand e-commerce web sites register with the

Commerce Commission, provided they meet certain criteria such as honor their policies and delivery times and have a secure server. As a result, that web site would be able to display an image showing proof of being registered with the Commerce Commission and providing a trustworthy service.

Risk

The concept of product category risk and financial risk was apparent to those interviewed. There was little difference in respondents view of financial risk, which is the risk associated with the Internet as a purchasing medium. Consumers are apprehensive about sending their credit card information over the Internet because it puts them at risk of credit card fraud (Fram & Grady, 1997; Jarvenpaa et al., 1999, 2000; Lynch et al., 2001).

However, it was felt that product category risk applied to not only the Internet, but the traditional 'bricks and mortar' environment. Product category risk refers to the risk associated with the product itself. It is the consumers' belief that the product will function according to their expectations (Fram & Grady, 1997; Jarvenpaa et al., 1999, 2000; Lynch et al., 2001). This was seen in the response by Participant 3:

P3: ...it's as if I went into a shop and picked up an appliance and I'd expect it to work a certain way, and until I get home and plug it in, I don't know that.

Further views of risk can be seen in the following:

P3: I always worry when I give my credit card details over, I wonder if someone can hack into their site and use it... but that was a risk I was prepared to take!

P4: Risk is the key factor, the risk of getting what you think you have ordered... as coupled with the risk of putting your payment details on an international highway. If those two risks were eliminated, then trust and reputation are almost irrelevant.

P7: I know that there is a risk factor, but in some ways, you sort of have to take that into account when you want to buy from the net. You're paying for the convenience more so than anything else.

Although the risk factor exists, the final purchase ultimately comes down to whether or not you want to take that risk. However, if this risk factor can be reduced or eliminated, then, as Participant 3 mentioned, "trust and reputation and almost irrelevant."

Reputation

The popular method of promoting the reputation of a web site is by publishing customer testimonials (Quelch & Klein, 1996). However, those interviewed tend to pay little attention to customer testimonials. Reasons included not knowing if they are real or how the person who wrote the testimonial based their judgements.

P1: They can be useful, although, sometimes you kind of wonder whether they really are customers.

P2: Mmmm, now the reputation of, I think I'm still people-based. The reputation of a web site doesn't come from the web site itself, it still comes from the people around me. So if I know people who order stuff off the net, say books, I'll go and ask them off which site they order , rather than, you know, oh this looks like a nice site, because it says so.

P3: ...this whole thing about reputation, I wouldn't place much emphasis on that, because I don't know they're valid testimonials, they could've been trumped up!

P4: No, not really. Unless the allocation of quality is carried out by an independent and highly regarded organization, it would mean nothing to me.

P7: It's a bit like when you read a newspaper and they have critics talking about certain restaurants, and it's like, for all I know, he could be tasteless! I don't know! This is where it comes back to that trust thing...if I got a comment from someone I knew, then that would mean a lot more than someone else.

P8: I tend to go with the supplier or service provider if it's been recommended to me by somebody else...it would have to be someone else I know.

Respondents prefer to speak to someone they know that has visited that site to see how they found that site, rather than trust a total stranger. The word-of-mouth parameter as shown in Figure 2 is important at this stage, for those interviewed. As shown in the above extract, Participant 7 would prefer a comment from "someone I knew, then that would mean a lot more than someone else", and again, this can be seen in the following extract:

P5: I know a lot of other people who have purchased the same product from that site, so I've seen the merchandise, and through that referral, I've got confidence in that site and the product.

This is the main difference between those interviewed and what the literature has to say regarding reputation. Rather than read customer testimonials left on the web site by unknown customers, the Mäori respondents prefer to seek and speak to someone they know and trust who has been to that web site and made a purchase from it.

Additional Features Relating to Mäori and Internet Shopping

During the interviews, participants were asked how they would feel in terms of trust towards a web site, with regards to the creation of web sites that were *Te Reo* Mäori (that is, web sites in the Mäori language). That is, would those interviewed be more trusting towards a web site in the Mäori language? As can be seen in the responses below, it was found that there would be an immense interest by the Mäori Internet shopper to "delve" into it and be "compelled" to view it. However, the same features are necessary to instil that sense of trust in the Mäori Internet shopper. That is, a good reputation from someone in their in-group.

P5: The same criteria would apply to sites that are in English…I think it would add to site interest…but as far as credibility and trustworthiness goes, the reputation would have to stand first.

P6: I'd still be looking for the same things that I'd be looking for in other sites…I would be very compelled.

P8: If the sites was in Mäori, and it had all those web-seals and the padlocks at the bottom and the price was reasonable, and you were able to access their service easily and quickly, then the thing would be awesome, but I think I would be looking for the same measures as I would on other sites, the safety measure and stuff like that before I started spending money on their site.

One possibility that arose in the interviews that could be applied to the practical environment is that New Zealand web sites may want to contain bilingual text. For example, some web sites, such as http://www.alibaba.com, have the ability to be viewed in either English, Chinese dialects or Korean. This may have more interest for the Mäori Internet shopper to at least visit the site.

An issue that was raised from the literature pertains to Mäori values and beliefs. Mäori prefer not to have personal information about them kept by a third party. Interviewee's were asked if such questions were raised when they entered their personal information and financial details into the web site. Although the concept of *taonga* was not apparent for all participants interviewed, there were some respondents, who felt that *taonga* was important, knowing that their information is kept on a system for an unknown period. Examples of *taonga* can be seen in these excerpts:

P7: Yes, because I know they keep this information for stats and hopefully to get some marketing information. I don't like the thought of it always sitting there and being accessible.

P8: ...as a Mäori, I am responsible, not just for my own personal information, but also details about my tribe, Iwi details, and other details about family and things like that, so there's a difference about what type of information can be entrusted to somebody else I think. Now if it's my own personal information, like address details, age and all other things, then those things are ok. But um, it's, it's historical information, or *whakapapa*...then that's where things get a little bit different. The nature of data exchange is a bit different there. As a younger person, I'm ok with entrusting information to somebody else, but I know that with other people, older people, other older Mäori people, it would be different...they just don't like shopping over the Internet and passing off their own, even their own personal details, bank account details, and things.

The above comment shows that Mäori are responsible for more than just their personal information. However, the degree of confidence varies when the respondent is performing a transaction via the Internet on behalf of their tribe, or *iwi*, as they are providing "historical information." The other difference is between the old and the young. Older Mäori do not like shopping via the Internet because they prefer to keep their personal details and bank details private, whereas the younger Mäori have fewer doubts with entrusting personal information to other people.

There are other features or factors that may help the respondents want to shop via the Internet. One feature includes the notion of anonymity that no one knows they are Mäori, and as a result will treat them no differently than non-Mäori. This can be seen in the comment below:

P6: There's also that whole thing of anonymity...I know when I go shopping with my sisters, there is this kind of people, the service people, the assistants, um, often they'll come up and say "Oh, can I help you with something?" and they'll be a particular way with us, that they're not like with other people, and I wonder if that's because we're Mäori...the anonymity that comes with the Internet and Internet shopping. As long as you've got the prerequisite, Visa card number, and a name and address to send the stuff to, you don't have to worry about that. Like everybody across the board is treated the same way…I can see that as being a really big attraction.

Essentially, everyone is the same when shopping on the Internet. That is, there is no cultural or racial discrimination. This can be a major influence to those that are treated differently whilst shopping in the traditional environment. Onc Internet shopper is treated exactly the same as another Internet shopper.

Photos of the people inside the organization on the web site gives the Mäori Internet shopper recognition that this organization does exist and they do have people working there, in other words, they are not a faceless organization.

P2: Being able to see a face [referring to the use of photo's of members of the organization on the web site], being able to contact that person, um, but then there's the whole *ahua* [look], the whole look of the site as well, does it have, you know, is it easy to navigate?

This also helps if the Mäori Internet shopper needs to call up for any reason, as they have a face to the name.

Finally, the association of recognizable Mäori names to e-commerce sites could also make a difference, as there is that reputation or word-of-mouth notion that if other recognizable Mäori trust the site, then the Mäori Internet shopper should do so.

P1: If Mäori see other recognizable names associated with e-commerce sites, it could well have a positive effect on their level of willingness to make purchases from that site.

Examples of recognizable Mäori names could be associations via tribes (*iwi*), sub-tribes (*hapu*), or family (*whanau*). If members of their tribe or family are willing to purchase goods and/or services from a particular web site, then this could have a positive effect on the Mäori Internet shopper to feel comfortable and trusting of that web site to purchase something themselves.

FUTURE TRENDS

The information provided in this chapter can help New Zealand (and possibly international) e-commerce businesses as it brings to light some issues that Mäori have that either hinder them or assist them to purchase via the Internet. As Mäori are classed as being a collectivist society (Gregory, 2001; Light, 1999; Patterson, 2000), this information could also be applied to other collectivist societies, such as Thailand or China).

As seen in the previous sections, the inclusion of photos of the organization and staff could give the Mäori Internet shopper recognition that this organization is not a faceless organization. That is, they do exist and they do have people working there. If the Mäori Internet shopper needs to call the organization for any reason, they have a face to the name. That is, "It's just as if you've walked into a shop" (P6). There is an association or link between the Mäori Internet shopper and the web site (and organization).

Another possible outcome of this chapter is the creation of a New Zealand web seal. As discussed above, an organization such as the Commerce Commission in New Zealand is seen as being a reputable source that those interviewed would trust. If New Zealand web sites are registered with the Commerce Commission, then this could help increase the consumers trust in the web site and make them feel more comfortable to make a purchase.

The association of Mäori names with a web site could also help the would-be Mäori Internet shopper trust the web site and is linked closely to the above suggestion of the web-seal. It is the recognition of a reputable association, and because the Mäori organization (*iwi, hapu, whanau*) trusts that associated name, the Mäori Internet shopper should then trust the web site.

Contact details should be made visible on the web site, as one participant states: "I like the thought of it being on every page. You know, usually down the bottom they'll have all that information, the help, the contact details" (P7). Displaying contact details creates a professional image that there is the ability to contact the organization.

Finally, displaying policies regarding shipping, returns and warrantees should also be made available on the web site. These policies should be visible and accessible for the consumer to read. The important feature is that these policies should be strictly adhered to by the organization. That is, if they say they are going to deliver in *x* number of days, they do so.

The study this chapter was based on also provides a base for future studies in the field of e-commerce and cultural values. The first and foremost area is the New Zealand Mäori. The study was an introductory investigation into the cultural differences of Internet shopping for Mäori. As a result, and possibly the first step for future studies is to investigate if and how the results of the current study compare to New Zealand Europeans.

Another extension would be to interview Mäori Internet shoppers in a New Zealand context, rather than a Wellington context. This would see if the results of this study are Wellington-specific, that is, only apply to Mäori Internet shoppers in the Wellington region. Another benefit of such an extensive study would create the ability to generalize the results New Zealand-wide, rather than concentrated on one specific city, Wellington. An investigation into other collectivist societies (Eastern countries, such as Japan, Thailand and China) could see if culture significantly influences the indigenous behaviors and attitudes of people.

The development of the trust pyramid (Figure 3) could be argued to include a fourth level, sensitive information. This level could be applicable to the Mäori culture as they have a strong sense of *taonga*, that is, a belief that their personal information is a treasure. Although this was not raised in the study, studies on levels of trust have identified sensitive information as another level (McCarthy & Campbell, 2001; Han & Maclaurin, 2002; Dawson, 2002). The term sensitive information can refer to the type of information that is extremely personal. One area in which this comes to mind is medical information, whereby a web site may ask when the last time a customer went for a check-up, and if any medical problems were found. Sensitive information could also refer to the type of product the customer purchased.

CONCLUSION

There are features of a web site that could be implemented that will help increase the sense of trust for the Mäori Internet shopper, however, completely removing the risk factor is a difficult task. The central concern of this chapter has been to gain some understanding of what issues of trust must be apparent to make the Mäori Internet shopper feel comfortable to shop online. The study this chapter is based on attempts to uncover some understanding of the associated factors that either help or inhibit Mäori from shopping on the Internet.

The study looked at eight Mäori Internet shoppers, consisting of five female participants and three male participants. All were full-time professionals in either the private or public sector in Wellington. Face-to-face interviews were performed to identify Mäori perceptions of trust and Internet shopping. The data was reviewed, which enabled the identification of issues that arose in either the interview or the background literature review.

As a result, this chapter tentatively suggests that trust for the Mäori Internet shopper in this demographic meant that the web site must have a good reputation, the ability to contact someone and the guarantee that the goods you order are actually the goods you receive in the delivery period as promised by the seller. There was also a sense of collectivism in the comments made. That is, participants want to see a contribution to Mäori society for any Mäori product they purchase, and the fact that they want to hear from someone they know and trust, typically someone from their in-group.

This chapter can also tentatively suggest that the current literature on trust in Internet shopping, risk and reputation applies to the Mäori Internet shoppers in this demographic to a certain extent:

- Participants interviewed claimed to pay no attention to assurance services such as web-seals as they claimed little knowledge of the groups or organizations supporting the web seals or what they stood for.
- In terms of risk, respondents felt that financial risk is important and the same as what the literature states, however, the product category risk equally applies to the traditional 'bricks and mortar' environment.
- Reputation is a major theme that was apparent in most of the interviews. Respondents prefer to speak to someone they know that has visited that site to see how they found that site, rather than trust a total stranger.
- There is the notion of anonymity, that is, no one knows they are Mäori, and as a result will not by treated any differently than non-Mäori.
- Photos of the people inside the organization can make a positive difference. It gives the Mäori Internet shopper the ability to put a face to the name and for the organization to show that they are not a faceless organization.
- The association of recognizable Mäori names to e-commerce sites could make a difference, as there is that reputation or word-of-mouth notion that if other recognizable Mäori trust the site, then the Mäori Internet shopper should do so.

This chapter has made a significant contribution to the body of trust in e-commerce knowledge by exploring the role of a collectivist culture (the New Zealand Mäori) and its influence on attitudes toward online shopping. By gaining more understanding of the role of the collectivist culture on trust, there is the prospect of future research projects into cross-cultural research, comparing other collectivist cultures in different countries, to better understand the role of culture and its influence on e-commerce.

The findings of the study, which this chapter is based on, assist both practitioners and researchers to understand the role of indigenous culture and values on online shopping. This chapter will assist practitioners in the planning and development of e-commerce where culture significantly influences the indigenous behaviors and attitudes. In summary, the social construction of a culture has an impact on the development of trust and success of B2C e-commerce web sites.

REFERENCES

Ah-Wong, J., Gandhi, P., Patel, H., Shah, U., Tran, T. & Targett, D. (2001). E-commerce progress: Enablers, inhibitors and the short-term future. *European Business Journal*, *13*(2), 98-107.

Anderson, E. & Weitz, E. (1989). Determinants of continuity in conventional industrial channel dyads. *Marketing Science*, 8, 310-323.

Applegate, L. M., Holsapple, C. W., Kalakota, R., Radermacher, F. J. & Whinston, A.B. (1996). Electronic commerce: Building blocks of new business opportunity. *Journal of Organisational Computing and Electronic Commerce*, 6(1), 1-10.

Ba, S., Whinston, A. B. & Zhang, H. (1999). Building trust in the electronic market through an electronic incentive mechanism. *Proceedings of the 20th International Conference on Information Systems*, 208-213.

Belich, J. (1996). *The Making of Peoples: A History of New Zealand from Polynesian Settlement to the End of the Nineteenth Century*. Auckland: Penguin Books.

Bhatnagar, A., Misra, S. & Rao, H.R. (2000). On Risk, Convenience, and Internet shopping behavior. *Communications of the ACM*, *43*(11), 98-105.

Bhawuk, D.P.S. & Brislin, R. (1992). The measurement of intercultural sensitivity using the concepts of individualism and collectivism. *International Journal of Intercultural Relations*, *16*, 413-436.

Bolin, S. (1998). E-Commerce: A market analysis and prognostication. *StandardView*, *6*(3), 97-105.

Camp, J. (2000). *Trust and Risk in Internet Commerce*. Cambridge: MIT.

Cashell, J. D. & Aldhizer III, G. R. (1999). Web trust: A seal of approval. *The Internal Auditor*, *56*(3), 50-54.

Chen, Y. A., Ingraham, L. R. & Jenkins, J. G. (2001). Creating value through e-commerce. *Strategic Finance*, *82*(7), 44-49.

Cheung, C. M. K. & Lee, M. K. O. (2001). Trust in Internet shopping: Instrument development and validation through classical and modern approaches. *Journal of Global Information Management*, *9*(3), 23-35.

Chiles, T. H. & McMackin, J. F. (1996). Integrating variable risk preferences, trust and transaction cost economics. *Academy of Management Review*, *21*, 73-99.

Choudhuri, A. & Holbrook, M. B. (2001). The chain of effects from brand trust and brand affect to brand performance: The role of brand loyalty. *Journal of Marketing*, *65*(2), 81-93.

Daft, R.L. & Lengel, R.H. (1986). Organisational information requirements, media richness and structural design. *Management Science*, 32(5), 554-571.

Das, T. K. (1998). Between trust and control: Developing confidence in partner cooperation in alliances. *The Academy of Management Review*, *23*(3), 491-513.

Dawar, N., Parker, P.M. & Price, L.J. (1996). A cross-cultural study of interpersonal information exchange. *Journal of International Business Studies*, *27*, 497-516.

Dawson, L.H. (2002). Trust me! It's safe! *Professional Safety*, *47*(2), 35-41.

Dedhia, N.S. (2001). E-commerce quality. *Total Quality Management*, *12*(3), 397-402.

Doney, P.M. & Cannon, J.P. (1997). An examination of the nature of trust in buyer-seller relationships. *Journal of Marketing*, *61*, 35-51.

Donthu, N. & Garcia, A. (1999). The Internet shopper. *Journal of Advertising Research*, *39*(3), 52-58).

Dowling, G.R. & Staelin, R. (1994). A model of perceived risk and intended risk-handling activity. *Journal of Consumer Research*, *21*, 119-134.

Dwyer, R.F., Schurr, P.H. & Oh, S. (1987). Output sector munificence effects on the internal political economy of marketing channels. *Journal of Marketing Research*, *24*, 347-358.

Egger, F.N. (2000). Towards a model of trust for e-commerce system design. *Proceedings of the CHI2000 Workshop*. Retrieved from the World Wide Web on May 13, 2001: http://www.zurich. ibm.com/~mrs/chi2000/contributions/egger.html.

Ernst & Young (1999). *The Second Annual Ernst & Young Internet Shopping Survey*. Retrieved from the World Wide Web on May 16, 2001: http://www.ey.com/publicate/consumer/pdf/ internetshopping.pdf.

Fram, E. H. & Grady, D. B. (1997). Internet shoppers: Is there a surfer gender gap? *Direct Marketing*, *59*(9), 46-50.

Gadamer, H. G. (1976). *Philosophical Hermeneutics*. California, University of California Press.

Ganesan, S. (1994). Determinants of long-term orientation in buyer-seller relationships. *Journal of Marketing*, *58*, 1-19.

Geyskens, I., Steenkamp, J-B.E.M., & Kular, N. (1998). Generalisations about trust in marketing channel relationships using meta-analysis. *International Journal of Research in Marketing*, *15*(3), 223-248.

Gray, G.L. & Debreceny, R. (1998). The electronic frontier. *Journal of Accountancy*, *185*(5), 32-38.

Gregory, R.J. (2001). Parallel themes: Community psychology and Mäori culture in Aotearoa. *Journal of Community Psychology*, *29*(1), 19-27.

Han, P. & Maclaurin, A. (2002). Do consumers really care about online privacy? *Marketing Management*, *11*(1), 35-38.

Harple, T.S. (1996). Considering the Mäori in the nineteenth and twentieth centuries: The negotiation of social identity in exhibitory cultures. *Journal of Arts Management, Law and Society*, *25*(4), 292-305.

Hawkins, K. (2001). Re: ACN, Main, Mäori Internet Statistics: Personal communication by e-mail to the author.

Heider, F. (1958). *The Psychology of Interpersonal Relations*. New York: Wiley.

Hoffman, D.L., Novak, T.P. & Peralta, M. (1999). Building consumer trust online. *Communications of the ACM*, *42*(4), 80-85.

Hofstede, G. (1980). *Culture's Consequences: International Differences in Work-Related Values*. Beverly Hills, California: Sage Publications.

Hofstede, G. (1991). *Cultures and Organizations*. London: McGraw-Hill Book Company.

Jarvenpaa, S.L., Tractinsky, N., & Vitale, M. (2000). Consumer trust in an Internet store. To Appear: *Information Technology and Management, 1*(1-2), 45-71.

Jarvenpaa, S.L., Tractinsky, N., Saarinen, L. & Vitale, M. (1999). Consumer trust in an Internet store: A cross-cultural validation. *Journal of Computer-Mediated Communication*, *5*(2). Retrieved from the World Wide Web on 5 April 2001 on: http://www.ascusc.org/jcmc/vol5/issue2/jarvenpaa.html.

Jones, S., Wilikens, M., Morris, P. & Masera, M. (2000). Trust requirements in E-Business. *Communications of the ACM*, *43*(12), 80-82.

Kalakota, R. & Whinston, A. B. (1996). *Frontiers of Electronic Commerce*. Addison-Wesley, Reading, MA.

Kim, K. & Prabhakar, B. (2000). Initial trust, perceived risk, & the adoption of Internet banking. *Proceedings of the 21st International Conference on Information Systems*, 537-543.

Klein, H.K. & Myers, M.D. (1999). A set of principles for conducting and evaluating interpretive field studies in information systems. *MIS Quarterly, Special Issue on Intensive Research*, *23*(1), 67-93.

Kovacic, Z.J. (2001). Positioning of Mäori Web sites in the space generated by the key concepts in Mäori culture. *2001 Informing Science Conference*. Retrieved from the World Wide Web on 12 May 2001: http://schedule.elicohen.net/.

Labour Market Policy Group. (2001). Closing the digital divide - Summary of stakeholder discussions. *Department of Labour*. Retrieved from the World

Wide Web on 17 May 2001: http://www. lmpg.govt.nz/publications/ stakeholder%20discussions%20final%20word97.pdf.

Lawrence, E., Corbitt, B., Fisher, J., Lawrence, J. & Tidwell, A. (2000). *Internet Commerce: Digital Models for Business*. (2nd ed.). Milton, Queensland: John Wiley and Sons.

Lewicki, R.J., & Bunker, B.B. (1995). Trust in relationships: A model of trust development and decline. *Conflict, Cooperation, and Justice*. San Francisco: Jossey-Bass.

Light, E. (1999). Market to Mäori. Key Mistakes: Key Remedies. *Marketing, 18*(6), 10-17.

Liu, J.H., Wilson, M.S., McClure, J. & Higgens, T.R. (1999). Social identity and the perception of history: Cultural representations of Aotearoa/New Zealand. *European Journal of Social Psychology, 29*, 1021-1047.

Lohse, G.L. & Spiller, P. (1998). Electronic shopping. *Communications of the ACM, 41*(7), 81-87.

Lynch, P.D., Kent, R.J., & Srinivasan, S.S. (2001). The global Internet shopper: Evidence from shopping tasks in twelve countries. *Journal of Advertising Research, 41*(3), 15-23.

Marshall, C. & Rossman, G.B. (1989). *Designing Qualitative Research.* Newbury Park, CA: Sage.

Martin, P.Y. & Turner, B.A.. (1986). Grounded theory and organisational research. *The Journal of Applied Behavioural Science*, 22(2), 141-157.

McCarthy, M.P. & Campbell, S. (2001). Taking E-security to a higher level. *Financial Executive, 17*(9), 50-51.

McKnight, D.H., Choudhury, V. & Kacmar, C. (2000). Trust in E-commerce vendors: A two-stage model. *Proceedings of the 21st International Conference on Information Systems*, 532-536.

McKnight, D.H., Cummings, L.L. & Chervany, N.L. (1998). Initial trust formation in new organizational relationships. *Academy of Management Review, 23*, 473-490.

Mehta, K.T. & Shah, V. (2001). E-Commerce: The next global frontier for small businesses. *Journal of Applied Business Research, 17*(1), 87-94.

Ministry of Economic Development. (2001). *Statistics on Information Technology in New Zealand: Updated to 2001*. Retrieved from the World Wide Web on 5 May 2001. http://www.med.govt.nz/ pbt/infotech/itstats2001/ itstats2001.pdf.

Moore, G.C., Deshpande, R. & Zaltman, G. (1993). Factors affecting trust in market research relationships. *Journal of Marketing, 57*, 81-101.

Myers, M. (1997). *Information Systems and Qualitative Research.* (Eds.). London: Chapman and Hall.

Ngwenyama, O.K. & Lee, A.S. (1997). Communication richness in electronic mail: Critical social theory and the contextuality of meaning. *MIS Quarterly, 21*(2), 145-167.

Nöteberg, A., Christiaanse, E. & Wallage, P. (1999). The role of trust and assurance services in electronic channels: An exploratory study. *Proceedings of the 20th International Conference on Information Systems*, 472-478.

OPRA Limited. (1998). Mäori Knowledge Assessment: Technical Support Manual. *OPRA Consulting*. Retrieved from the World Wide Web on 16 July 2001. http://www.opra.co.nz/downloads/manuals/ MKAManual.pdf.

Patterson, J. (1992). *Exploring Mäori Values*. Palmerston North: Dunmore Press Limited.

Patterson, J. (2000). Mana: Yin & Yang. *Philosophy East & West, 50*(2), 229-240.

Perrett, R.W. & Patterson, J. (1991). Virtue ethics and Mäori ethics. *Philosophy East & West, 41*(2), 185-203.

Peszynski, K.J. (2001). Trust and the Mäori Internet shopper: An exploratory study. *Honours Thesis (unpub.)*, Victoria University of Wellington, Wellington.

Peszynski, K.J., & Thanasankit, T. (2002). Exploring trust in B2C E-Commerce - An exploratory study of Mäori culture in New Zealand. *Paper presented at the 10th European Conference on Information Systems*, Gdansk, Poland.

Quelch, J.A. & Klein, L.R. (1996). The Internet and international marketing. *Sloan Management Review, 37*(3), 60-75.

Resnick, P., Zeckhauser, R., Friedman, E. & Kuwabara, K. (2000). Reputation systems. *Communications of the ACM, 45*(12), 45-48.

Riggins, F.J. & Rhee, H.S. (1998). Towards a unified view of e-commerce. *Communications of the ACM, 41*(10), 88-95.

Schneider, G. & Perry, J. (2000). *Electronic Commerce*. Cambridge, MA: Thomson Learning/Course Technology.

Schurr, P.H. & Ozanne, J.L. (1995). Influences on exchange processes: Buyers' preconceptions of a seller's trustworthiness and bargaining toughness. *Journal of Consumer Research, 11*, 939-953.

Sklar, D. (2001). Building trust in an Internet economy. *Strategic Finance, 82*(10), 22-25.

Smith, A.G. (1997). Fishing with new nets: Mäori Internet information resources and implications of the Internet for indigenous peoples. *Paper presented at INET'97*.

Smith, A.G. & Sullivan, R. (1996). Mäori electronic information: Issues and resources. *New Zealand Libraries*, *48*(6), 111-118.

Starr, P. (2000). The electronic commons. *The American Prospect*, *11*(10), 30-35.

Statistics New Zealand. (1998). *New Zealand now Mäori*. Wellington, New Zealand: Statistics New Zealand.

Steinauer, D.D., Wakid, S.A. & Rasberry, S. (1997). Trust and traceability in e-commerce. *StandardView*, *5*(3), 118-124.

Stewart, K.J. (1999). Transference as a means of building trust in world wide web sites. *Proceedings of the 20th International Conference on Information Systems*, 459-464.

Te Puni Kokiri. (1994). *Privacy of Health Information: Te matatuakiri me te matatapu o ng kMrero hauora*. 1994.

Tesch, R. (1990). *QualitativeRresearch: Analysis types and software tools*. New York: Falmer.

Thanasankit, T. (1999). Exploring social aspects of requirements engineering – An ethnographic study of Thai software houses. *PhD Thesis (unpub.)*, University of Melbourne.

Thibaut, J.W. & Kelley, H.H. (1959). *The Social Psychology of Groups*. New York: Wiley.

UMR Insight, Ltd. (1999). *Internet Use Statistics*. Retrieved from the World Wide Web on 17 May 2001: http://isocnz.org.nz/help/help010516omni.html.

Wilkins, L., Swatman, P.M.C. & Castleman, T. (2000): What's in a name? Conceptual issues in defining electronic commerce, *Proceedings of the 8th European Conference on Information Systems*, *1*, 11-16.

Yamagishi, T. & Yamagishi, M. (1994). Trust and commitment in the United States and Japan. *Motivation and Emotion*, *18*, 129-165.

Zwass, V. (1996). Electronic Commerce: Structures and issues. *International Journal of Electronic Commerce*, *1*(1), 3-23.

Chapter IX

The E-Commerce of SMEs in Thailand

Arunee Intrapairot
Rajamangala Institute of Technology, Thailand

Anongnart Srivihok
Kasetsart University, Thailand

ABSTRACT

Small and medium enterprises (SMEs) in Thailand are fundamental business units spread all over the country. Since the severe economic crisis (i.e., Tom Yum Kung disease) in 1997, thousands of SMEs have gone bankrupt and so dropped out of the Thai economy each year. One key means of enhancing the viability of SMEs and assisting in economic recovery of the country that has been suggested is to transform them from a traditional to digital business using the Internet and e-commerce.. The expected advantages of e-commerce strategy include decreasing costs, expanding marketplaces, enhancing competitiveness, improving business image, and increasing revenues.

However, there are snares and hidden pitfalls in the backend of this business. This chapter presents an overview of e-commerce of SMEs in Thailand. The first part introduces fundamental background of SMEs in Thailand including types and characteristics. The second part investigates advantages and disadvantages of e-commerce implementation. Finally, the third part discusses SMEs and e-commerce in Thailand in the case of e-tourism.

INTRODUCTION

In the past, Thailand aimed at being an industrialized country. The country's development schemes highlighted large investment depending on foreign capital, labor-intensive production and advanced technology while neglecting the skills and know-how of local people. The severe economic crisis in 1997 brought Thailand to realize that small and medium sized enterprises (SMEs) are important as a mechanism that may help the country to survive and compete in a highly competitive globalized world.

Intense competition and the advent of information technology have stimulated SMEs to invest in and integrate technological infrastructure. They expect that this will attract customers because of greater convenience, better access to information, more efficient transactions, and more attractive variety of products. E-commerce has become the most sought-after technology because it allows SME customers to conduct real-time, remote transactions without limitations imposed by time or geography and to access more up-to-date and transparent information, which helps them to make appropriate decisions and fulfill their requirements (WebAustralia, 1996).

In turn, SMEs themselves may gain fundamental benefits from e-commerce in terms of reduction of costs for office establishment and operating costs (e.g., personnel and equipment). The cost of setting up a full-service e-commerce web site is quite similar to that of opening a single physical storefront, but it can reach more customers. Furthermore, e-commerce customers, who tend to be young, affluent, and highly educated, may create a high demand for products and services and opportunities for cross-selling and up-selling (Phillips, 1998). The low operating costs and low technology they employ enable SMEs to offer reasonable prices and effective service to not only domestic but also world markets.

Benefits from e-commerce are contingent upon the completion of telecommunication infrastructure, confidence in the security of the system, and acceptance by customers. Therefore, SMEs wishing to implement this technology need to extend infrastructure, improve the skills of their personnel, and strengthen their security systems (Laudon & Laudon, 2000; Smith, 1997).

However, engaging in e-commerce may increase overall costs unless SMEs reduce expenditures along conventional channels by closing physical branches, downsizing staff, and re-engineering operation systems. E-commerce alone may not reduce costs because SMEs are unable to conduct typical transactions and to undertake back office workload via the Internet. Additionally, while SMEs may save costs for customer support due to front-end self-servicing systems, they have to make expenditures on technology devices, communications support, and product or service support (e.g., delivery, on-line payment and certified security).

Initially, adoption of e-commerce may not necessarily be aimed not at making money but rather at public relations, i.e., maintaining an image as an innovative organization, defending a market position against competitors, and building relationships with customers. Such intangible benefits aside, potential revenues from e-commerce are yet unproved by many SMEs

SMES IN THAILAND

SMEs are small and medium-sized enterprises that are driven by services or agricultural or manufactured products involving unique skills. They produce products and provide services using mainly domestic raw materials and employing local people to serve the world market demand. With minimal initial investment, they are able to generate incomes from both domestic and overseas sources that are then distributed back to local communities.

Organizations concerned with SMEs in Thailand use various criteria in defining them. According to the Department of Industry Promotion Thailand, for example, an SME is an enterprise with fixed assets of 20 to 100 million bahts and 20 to 100 employees, whereas the Industrial Finance Corporation of Thailand (IFCT) requires fixed assets of 100-500 million bahts but does not specify a number of employees.

SMEs have advantages over large enterprises because of their independent management, affordable business establishment, and close communication with customers and staff (Hirunkitti, 1999). For their part, SMEs entrepreneurs expect various opportunities and benefits from running their business, including gaining control over their destiny, differentiating products or services to serve individual customers (i.e., mass customization), reaching their full potential, reaping unlimited profits, contributing to society, and doing what they enjoy (Scarborough & Zimmerer, 1996).

Thai SMEs represent 80 percent of the country's industrial producers and account for 70 percent of all employment (Bunyamanee, 2001). They thus may be able to give a great boost to the Thai economy in many ways. In addition, the demand for handmade and natural products is increasing. According to the WTO (1999), consumer products such as ceramics, hand-woven cotton and silk textiles, wooden toys, and leather products are valued at over 81 million dollars per year, with a growth rate of 15 to 20 percent. Ceramics and hand-woven textile are two main export products, with a value of $173M per year (i.e., 3.5 percent of the world market). Although the market shares of other products are about 0.5 - 1.0 percent, their potential growth rates are promising.

SMEs have been promoted as a means for Thailand to penetrate global markets with products and services involving unique skills despite the country's lack of capital for large investments and of human resources for technology-intensive production. SMEs seem to offer a way to tap the country's rich local wisdom and cultural heritage to produce various unique high quality products.

The Prime Minister advocates SMEs as a mechanism to drive the Thai economy, especially in prominent industries such as agriculture, gems, and tourism. He has a vision of the Thai product, which incorporates both high technology and local wisdom. Such products will strengthen Thai SMEs and help them gain sustainable growth and so support the Thai economy.

Thus, it is vital for SMEs to adapt themselves to new technology and apply it with local wisdom to generate distinctive products, which entirely fit world demand for products of nature and the human spirit. SMEs can be developed with the support of the public sector by such means as creating a greater variety of products, reducing costs by using technology, conducting research and development, decreasing dependencies especially for software, and creating recognized brand names.

Characteristics of Thai SMEs

As previously mentioned, definitions of SMEs vary according to an organization's perception. According to the Committee for Economic Development, SMEs should have at least two of the following characteristics: their management is independent (i.e., they are managed by their owners), they obtain capital funds mainly from their owners or their relatives, they operate within domestic markets, and they are small compared with other enterprises in the same industry (Ryan, Roberth & Hiduke, 1999). The specific characteristics of Thai SMEs are as follows:

- Thai SMEs have few employees and these are flexible and able to change product lines and production processes and so are able to adapt themselves well to customers' requirements.
- SMEs are able to initiate their business with low investment leading to low capital requirements, low burden of debt, and less relation to commercial banks.
- SMEs use skill, mainly manual, in production, blending their own wisdom with new technology to produce diversified products to meet the world demand and world-class standards.
- SMEs use local or domestic materials and the skills and expertise of local people. The use of imported materials and machines is minimal and limited to only where essential to enhance value and product lines.

- Products are made based on mass customization rather than mass production to cope with a current situation and serve individual requirements. Products are unique, high quality, and meet the standards, health regulations, and laws of many countries.
- SMEs perform an active part in their communities by employing local resources such as funds, people, and material.

Apart from the above characteristics, the usual stereotypes of SMEs are self-ownership, close communication with staff and customers, simple organizational structure, high responsibility of the owner, and the relatively high failure rate (approximately 35 percent fail within six years of establishment) (Scarborough & Zimmerer, 1996).

Obstacles SMEs Face

Thai SMEs still confront many difficulties in competing with large enterprises and striving for a sustainable growth. The main obstacle is severe financial difficulties, including a shortage of working capital and unsustainable debt burdens. Many SMEs, especially those making handcrafted products, have deficient fixed assets and do not use standard accounting procedures. As a result, they have difficulty obtaining credit from domestic financial institutions, and they have limited or no access to other sources of capital because they cannot afford the services of international investment banks (Asian Development Bank, 2000). Apart from financial problems, SMEs lack designers who are able to create products in line with world market demand, and their expertise in accounting and global marketing are deficient. Furthermore, the government realizes the importance of SMEs, but its policies to support them are still vague.

Supportive Measures to Help SMEs Overcome Obstacles

Since capital shortage and lack of liquidity are main hindrances to their growth, SMEs have called for prompt action by the government in launching more credit packages through public financial institutions, supporting sound management and effective marketing operations, and promoting the use of modern technology.

The former government launched many programs to help SMEs. It passed the SME Promotion Act on February 18, 2000, and set up a venture capital fund to support promising SMEs. In 2000, the government established the Small and Medium Finance Corporation to increase its capital from 400 million to 4.4 billion bahts for the financial support of SMEs. Other public financial institutions were also encouraged to provide loan packages to SMEs such as the Bank of Thailand (6.57 billion), IFCT (9.23 billion), Bank for Agriculture and Agricultural Co-operatives

(3.66 billion), Government Savings Bank (950 million), and Small and Medium Finance Guarantee Corporation (642 million). In addition, Small and Medium Enterprise Development was established to provide technological support and advice (Bunyamanee, 2001).

The present government is also a strong SME supporter. Many programs have been initiated such as the national asset management scheme (AMC), the setting up of an SME Bank, the one-product-per-*tambon* project, credit loans, and the one million baht circulating fund for each village. These programs will create a variety of niche markets, and strengthen SMEs, enabling them to become the backbone of the Thai economy (Bangkok Intelligence News, 2000; Krairiksh, 2001).

Assistance also comes from overseas. For example, the Asian Development Bank (ADB) has approved a US$25 million equity investment for Thai SMEs. The fund is a part of the ADB's strategy to assist crisis-affected economies by restoring investors' confidence in Thailand, reducing the high debt-to-equity ratios of SMEs, and stimulating the Thai banking system to expand credit or provide new loans (Asian Development Bank, 2000).

ADVANTAGES AND DISADVANTAGES OF E-COMMERCE

Applying the e-commerce strategy to SMEs in Thailand is in its infancy. Few enterprises use Internet technology and the World Wide Web for their business either for communication, as a marketing medium, or for transactions. Small and medium-sized firms have suggested both advantages and disadvantages.

Advantages

Electronic commerce (e-commerce) refers to all forms of transaction relating to commercial activities of both organizations and individuals that are based the processing and transmission of digitized data including text, sound, and visual images (United Nations, 2000).

The e-commerce strategy is perceived to offer many advantages. One great benefit of online business is that it lowers the cost of information delivery and transfer. There are no expensive brochures, so publishing and postage costs are reduced.

Another advantage is that Internet technology can be used as a marketing tool. It is an inexpensive way of providing catalogs, and new products or services can be immediately advertised on the Internet. Customers can access business content provided on the WWW instantly, an unlimited number of times, any time—day or night. The Internet lowers the cost of market research. Potential or target customers can be reached in both local and international markets. Furthermore, an effective web site that entertains and contains the information needed for buying decisions quickly enhances an organization's image and public recognition.

E-commerce offers greater returns on investment. Traditional storefronts are costly to build. The expenses include the purchasing or renting a premises, store decorations, labor, and products. On the other hand, the main expense in setting up an online storefront is the fee paid to web designers for developing web sites. The amount involved in the latter case is substantially less than the former.

Further, online business may lower costs in the long run such as lower costs for business transactions and lower cost for customer services are suggested. From the service perspective, product support or customer services on the Internet can be accessed instantly, 24 hours a day. Web technology can be used to improve customer services and reduce costs. Typically in the US, a live call agent of service transaction costs 5 dollars, while a voice responding system costs 50 cents, and service via a web-based system might cost only a few cents. A company may publish a web site detailing its products open for customers to access 24 hours a day, including customer service systems that capture online customer action and provide assistance if customers have problems.

Disadvantages

Various disadvantages are cited by enterprises experienced in using e-commerce. These include technology problems, lack of resources to fully exploit the Web, lack of expertise in legal issues, lack of brand name recognition, the high cost of setup and maintenance, disadvantages when the product is a commodity, lack of personal contact, and no advantage of being part of a local community.

Low sales figures after e-commerce implementation might be due to many factors related to competency, time, finance, marketing and technology. Most SMEs have limited experience with information technologies. Since there is a shortage of IT personnel and some firms are unable to update the web sites, they are dependent on web designers and Internet service providers, who may not be responsive to their particular problems. Some companies have encountered difficulties in designing web sites that are customer oriented. Further, some customers cannot find company web sites via search engines, decreasing the company's opportunity to establish contact with potential customers who are looking for their goods or services through the Internet.

Generally, the costs of e-commerce set up and maintenance include infrastructure establishment, initial web design fee, and web site maintenance. Additional costs may include research, development, staffing, and promotion.

In Thailand, there is a shortage of expertise in legal issues. At present, there are a few guidelines, laws or regulations concerning e-commerce or online business. In 2002, the Thai members of Parliament have passed two laws for information and technology. They include Electronic Transaction and Electronic Signature Laws (NITCS, 2002). The other two Computer Crime or Electronic Transfer laws have not been passed the Government meeting. Thus, online customers or suppliers still risk facing computer crimes (e.g., illegal access and use, data alteration and destruction, information and financial losses, and fraud).

Newcomer SMEs on the Internet may encounter online competitors who are the first movers. The web pioneer or large firms already have brand name recognition, cost advantages, and more experience in personnel training and web management, and they may have a major market share. Newcomer SMEs have less chance to capture customers or to compete directly with them.

Traditionally, SMEs have advantages over larger firms in terms of having personal contact with customers, making specialty products or services for customers, being in a local community, and targeting niche markets. An SME might for example produce or market a single product in one geographical area. These markets are protected to some extent because their size is not big enough to be cost effective for large firms. Turning to online business might ease larger firms in penetration to local community and potential customers. Essentially, the Internet allows online business to enter niche markets at low cost. Niche market invasion occurs when the transaction costs are low. This will cause firms with large overheads to go into the markets.

SMES AND E-COMMERCE IN THAILAND

SMEs perceive the Internet as a powerful technology that can be used as a sales vehicle. Therefore, e-commerce is not only an additional storefront, but also a must for competitive strategy and business survival because it helps SMEs to expand their marketplaces nationally and internationally without limitation of time and geographical boundaries. This capacity for conducting transactions between firms across geographical space presents new opportunities for SMEs in many respects ranging from public relations, network creation to income generation (Fariselli, Oughton, Picory, & Sugden, 1997).

However, adoption of e-commerce technology is not easy for SMEs because of they lack essential information and support to get started. Therefore, e-commerce implementation requires the provision of information regarding potentials and advantages of e-commerce development, costs, procedures necessary for implementation, and prospective customers (Araujo & Machado, 2001).

E-commerce in Thailand may be initiated by Internet Service Providers (ISP). There are at least seven ISPs providing online shopping services dedicated exclusively to electronic shopping malls (e-malls) such as GoldSite (www.goldsite.com) of KSC, Shopping Thailand (www.shoppingthailand.com) of Loxinfo, and Hot Zone/Shopping (www.samart.co.th) of Samart, for instance. These e-malls aim at facilitating additional services to their customers who use web-hosting services.

A survey of 656 participants from almost all Thai industries, attending a seminar on 22-24 July 1999, revealed that only 28.94 percent of participants had developed e-commerce capability for business transactions, whereas 71.06 percent of them had not. However, approximately 92 percent of them had a positive view of the importance of e-commerce implementation. Since this seminar was held at the beginning of the adoption of e-commerce in Thailand, despite the potential benefits, most participants were unsure about many things. Therefore, they demanded that the government provide training programs dealing with security systems, technology use, law, and homepage construction. The main obstacles that must be resolved included increasing security of ordering systems, enhancing awareness, increasing network systems, issuing laws and rules on online transaction, and intensifying government support (Electronic Commerce Resource Center, 1999).

On the consumer side, what Thai customers purchase online are products that are otherwise unavailable, recently placed on the market, or tax-free. The main products are books, CDs, tapes, tickets and accommodations. Many Thais still hesitate to purchase online because they are not able to inspect products, lack confidence in payment and security systems, and feel uncertain whether they will receive what they order (Mayongpong, 1999).

Thus, enhancing motivation for online purchasing is crucial. The important motivational factors are consumer needs, product utility and product characteristics. First, consumer requirements can be fulfilled by reducing time for product selection and increasing convenience in searching, diversification, and availability of products and services. Second, utility factors consist of 24-hour trading, order tracking, and information comparison. Third, product characteristics in demand are famous brand names, image, reliability, new ways of ordering, convenience in payment, security in payment, and competitive prices (Mayongpong, 1999).

Many surveys have been conducted to find out about the characteristics of e-commerce developers and users, readiness in e-commerce implementation, obstacles, and supportive factors. Private sector organizations, government agencies, and research institutes have applied this information to accelerate the diffusion rate of e-commerce to help Thai SMEs. Information on the three main industries in

Thailand: tourism, agriculture, and handicrafts, gives a broad picture of the e-commerce of Thai SMEs (Electronic Commerce Resource Center, 1999). According to the surveys, SMEs are in the process of web site development. The tourism industry is the most active compared with agriculture and handicraft; nearly half (50.05 percent) of the SMEs in the tourism industry already have web sites. This may result from the fact that intangible information-based tourism products and services are more suited to e-commerce transactions than the bulky tangible products of agriculture and handicrafts (see Table 1).

SMEs develop web sites for four main activities: advertising, ordering, payment and delivery. In all three industries, it is obvious that advertising plays an important role (see Table 2).

SMEs perceive various advantages from e-commerce. Market and customer expansion is the most widely perceived advantage especially by respondents in the field of agriculture (90.74 percent). Other expected benefits are advertising and

Table 1: Progress in Web Site Development by SMEs in Various Industries

Web site activities	Agriculture	Tourism	Handicrafts
Operational	32.41	50.55	27.33
Work in process	31.02	27.47	29.33
No activity	33.33	14.29	38.67

Source: Electronic Commerce Resource Center, 1999; 2000; Koanantakul, 1999.

Table 2: Web Site Activities of SMEs Engaged in E-Commerce

Web site activities	Agriculture	Tourism	Handicraft
Advertising	91.43	16.48	82.93
Ordering	14.29	6.60	34.15
Payment	8.57	11	12.20
Delivery	5.74	N/A	N/A

Source: Electronic Commerce Resource Center, 1999; 2000; Koanantakul, 1999.

public relations, decreased operational cost, increased sales and income, increased competitiveness, convenience, reduced work process, and image promotion (see Table 3).

The main obstacles to e-commerce development are lack of awareness, unsecured product ordering process, uncertainty about payment systems and security systems, lack of law support, poor communication infrastructure, no certification authority, and language problems. Lack of awareness is the main hindrance. Most participants revealed that they did not understand and lacked knowledge to develop e-commerce (see Table 4).

The success of e-commerce is contingent upon Internet usage. Although the number of Internet users had increased substantially, the participants perceived that Internet was not in readiness for e-commerce. Main problems concerning Internet use were low access speeds, insufficient relevant information, the lack of search engine systems, unattractive design, and the lack of systems for ordering and payment (Electronic Commerce Resource Center, 1999).

Recommendations for promotion and support e-commerce are to provide training and seminars, to increase staff competence, to secure support from the government in terms of policy and funds, to enhance security of the system, to develop portal sites, and to establish e-commerce branch offices in other regions to diffuse e-commerce knowledge (Electronic Commerce Resource Center, 1999).

Table 3: Expected Benefits of E-Commerce

Expected benefits	Agriculture	Tourism	Handicraft
Market & customer expansion	90.74	69.23	85.33
Public relations and advertising	69.44	53.85	68.67
Reduced operational costs	63.43	47.25	55.33
Increased sales and revenues.	62.50	49.45	55.33
Increased competitiveness	60.65	50.55	47.33
Convenience and reduced work	57.87	52.75	56
Image promotion	55.56	48.35	46

Source: Electronic Commerce Resource Center, 1999; 2000; Koanantakul, 1999.

Table 4: Major Obstacles

Major obstacles	Agriculture	Tourism	Handicrafts
Lack of awareness	79.17	58.24	84
Unsecured product ordering process	68.06	49.45	47.33
Unsecured payment system	55.09	50.55	42
Lack of law	52.31	50.55	37.33
Poor telecommunication infrastructure	49.54	31.87	45.33
No certification authority	49.07	24.18	29.33
Internal impromptu	35.19	29.67	35.33
Language problems	26.39	31.87	44.67

Source: Electronic Commerce Resource Center, 1999; 2000; Koanantakul, 1999.

A CASE STUDY OF E-TOURISM IN THAILAND

This case study of e-tourism in Thailand is partly derived from the research conducted by the Thailand Development Research Institute (TDRI) in order to develop an e-commerce master plan for the tourism industry for the Tourist Authority of Thailand (TAT). The study aims at providing general information on e-tourism, business models of e-commerce for Thai SMEs, and impacts of e-commerce on SMEs (Kao-Saad, Intrapairot, Tangkitvanitcha, Plangpraphan, & Kaewmesri, 2001).

General Information for SMEs E-Tourism

Thailand's technological structure is at the beginning stage. In 2000, there were approximately 1 million Internet users (Tangkitvanitcha, 2000). A survey of tourists found that 24 percent of respondents used the Internet as a source of information for tourism. The Internet was third in rank, behind word-of-mouth and guidebooks. The most popular web sites were www.sanook.com, www.hunsa.com, and www.thailand.com, while the official web site of the Tourism Authority of Thailand (http://www.tat.or.th) ranked eighth among the tourism web sites. Approximately 80 percent of Internet respondents used the Internet to search for data, while 8.15 percent used it for online booking. Less than three percent used it for online payment (e.g., accommodations, air tickets, and package tours).

Approximately 90 percent of 512 foreign tourists used the Internet, and 22 percent of these Internet users used it to search for information before visiting Thailand. The Internet ranked third behind guidebooks and word-of-mouth as a source of information. The most popular web sites were www.lonelyplanet.com (53 percent), www.travelocity.com (11 percent), and www.expedia.com (9 percent).

E-tourism entrepreneurs in Thailand can be divided into two groups. The first group are those who run their traditional tourism businesses and developed web sites for public relations, providing information provision, and establishing additional storefronts. The second group are pure online tourism companies using the Internet to connect with their customers.

A study of Thai entrepreneurs indicated that most of them are not ready to develop a complete e-commerce. Most web sites are for presence only. Few online reservation forms are provided because most SMEs still prefer making reservations via e-mail and facsimile to real-time e-commerce. A survey of 206 tourism businesses revealed that many small and medium sized tourism enterprises did not have web sites (67.6 percent and 52.9 percent, respectively). The web sites were used for public relations (35.4 percent), reservation services (23.3 percent), and online payment (4.9 percent). Problems and obstacles for tourism e-commerce were for the most part similar to those identified by previous research: lack of knowledge and technique for improving web sites, high costs, insufficient competence of IT people, lack of confidence in online payment, fear of imitation (e.g., routes, products, and services), legal problems, and difficulties with language and communication (Kao-Saad, Intrapairot, Tangkitvanitcha, et al., 2001).

An analysis of 150 Thai tourism web sites revealed that half of them were incomplete, inactive, or contained few data. The web sites only facilitated contact via telephone, facsimile and e-mail. Most interactive web sites were those of travel companies (80 percent), the rest being those of accommodation and car rental concerns. The main purpose for web site development was for public relations (71 percent) (Kao-Saad, Intrapairot, Tangkitvanitcha, et al., 2001).

Business Models of Electronic Commerce in Thailand

SMEs adopt e-commerce based on their required business models such as e-shop, e-mall, e-auction, and third-party marketplace. An e-shop is established to promote a company's profile, goods and services, then provide products directly to customers. An e-mall is virtual collection of shops providing various kinds of products and services. An e-marketplace is a common marketing front-end and transaction support to a number of businesses. Information brokers add value in searching, providing and packaging information and consultancy. In such virtual communities, value is added through communications and exchange of information between members or partners (Pereira & Fife, 2000).

The information derived from the study of Thai SME e-tourism can be classified into the following business models tours (Kao-Saad, Intrapairot, Tangkitvanitcha, et al., 2001).

Direct Marketing. SMEs tend to develop their web sites in order to present and offer their products or services via electronic shops, apart from their traditional storefronts or distribution channels. Large enterprises not only sell their own products and services but also collect products from other suppliers or providers and resell to consumers under their trademarks (e.g., www.phuket.com). This business model gains income from sales and advertising.

Indirect Marketing. SMEs who are unsure about their products and goodwill or lack marketing or technological knowledge develop their web sites by using the service of virtual malls or portal sites. E-malls and portal sites act as intermediaries between their members and customers. For example, many budget hotels in Thailand have their web pages hosted by www.thaihotel.com.

E-Distributor. Some businesses develop portal sites or e-malls as a centre for transactions between their members and customers. Customers are able to order via the web sites. The sites provide information, certify products, and are responsible for payment and delivery. Therefore, the web site hosts have expertise in their business lines. The expected income comes from brokerage fees, and advertising.

E-Broker. These businesses develop web sites as portal sites or e-malls the same as e-distributors do. However, they are not responsible for transactions between members and customers, certifying products, or payment. The web sites are only virtual intermediaries to introduce members to customers. In general, members are responsible for transactions themselves. E-brokers receive commission fees from transactions and advertising. The major web sites in Thailand prefer to be e-brokers to e-distributors (e.g., www.Thai.com, www.Siamguru.com, and www.Thailand.com).

E-Marketplace, or Virtual Corporation, or Networking Between Business Partners. An e-marketplace is collaboration among many companies or partnerships in which costs, resources, and expertise are shared in order to achieve success in selling products and services. The companies may be in the same or different industries. For example, tour operators may be in alliance with travel agencies or suppliers and at the same time cooperate with banks and credit companies for payment facilitation, with insurance companies for security, and with transportation companies for delivery. The e-marketplace is an ideal business model of SMEs for each industry in the future (e.g., www.tourismthailand.org for the tourism industry, and www.thaiecommerce.net for export).

Content Creation. The main purposes of this business model are public relations, advertising, and providing correct and up-to-date information. Thai content creators may not aim at selling their content because of low quality content for sales and easy imitation. For example, the official web site of TAT (i.e., www.tat.or.th) and www.sabuy.com provides useful content for tourists. Many SMEs develop their web sites based on this business model.

Most SMEs develop their web sites by becoming a partner or a member of a reputable portal or e-mall. A portal is a web site or service providing an initial point of entry to the web. It offers services and resources such as e-mail, search engines, and discussion forums so that members are able to provide visitors with updated information and services (Laudon & Laudon, 2000).

Portals and e-malls in Thailand are quite similar. Portals acquire members by providing information and facilitation for communication. E-malls provide members with trading facilitation. In the long run, portals and e-malls have to facilitate everything to enhance traffic and business opportunities. Popular general portals are www.sanook.com and www.hunsa.com whereas www.Sabuy.com is a well-known tourism portal site. The recognized e-malls for general products are www.Thai.com, www.thailand.com, and www.shoppingthai.com whereas www.phuket.com serves visitors mainly with tourism products or services.

The success of e-commerce requires the study of business models to analyze directions for profit creation, trust enhancement, risk mitigation, and effective distribution of products and services. However, business models are always evolved based on many factors such as community expansion, technological progress, increased content, experience, and opportunities (Turban, Lee, King, & Chung, 2000). Therefore, there is no fixed criterion for the best e-commerce business model. The most suitable one should fit organizational competencies in terms of human resources, level of technology, financial support, and business tasks.

Impacts of E-Commerce on SMEs

It is estimated that the value of e-commerce for the tourism industry will be no less than US$10.8 billion US dollar in 2002. This amount will come from three main sectors: online airline tickets, accommodations, and package tours (IDC, 1999). According to WTO Business Council (1999), the Internet is widely used in four countries: USA, Germany, Japan and the United Kingdom (representing about 79 percent of 129 million worldwide Internet users). Since these countries are the major tourism markets of Thailand, there are good prospects for e-commerce in the tourism industry.

There are, however, external factors that will have a negative impact on the Thai tourism industry unless it adapts itself to the new changing environment. Among these factors are changing consumer behavior and taste of foreign tourists, advances in information and communication technology, and the intrusion of large major online tourism companies.

Young, well educated, and informed tourists seem to have new types of behavior and tastes. They use the Internet more intensely than other groups. Data and information, then, will become important factors for the tourism industry because customers will make decisions based on information. Since information becomes transparent, the low cost strategy, which is the major problem of Thai tourism, does not work well, compared with the strategy of product differentiation.

The advance of information and communication technology (ICT) will result in a market expansion leading to a change in the structure of tourism industry that will see the emergence of online tourism, bankruptcy of traditional travel agencies, and business alliances sharing information and resources. Technological change will provide good opportunities for tourism entrepreneurs to access numerous world-wide customers, directly accumulate products and services from various sources, customize their products to meet customers' requirements, and supply their customers within a short time. Yet, these innovations will expand the gap between large enterprises and SMEs.

Large online companies from overseas are expanding worldwide, and this will have direct impact on the Thai tourism industry, especially SMEs. Although large online enterprises such as Expedia (www.expedia.com) or Travelocity (www.travelocity.com) have as yet to expand to Thailand, medium-sized online companies such as Chan Brothers (www.bookntravel.com) and Asiatravel (www.asiatravel.com) have already set up affiliated companies in Thailand.

The evolution of the tourism industry affected by e-commerce will have impacts on tourism businesses. The World Travel Organization (WTO) indicates that many conventional tourism companies will change in the future (WTO, 2000). For example, travel agencies and tour operators, who act as traditional intermediaries, may be impacted if suppliers (e.g., hotels or transportation) employ e-commerce for direct sales (i.e., disintermediation), or switch to use the service of major online tourism companies such as Travelocity (i.e., reintermediation). This may lead to decreasing market shares, fees, and revenues. Without preventive strategies, SMEs may lose their business in the end, a situation similar to the Thai retail industry, where domestic SMEs are losing their market share to large multinational companies (e.g., Carrefour, Lotus and 7-11).

Therefore, SMEs have to adapt themselves to the e-tourism environment. First, they have to focus their business to serve niche markets such as trekking tours, eco-tourism, or cultural tourism instead of competing directly with large enterprises for general markets (e.g., air tickets, accommodations, and car rental). Second, SMEs may have to join with large enterprises as subsidiaries to help them handle domestic business or niche products. Third, they must emphasize e-commerce development, customer relationship management, mass customization, product differentiation, and community involvement.

SMEs need to develop strategic plans specially for adopting e-commerce. The plan should address issues like: customer patterns and customer behavior on online shopping, choices of technology, policies and regulation, returns on investment, competition and globalization.

In addition, SMEs have to beware many issues for e-commerce development. All online products should be available in the physical store to prevent delivery delays that may irritate customers. Customers must be cared with good services because they demand for careful, interactive, and useful communication all the time. This requires Thai SMEs to train themselves in good Internet etiquette and in English for communication. Creative promotion, ease of use, and simple functions are also highly demanded (Lohse & Spiller, 1998).

Since the revolution is ubiquitous, the government should set policies for e-commerce development and create an environment for the private sector to flourish and survive in the competitive new economic climate. The policies include development and amendment of laws in such areas as electronic transactions, authentication, certification, security, fraud, and consumer rights, effective facilitation in the areas of telecommunication, finance, and interaction of commercial entities, and cultivation of confidence in e-commerce use (Walters, Clayton & Greenwood, 2001).

Furthermore, the government should provide opportunities for SMEs to set up their web sites without cost and to develop portals for Thai industries. The portals will be used for group discussion, directories, public relations, information provision, and ultimately transaction (Tangkitvanitcha, 2000). For example, Tourism Authority of Thailand (TAT) must develop a portal site to provide information for tourists and to support SMEs in the tourism industry.

The threat from e-commerce has forced TAT to set a strategic plan to cope with e-commerce in the future, and prevent Thai SMEs from losing their markets to the world class e-commerce web sites. TAT has to be an intermediate for the Thai SMEs because they cannot afford for the set up cost of e-commerce and lack knowledge for e-commerce implementation.

In line with the vision of the "World-Class E-tourism" in the year 2112, TAT will issue a development plan for e-tourism to support SMEs. The plan will be implemented based on the following three main phases: a complete content provider web site within one year, a complete e-mall within three years, and an e-marketplace) within five years.

CONCLUSION

This chapter discusses the e-commerce of SMEs in Thailand. SMEs are vital to the Thai economy, not only because of their numbers but also because of their ability to perfectly blend technology and local wisdom in a way befitting the nature and resources of the country.

The rapid change of information and communication technology is forcing SMEs entrepreneurs to make crucial decisions with regard to adoption of e-commerce despite uncertainty of its actual benefits. SMEs are sometimes placed in a dilemma. If they do not provide e-commerce, they may lose market share to rival online enterprises. However, the provision of e-commerce does not assure complete success. A better understanding of the advantages and disadvantages would aid entrepreneurs who are going to start up web sites to make proper decisions.

At present in Thailand, the level of acceptance of using e-commerce for business transactions is low because there are few developed web sites. However, SME entrepreneurs realize the importance of e-commerce as a competitive tool and are in the process of developing web sites. Therefore, there is reason to believe that e-commerce may increase in the end.

Thai SMEs develop web sites for four main activities: advertising, ordering, payment, and delivery. The main initial objective of Web presence is public relations. Beyond this, most SMEs hesitate to develop their web sites because they cannot cope with the many obstacles. These include lack of awareness and of law support, unsecured product ordering processes, payment systems and security systems, poor communication infrastructure, lack of a certification authority, and poor language competence.

The case study of e-tourism in Thailand reflects the e-commerce of SMEs in Thailand clearly. From on the demand side, foreign tourists use e-commerce as a common tool for searching information before visiting Thailand. However, based on the supply side, Thai SMEs are not ready to develop a complete e-commerce. Most web sites are used only for web presence with few online reservation forms.

The evolution of e-tourism will exert a negative impact on the Thai SMEs. Suppliers will tend to employ e-commerce for direct sales or replace their traditional intermediation with major online tourism companies. Thus, SMEs may lose their business to their competitors in the long run.

Therefore, SMEs have to adapt themselves to suit the e-tourism environment by serving niche markets, becoming subsidiaries of large enterprises to handle domestic business or niche products, and focusing on customer relationship management, mass customization, product differentiation, and community involvement.

In addition, support from the government will accelerate the e-commerce development. The government should provide space for SMEs to set up their web sites at low cost, develop portals for Thai industries, provide sufficient facilities, training, and information, and resolve the macro problems such as law, tax, and security.

REFERENCES

Araujo, J. & Machado, V. (2001). *Adopting E-Commerce in SMEs: The Common Problems and Training Needs.* Paper presented at the BITWORLD Conference, Egypt.

Arminas, D. (2000). UK firms slow to make use of e-procurement. *Supply Management 5(4)*, 12.

Asian Development Bank (2000). *Investment fund to support small and medium-sized firms in Thailand* [Online]. Retrieved on March 16, 2000 from the World Wide Web: http://www.adb.org/Documents/News/2000/nr2000024.asp.

Bangkok Intelligence News (2000). *Thaksin's trio plays entrepreneurs tune* [Online]. Retrieved on May 18, 2000 from the World Wide Web: http://members.tripod.com/thanong/05182000.htm.

Bonk, E.T. (1996). The information revolution and its impact on SME strategy: The Asia Pacific Economic Co-operative forum as a model. *Journal of Small Business Management, 34*(1), 71-77.

Bunyamanee, S. (2001). *Small Business: Squeeze Remains Tight for Most.* Bangkok Post, Economic Year-End 2000.

Electronic Commerce Resource Centre. (1999). Awareness and requirement of E-commerce [Online]. Retrieved on March 12, 2001 from the World Wide Web: http://www.iecommerce.or.th.

Electronic Commerce Resource Centre. (2000). ECRC survey: E-commerce and tourism. *Electronic Commerce Newsletter*, *2*(3),4-5.

Fariselli, P., Oughton, C., Picory, C. & Sugden, R. (1997). Electronic commerce and the future for SMEs in a global market place: Networking *opportunities and public policy* Retrieved from the World Wide Web: http://europa.eu.int/ISPO/ecommerce/sme/ reports/ecfuture.htm#conclusion.

Hirunkitti, S. (1999). *Small Business Management*. Bangkok: Teera Film and Cytext, Ltd.

IDC. (1999). *IDC forecasts strong growth in e-commerce for travel industry* Retrieved on December 17, 2000 from the World Wide Web: http://www.idc.com/eBusiness/press/EBIZ022201pr.htm.

Kao-Saad, M., Intrapairot, A., Tangkitvanitcha, S., Plangpraphan, J. & Kaewmesri, T. (2001). *The Master Plan of E-Commerce for Thai Tourism Industry*. Bangkok: Thailand Development Research Institute Foundation.

Kleindl, B. (2000). Competitive dynamics and new business models for SMEs in the virtual marketplace. *Journal of Developmental Entrepreneurship, 5*(1), 73-85.

Koanantakul, T (1999). *Readiness of Thai Business in Electronic Commerce Activities*. Bangkok: National Electronic Computer Technology Center (NECTEC).

Krairiksh, S. (2001). *Japan-Thailand trade and economic committee* [Online]. Retrieved on February 2, 2001 from the World Wide Web: http://www.thaiembassy.or.jp/economics/j-keidanren.htm.

Laudon, K.C. & Laudon, J.P. (2000). *Management Information Systems* (6th ed.) London: Prentice Hall.

Lituchy, T.R. & Rail, A. (2000). Bed and breakfasts, small inns, and the Internet: The impact of technology on the globalisation of mall business. *Journal of International Marketing 8*(2), 86-97.

Lohse, G.L. & Spiller, P. (1998). Electronic shopping. *Communications of the* ACM, *41*(7).

Mayongpong, A. (1999). *Factors Affecting Motivation of Buying Products via Internet.* Master's thesis, King Mongkut's Institute of Technology, North Bangkok.

McCue, S. (1999). Small firms and the Internet: Force or farce? *International Forum 1,* 27-29.

NITCS. (2002). Thai Information Technology laws. National Information Technology Committee Secretariat. Retrieved on August 2, 2002 from the World Wide Web: http://www.nitc.go.th/itlaws/itlawss1/head1-3.html.

Pereira, F. & Fife, E. (2000). *Meeting Consumer Needs on the Internet: Successful Business Model*. Center for Telecommunication Management, DCC217 Marshall School of Business, University of Southern California and University Park Los Angeles, CA.

Phillips, W. (1998). Catering to divergent customers. *ABA Banking Journal, 20*(2), S3-5.

Ryan, J.D., Roberth, J.R. & Hiduke, G.P. (1999). *Small Business: An Entrepreneur's Plan (5th ed.).* Fort Worth: The Harcourt Brace College Publisher.

Scarborough, N.M. & Zimmerer, T.W. (1996). *Effective Small Business Management (5th ed.).* Upper Saddle River, NJ: Prentice Hall.

Smith, M. (1997). Technology and trust. *Canadian Banker, 104*(6), 34-35.

Tangkitvanitcha, S. (2000). *Creating Capacity for Competition of e-Commerce: Policy recommendations* (Research Report). Bangkok: Thailand Development Research Institute Foundation.

Turban, E., Lee, J., King, D. & Chung, H.M. (2000). *Electronic Commerce: A Managerial Perspective.* London: Prentice Hall International, Inc.

United Nations (2000). *Building Confidence: Electronic Commerce and Development.* Geneva, United Nations Publication.

Walters, D., Clayton, T. & Greenwood, A. (2001). Government support for e-business in SME's: A tool for regional development? *Communications of the ACM, 41*(7).

WebAustralia. (1996) *Internet banking* [Online] Retrieved on August 3, 1996 from the World Wide Web: http://www.webaustralia. com.au/ banking/ brochures/folder/comm2.htm.

WTO Business Council. (1999). *Marketing tourism destinations online*, the World Tourism Organisation.

Chapter X

Micropayments and E-Commerce Transactions: Thailand[1]

Amnuay Ekasdornkorn and Utomporn Phalavonk
King Mongkut's Institute of Technology North Bangkok, Thailand

Brian Corbitt
Deakin University, Australia

ABSTRACT

Online payments in electronic commerce (e-commerce) are usually carried out with credit cards because they are the most convenient to use. Websites that do not accept credit cards risk losing their customers. Yet potential customers do not include only credit card holders. There are a lot of potential customers who do not have credit cards, some for cultural reasons, others because of trust implications and others because of cost. Even among those who have credit cards, some do not buy online just because they do not feel that the system is secure enough to give away their credit card information over web pages. More importantly perhaps, credit card payments are not suitable for small-value purchases due to their high-incurred overheads to merchants.

This research project presents an alternative concept and the resultant advantages of an online payment system known as "Micropayments." A model named "NEZcard," which resulted from requirements gathering survey, is proposed. The NEZcard model takes into account the factors of convenience, anonymity, security, and continuity of use.

INTRODUCTION

Electronic payments (or e-payment) have become a vital part of e-commerce and the emerging realm of e-business. However, in Thailand very few Websites accept payments online. The only online payment method available for Thai e-commerce merchants is credit cards. The problem in this is that not everyone owns a credit card in Thailand and there is also a serious antipathy towards using credits cards online because of mistrust and potential fraud.

The obstacles for e-commerce payments in Thailand are based on the following assumptions:

- Merchants find it difficult to enlarge their customer base. People who own credit cards usually abandon their purchases when they find that the vendor does not accept credit cards.
- People who do not own credit cards find it too troublesome to buy online but rather pay offline, e.g., at a 7-11 store where the goods have been sent for collection and payment, or they just go to the nearest shopping centers and physically buy the goods.

These two extremes leave the e-commerce environment in Thailand with large gap between expectations and deliverables that need to be filled by some payment methods. These methods should be as convenient as using credit cards, as anonymous as using cash, and secure.

Micropayments have been discussed by many researchers. Rivest and Shamir (1996) invented *Payword* and *Micromint*. Both schemes relied on hash calculation to produce unique chains of "tokens" or "coins." Chi (1997) worked on evaluation and comparison of many schemes including *Millicent, Payword* and *Micromint*. Each of these schemes incorporated mechanisms to deal with anonymity, and security. In other research, Schmidt and Muller (1999) proposed the framework for evaluation of micropayment schemes, including taking into account the impact within economic, technological and social areas and was used to develop the data which supports the proposed model.

This research project has the following objectives:

- To discover the reasons which prevent Thai people from buying online.
- To discover if there is a demand for micropayments in Thailand.
- To discover the characteristics of micropayment suitable to Thai people.

This research then will benefit three parties:

1. E-merchants, who can expand their customer base to include those who do not have credit cards or feel reluctant to use credit card to purchase electronically. Mitchel (1999) suggested that content providers also rely less on sponsors as micropayments allow easy payments for small valued items. Accepting micropayments also incurs less overheads than accepting credit cards;
2. E-shoppers, who do not have credit cards, can make purchases with micropayments. Those who have credit cards but do not like to reveal credit card information on the web may also find micropayments a more trustworthy substitute; and
3. Payment processors or micropayment service providers such as banks, who can participate more in e-commerce. Methods of payment are not as important as the volume of payments that pass through their systems because they earn transactions fees.

LITERATURE REVIEW

A survey by the authority responsible for policy development and ICT implementation in Thailand, NECTEC (2000), reveals wide popularity for e-commerce among Thai Internet users. Internet Purchasing or e-shopping in Thailand has increased from around 18% in 1999 to around 19% in 2000 (an increase of nearly 700,000 users in one year). A successful B2C (Business-to-Consumer) e-commerce transaction means a customer actually pays online.

Credit Cards and Online Payments

In the USA, most e-commerce payments are made with credit cards. Micropayments have more chance to grow in Asia because credit card usage rate in Asia is still much below that in the USA (McLaughlin, 2000). For an e-commerce Website, deciding on which payment options to provide to potential customers is very important. Most e-commerce Websites across the world accept credit card payments. If the merchant's web business is not well known, the only way to be appealing to customers' need for security is to accept credit cards. Merchants can either directly accept credit cards online or outsource the function to a third party.

Costs to merchants will be reflected in the prices that they charge. Although accepting credit card payments is really a convenient service to customers, it is an expensive solution for vendors. The company needs a merchant account in order to be able to accept online credit card payments. Most merchants are charged by banks and credit card-issuing firms on a transactional basis. Low-priced items usually fetch so small a margin that they cannot afford the transactional overheads. Any financial institution, like banks that offer credit card services, will collect payments on each transaction and credit the vendors' accounts, at costs of between 2.5% and 5% plus a flat fee of US$0.30 – 0.50 per transaction (Apicella, 2000).

Is Paying With Credit Cards the Best Method?

E-commerce payments are mostly accomplished with credit cards. There are, however, a few cases for which credit cards do not seem practical. Online payments with credit cards can be risky. Some customers may find that, when the credit card statement comes, many entries have been made without their consent or even their knowledge at all. Credit card fraud can be a threat to both e-merchants and e-shoppers alike. More than ten million US citizens do not have credit cards (Western Union, 2000) and this was one of their main reasons for not doing online purchases.

Users want more options for online payments (Koprowski, 1998). Merchants, we would argue, should offer a number of payment options for customers because convenience is one of the key success factors for online trading. The other key factor, especially in the Thai context, is that any payment systems must be designed in such a way as to minimize fraud.

THE SITUATION IN THAILAND

In the context of e-commerce for Thailand, some interesting points to note include:

- There are significant numbers of people in Thailand who do not own credit cards (NECTEC, 2000). These people have to pay offline (at banks or post offices, for example)
- Some credit card owners feel reluctant to disclose their credit card information (i.e., credit card number, expiry date, and cardholder's name) on any web page/site, even though that page/site is secure through one means or another (NECTEC, 2000).
- Some e-commerce sites, claiming to provide the convenience of a one-click purchase, store the credit information themselves and are exposed to risk of

hacking. There is also a possibility that these vendors may sell that information to other organizations.

- Goods such as online magazines, newspapers, articles, reports, or software, offered as downloadable files or browsing permission for small fees on many e-commerce sites, do not justify the burden of paying for them with credit cards.
- Local Thai credit cards are usually not acceptable to international Websites.

So What is the Solution?

There is a demand for alternative methods to credit cards for e-commerce payments and micropayments, we would argue, can be one of them. This demand is supported by the results of a survey of over 200 e-commerce participants in Thailand. The survey sought to collect data about the habits and practices of people engaged in Thai e-commerce and to understand what they perceived as barriers to the use of web businesses for purchasing. The emphasis in the survey was on Thai consumer, rather than business, activity. The data was summarized and the key propositions or generalizations that emerged from that data are summarized below.

1. There is a strong awareness of fraud and other security issues concerning e-payments by credit cards. There is a decided fear that information may be intercepted or altered during transmission; that the information may be stored on vendors' servers and they may fall victims to hackers who may later sell the information or use the information to make illegal purchases; and that dishonest vendors may sell the information. Under the regulations of the Thai banking system, each of these threats exposes credit card holders to the risk at their remaining credit line. Credit card holders are not informed of these losses until their monthly statements arrive.
2. Because of the above, some credit card holders do not like to enter their credit card information on web pages or through Internet connections. A less risky method would make them comfortable in making Internet purchases.
3. Paying by credit cards reveals the payers' identity to providers and vendors. Some users do not want other parties to know which items they have bought or which Websites they have visited. The trails usually show up on the monthly statements. There is a need for payment models where users appear anonymous, at least to vendors and perhaps also to providers.
4. Credit card payments do not include any measure to limit spending at each vendor. Spending limit settings need to be built into payment systems to prevent unscrupulous vendors from replaying a transaction to get paid twice.

5. Credit card payments do not include setting of daily limits. The only limit is the cardholders' remaining credit line. Daily budget setting to prevent inadvertent overspending should be built into payment solutions.

MICROPAYMENTS

Micropayments according to Schubert and Zimmermann (1998) are anonymous payments of amounts smaller than approximately US$10. Lawrence et al. (1998) suggest that micropayments are fractions of a cent or a very small amount that may be charged for on-line usage or connection time. The RSA Report of more formal and define it I this way, "Micropayments are payments of small sums of money, generally smaller than those in which physical currency is available. It is envisioned that sums of as little as US$0.00001 may someday be used to pay for content access or for small quantities of network resources" (RSA, 2000). Micropayments are designed:

- To minimize transaction overheads including costs for risk management, communications, processing, and setup (Mitchel, 1999).
- To be used in place of credit cards for certain sorts of e-commerce transactions. The prices of such items as pay-per-view content or pay-per-use software rental are too low to justify payments by credit cards.
- To provide users with more options for online payments (NECTEC, 2000). Web surfers have different backgrounds and attitudes to the use of credit cards. Websites/e-businesses that provides more options have a higher chance of gaining a wider customer base.
- To enable convenient online payments for people with no credit cards.
- To provide an alternative for people who are not willing to fill in credit card numbers on web pages.
- To free content providers from relying on sponsors or advertisements so the quality of contents directly reflects the demand of customers. There is no need to put on annoying banners or pop-ups if contents can be sold. Content providers have a duty to fulfill their clients' needs by providing high quality (not 'junk') contents. Consumers will no longer be passive. They will choose the content, based on their interests, and they will pay for a product or service instead of viewing the Website for free, but with the annoyance of interruption from advertisements. They may pay for a download of one CD track, or they may choose to subscribe on a monthly basis for unlimited playback or downloads.

A Brief History of Micropayments

Micropayments were introduced in the early 1990's (Solomon, 2000) but were never widely adopted. People did not need separate billing systems while they were already familiar and comfortable with credit card systems. Subsequently, a great number of micropayment providers went out of business. No one denied that micropayments were necessary and could attract non-credit-card-holding customers but vendors were not prepared for the difficulties and burdens of dealing with a second system, which usually involves installing a proprietary software package from the provider.

Micropayments were predicted to be a new revenue stream for Websites that would not rely on advertisers' support. Prediction was made that micropayments should have been prevailing in the payment marketplace by 2000 but that prediction has not been realized (Shirky, 2000). There have been a number of attempts to implement micropayments, and they have not been popular. Examples of failed systems included FirstVirtual, Cybercoin, Digicash, Internet Dollar, Pay2See, MicroMint and Cybercent. They have all failed to persuade Internet shoppers to use new so-called "e-cash" for online payments. The word "micropayment" was practically unknown. The barrier to micropayments, besides the problems of technology and interfaces, was and still is *user approval*.

One of the reasons micropayments are not widely used is that most systems require that consumers download the plug-in for their browsers. If micropayment systems were all following the same standards (like credit cards do with SET, SSL etc.), consumers would have been more willing to have those systems. But now the micropayment systems on one Website can be different than those of other Websites which a consumer would want to access. In this case, it means the consumer needs several plug-ins or client software packages. These added problems discourage the growth of micropayments.

To be successful in the competitive marketplace of payments systems, micropayment schemes should provide users with the following:

- Simple, predictable and measurable solutions (Shirky, 2000).
- The micropayment links on a web page must be simple. Micropayment users just fill in the account IDs and passwords. As the owner alone knows the password, it is more secure than credit card numbers.
- Micropayments must minimize network traffic with regards to computational resources and transmitted data.
- Micropayments should rely on existing transportation/security mechanisms already implemented on standard Internet protocols.
- A micropayment scheme should be consistent throughout the whole scheme. It is very desirable that all micropayment providers agree on a standardized set of procedures.

Using these criteria we propose that a system can be scoped and developed to meet these requirements.

NEZCARD MICROPAYMENT SYSTEM

NEZcard is the name of the model proposed after a survey conducted in Bangkok, Thailand during November and December 2001. The survey results have been integrated into the model. The model has been designed to meet the requirements identified in the survey and to meet the known critical success factors for payments systems and to meet identified criteria about earlier failed micropayment systems.

NEZcard is a micropayment model that integrates features from several existing schemes plus the characteristics obtained from the survey results discussed earlier. This model involves three parties as other models do: customers, vendors, and brokers. Many names can be given to each party. A customer may be called a user, a buyer, or a payer. A vendor can be referred to as a merchant, an e-merchant, a seller or a payee. A broker may be called a processor or a provider. The NEZcard model includes the following concepts and logics:

- *Simple to use*: NEZcard model uses a prepaid account model but no hardware is involved on the user's part. A simple paper card contains the information for use when entering PIN and password. The card is, in fact, not a vital part of the system but can provide a convenient way to carry the information about.
- *Universal*: Although the model results from a survey in Thailand, the model can be used anywhere. To be universal, a neutral measuring unit called "NEZ Point" is introduced. "NEZ Point" makes it easy for both vendors and buyers to compare products from all parts of the world. For international use, the unit for pricing can be mapped to U.S. dollars.
- *Secure*: The model does not allow duplicate transactions and only honors complete transactions. The model would be implemented on a secure server with SSL infrastructure. Each transaction must be complete before any balance is deducted from the account.
- *Anonymous*: Since no registration is required on the payer's part, the model is cash-like. Although anonymous, the payer is protected. Each transaction is logged and any disputes can be verified against the log. Normally, the rightful card owner is the account holder, so the weakest point of this system lies in the fact that the information on the card is exposed to others.
- *Mobile*: Because the model does not require any special hardware or software, users can simply buy with a NEZcard from any Internet-capable public computer, fixed or mobile.

This model features the use of NetEZ Micropayment Card (NEZcard). This is a stored-value card but not a smart card. It can also be regarded as an e-wallet. The paper card just makes it convenient to carry the necessary information about to access the e-wallet.

NEZcard's Simple Mechanism

The functionality of NEZ card is illustrated in Figure 1 below. Each NEZcard account has been pre-created on B's server. NEZcard comes, fictitiously in this paper, in THB200, THB500 and THB1000 variations. C purchases a NEZcard package from one of the authorized outlets. (Hint: the same places where Internet kits are sold.) A NEZcard kit is an envelope containing just a card and a booklet. C should ensure that the envelope is properly sealed prior to purchase. The front of the card is B's logo (which is meaningless in this context, but may become a good advertising space), 16-digit PIN ("9999-9999-9999999-9" format) and the face value.

The back contains B's URL and the initial password. The booklet contains all the information C needs to know when refilling the card, making payments, claiming refunds, etc. There is also a section that lists all the sites that are part of B's network of vendors. The section may not be up-to-date due to fast changes in the Internet world but the list keeps growing. The most current list can be found in B's Website with direct links to specific vendors.

Figure 1: Message Communication During NEZcard Transaction

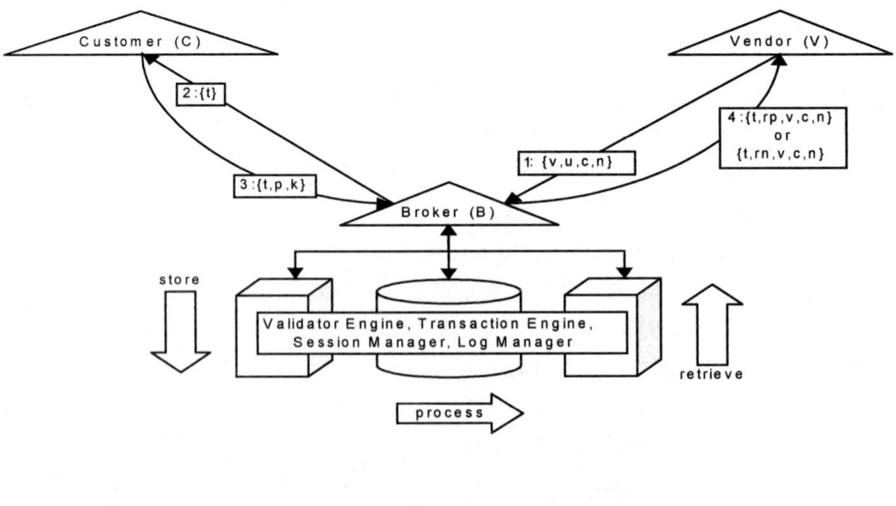

C has to activate the account before spending money out of it. Activation is easy. C just goes to B's Website (by the URL shown on the card) and selects "Activate New Account." Then he or she just fills in the PIN and initial password. For strengthened security, C must also fill in a new password and confirm it.

B's Website also has an up-to-the-minute directory of vendors which support NEZcard. C can browse all of them and may find something of interest. When C spots an interesting item (the categories or nature of goods will be discussed later), C would click on the "Pay with NEZcard" link. Paying with NEZcard is easy. C just fills in his or her 16-digit PIN and his or her password (not the initial password, but the one he or she has changed to.)

The NEZcard model has the following characteristics:

- The optimal range for NEZcard micropayment system is from THB 100 to 5,000. However, the model is flexible to support any amount.
- Prepaid card model. Users buy prepaid cards of various face values from NEZcard authorized outlets. They then register the cards on NEZcard system Website to activate their accounts. (Alternatively, NEZcard may sell these virtual cards online.)
- NEZcard points can be spent on anything from NEZcard member merchants. Merchants has their catalog posted on the NEZcard system.
- Typical products include downloadable news articles, CD tracks, MP3 songs, stock quotes, in-depth decision guide for other products, etc.
- NEZcard account holders select an item. The points are deducted and the item can then be downloaded.
- Users can buy new NEZcard account cards when old ones are finished.
- Users can also buy NEZcard refill cards if they decide to continue using existing accounts. Refilling is also performed on NEZcard system Website.
- Users have the options to set limit on daily spending or to set limit total points spent on each vendor.

It is technologically possible to have automatic payments for the click of a news title (full "click and pay" functionality instead of a more obvious "Pay with XXX" button or link.) Micropayment providers should be careful about their partners. Some less-than-honest ones may cheat users by refreshing the page frequently.

Selling articles piece by piece is not difficult. Each NEZcard-ready site has to reach a common agreement with its customers (especially those holding NEZcard accounts). A customer who agrees to the automatic mode will have to log in for that session. To log in, the customer will be presented with NEZcard login page that binds with the merchant. Then a click on each "for-sale" link will create a micropayment transaction.

There are problems selling article by article. This could affect academic people like students, teachers, and professors because they need only useful articles and would probably not know their real usefulness until reading through them. If they had to pay for each article (which is the possibility introduced by micropayments), they end up doing a lot more reading, just in the process of deciding whether or not an article is worth the fee. The time involved is a cost over and above the actual cash payment being made. It is a cost paid for each and every article, whether or not they decide to buy. The better concept is the zoo-ticket model. You pay at the gate and explore your way in the zoo until closing time. The same works for content site, users pay for "one-day" tickets (or passes) and browse or download articles as needed. Of course, big articles or important reports may be in the site. They can be treated like normal items so they are priced explicitly and have their own "buy" buttons.

NEZcard Message Communication Model

Making a micropayment is simply created by sending a series of secure messages (requests and responses.) The messages in this context are at the same level as CGI calls. Secure HTTP can be employed to strengthen the already in-place security model. Therefore, NEZcard is lightweight and consumes no more traffic than any other web-based applications.

The first message, generated when the customer C clicks on the "Buy" button, goes from the vendor to the micropayment provider:

$V \rightarrow \{v,u,c,n\} \rightarrow$ (4-1)

where
v = vendor's ID,
u = Return URL,
c = Order Code, and
n = Order Amount.

u is a string containing two actual URLs, separated by a semi-colon (;). The first one is used when a positive result is obtained, the second for a negative result.

When the server of B receives a message, it stores all the parameters passed from V, generates a unique transaction ID, and responds by sending the user authorization page to C's browser screen:

B $\rightarrow$ {t} $\rightarrow$ C (4-2)

where t = transaction ID.

The next message is generated when C clicks "Authorize NEZcard Payment" after filling in the PIN and password:

C $\rightarrow$ {t,p,k} $\rightarrow$ B (4-3)

where
p = PIN and
k = password (secret key).

The request triggers automatic validation and balance checking procedures of C's account on B's server.

The response (B$\rightarrow$V) can be either positive or negative.

B $\rightarrow$ {t,rp/n,v,c,n} $\rightarrow$ V (4-4)

where
rp = positive result code; and
rn = negative result code.

V's script determines which page to present to C. If rp is returned (positive), the page should be the "Thank you" page, which includes the message thanking C and the shipping confirmation. If the item just paid for is a downloadable piece of information, then this page should give C enough instructions so that C knows how to download immediately, download sometime later (within a limited time frame), or to receive the file via e-mail. C may simply shop for new items at will.

If rn is returned, the script would inform the redirect to a page that should also thank C and invite C to continue shopping after informing C of the unsuccessful payments.

Scalability of NEZcard Micropayments

The NEZcard model is scalable. If the number of transactions increases so that the existing NEZcard servers are too busy to support concurrencies, NEZcard can be scaled up to have their servers located in different parts of the world to handle area-specific NEZcard. This can be effectively handled because the first four-digit field of the PIN has already been designed to accommodate ten thousand servers. In fact, at the same server root, the physical servers can be clustered (into server farms). Each server in the farm may handle a number of series, and so on.

Extended Features of NEZcard

1. Peer-to-Peer payments. NEZcard can be used for peer-to-peer (or P2P for short) payments. P2P payments are transactions between two NEZcard account holders. The algorithm has not been demonstrated here but the concept is relatively simple. P2P can be used to settle small debts. Individuals offering online services also benefit from this feature because they do not involve any vendor registration process. However, the risk totally falls on the payer, because the NEZcard network cannot trace the identity of either side. Making a P2P payment is easy. The NEZcard account holder just browses to the NEZcard Website, enters the PIN, the password, and the payee's NEZcard PIN.
2. Payment through e-mail. Another variation is to use e-mail as the medium. This variation offers higher security for buyers. A NEZcard account holder pays to the vendor's e-mail address. In this case, the vendor needs to be a NEZcard account holder but request to publish his/her identity with his/her valid e-mail address for accepting NEZcard payment. Below is a scenario to clarify the concept.
3. Mr. A holds a NEZcard account. He wants to make payment to hire Miss B, a professional web designer, who states that she accepts NEZcard payment via e-mail. Mr. A points his browser to the NEZcard Website and chooses payment through e-mail link. He enters the PIN, the password, the receiver's e-mail address, the reference or order number and his own e-mail address. The transaction is logged (and can be viewed at any time). An e-mail message is sent to Miss B containing the order reference and the system-generated key to retrieve the money. An e-mail message is also sent to Mr. A, stating the details of the payment, which he keeps as a reference.

DISCUSSION

NEZcard micropayment model is applicable to Thai e-commerce sites that offer such items for sale including telephone directory information, traffic guidance (key information domain in Thailand), weather reports, economic and statistical reports or databases, the placing of small advertisements (such as banners on a web page), tour or hotel reservations, deposits for goods, donations, downloads, forms, software, music, videos, SMS-services, graphics and pictures, etc.

Some items may seem impractical to Thai people; for example, the weather forecast, but here it refers really to a value-added weather forecast service such as predicting upcoming storms for yachtsmen/women with detailed graphics from satellites all over the world.

How then does NEZcard compare to credit cards as a solution for e-business payments? Firstly it can be compared on their prepaid and postpaid nature. NEZcard accounts must be prepaid. However, they can be bought with cash or credit cards. NEZcard is simple to use. No hardware or software is needed. Users can, therefore, make purchases on any internet-ready computers. NEZcard is universal, like credit cards. Points can represent any currencies. NEZcard is secure. The system is based on account codes/passwords pair verification. Vendors and their products are listed on NEZcard system so duplicate transactions can be prevented. Credit card processors do not care about this. If you click pay twice, you may lose your money more than necessary. Moreover, only complete transactions are honored. Points are deducted from user accounts and added to vendor accounts. NEZcard user identity is not revealed because no private information is asked for at any stage. While credit card users must be verified for each transaction, NEZcard users make their purchases as if they pay in cash.

This paper has proposed an alternative payment system for e-commerce which, because of its simple and internal logic, provides a viable alternative to credit cards in contexts like Thailand where large proportions of the population either do not have credit cards or there is a lack of trust in the security features of credit cards used over the internet.

Across the world where students, particularly university students, also have lesser access to credit card acquisition, there is a also the possibility for them to muse this type of system. The needs of demand are addressed and the need for security becomes self-evident. In the payment systems market there is again the need to revisit the alternatives to credit cards. This solution offers one choice.

ENDNOTE

[1] An earlier version of this paper was presented at the CollECteR conference (2002), Deakin University.

REFERENCES

Apicella, M. (2000). Worry-free payment processing keeps the customer satisfied [Online]. November 10. Available from: http://www.infoworld.com.

Asokan, N., et al. (1999). *The State of the Art in Electronic Payment Systems.* Nokia Research Center, Helsinki, Finland.

Chi, E. (1997). *Evaluation of Micropayment Schemes.*

Forbes (1999). New Internet payment system launching [Online]. August, Available from: http://www. forbes.com/1999/08/11/ mu2_print.html

Koprowski, G. (1998) Cache and carry [Online]. Available from: http://www.business2.com/ articles/mag/print/0,1643,12731,FF.html.

Lawrence, E., et al. (1998) *Internet Commerce: Digital Models for Business.* John Wiley & Sons Australia, p. 242.

McLaughlin, K. (2000). The race to rule e-payments in Asia [Online]. Available from: http://www. business2.com/articles/web/ print/0,1650,16107,FF.html.

Mitchel, T. (1999) Common markup for micropayment per-fee-links. *World Wide Web Consortium (W3C).* Available from: http://www.w3.org/TR/1999/WD-Micropayment-Markup-19990825.

NECTEC (2000) Reasons against Internet purchase, *Internet User Profile of Thailand 2000.* National Electronics and Computer Technology Center, Bangkok, Thailand.

Rivest, R.L. & Shamir, A. (1996). *PayWord and MicroMint: Two Simple Micropayment Schemes.* MIT Laboratory for Computer Science.

RSA Security. What are micropayments, RSA Security Crypto FAQ. Available from: http://www. rsasecurity.com/rsalabs/4-2-5000.htm.

Schmidt, C. & Muller, R. *A Framework for Micropayment Evaluation*, Institute fur Wirtschaftsinformatic, Humboldt-Universitat zu Berlin.

Schubert, P. & Zimmermann, H-D. (1998). *Electronic Commerce Transactions: The Deployment of Chip Cards for Micropayment Settlements*, Institute for Information Management, University of St. Gallen, Switzerland.

Shirky, C. (2000). The case against micropayments [Online]. Available from: http://www.openp2p. com/lpt/a//p2p/ 2000/12/19/micropayments.html.

Solomon, M. (2000). Micropayments [Online]. Available from: http://www.computerworld.com.

Western Union MoneyZap [Online]. (2000). Available from: http://www.monzap.com.

SECTION IV:

E-LEARNING AND CULTURAL VALUES

Chapter XI

Factors Influencing the Acceptance of Web-Based Online Education for Thai Educators: Impact of Thai Culture and Values

Orasa Tetiwat
Victoria University of Wellington and Naresuan University, New Zealand

Sid L. Huff
Victoria University of Wellington, New Zealand

ABSTRACT

Online education has become widely used and accepted in many universities, especially in North America and Europe, since in the early 1990s. However, its adoption and use in developing countries such as Thailand is at an earlier stage. Many Thai educators are still hesitant to deploy online education for their courses. Many factors affect their decisions to accept online education. Thus, there is a need for research in this area so that educators can plan and prepare in deploying online education. The main objective of this chapter is to investigate the factors that influence Thai educators in accepting online education and highlight how Thai culture and values have an effect on these influencing factors. The framework of this study is based on three adoption and acceptance theories: the Diffusion of Innovation theory (DOI), the Technology Acceptance Model (TAM), and the Theory of Planned Behavior (TPB).

In-depth interviews were conducted with 22 Thai educators who have used or managed online courses in 12 Thai universities. The findings indicate that the five most influential factors are control beliefs regarding availability of technology, cost of computer technology and Internet access, *and* accessibility to technology *and behavioral beliefs regarding* compatibility, and relative advantage. *Other important factors (from top six to top ten ranking) include the user's attitude towards IT, the behavioral beliefs concerning* student demand, complexity of online education and trialability, *as well as the control belief concerning* institutional policy. *Less influential factors include control beliefs regarding* government policy, management support, ethical considerations, and language barrier, *as well as the normative beliefs regarding* group influence. *Influencing factors that are impacted by Thai culture and values are compatibility, group influence by supervisors, management support and institution's policy, government policy, and language barrier.*

INTRODUCTION

Due to the expansion of communication technology, and especially the Internet, many institutions have begun using the World Wide Web in order to deliver online education. However, web-based online education (hereafter referred to as online education) is still at an earlier stage in Thai institutions. Thai educators are still hesitant to deploy online education for their courses. A variety of factors affect their decisions regarding whether or not to accept online education. Research is needed to identify and understand these factors, so that educators and leaders of educational institutions can better plan and prepare deployment of online education. The main objective of this chapter is to investigate the factors that influence Thai educators in accepting online educational mechanisms, and the ways in which Thai culture and values influence these factors.

This chapter is organized into seven sections. The first section introduces the concept, components and functions of online education, and how it can be used in higher educational institutions. The second section covers Thai culture and values.

The third section explains education system and online education in Thailand. The fourth section describes three based theories of technology adoption /acceptance: Diffusion of Innovation theory (DOI), the Technology Acceptance Model (TAM), and the Theory of Planned Behavior (TPB), and also proposes the research framework used in the study. The next section explains research methodology, respondent profile, research findings and discussion. The sixth section discussed impact of Thai culture and values on the factors influencing the acceptance online education. The final section summarizes and concludes the chapter.

THE USE OF ONLINE EDUCATION IN HIGHER EDUCATIONAL INSTITUTIONS

Online education is a teaching and learning environment that provides students and instructors a medium for teaching and learning via the Internet. Students and instructors can use online education as a supplement to the existing traditional classroom, or as a substitute for the traditional classroom. Instructors can deploy online education as a tool for delivering or enhancing learners' learning. In an mixed online learning environment, learners usually meet with their instructors in the traditional face-to-face classroom, and the instructors augment classroom sessions by posting their class materials, notes, presentations, assignments or useful links to a website for their students' use. Online education can also be used to deliver instruction to distant students (Khan, 1997).

It provides many benefits for both instructors and students. Examples of these benefits are that instructors can use or reuse their prepared course materials; students can study at their own convenient time, place, and pace; it can help students to reduce their cost of study; both faculty and students can use online education to communicate with each other effectively. This can help both the faculty and students to save time and costs of travel for face-to-face meetings (Tetiwat & Igbaria, 2000).

Online education can replicate many of the features of a traditional classroom such as lecture notes, student participation, feedback and evaluations by using video, audio, and high speed Internet to enable synchronous and asynchronous communication (Aggarwal & Bento, 2000). Khan (1997) explains that online education should consist of the following components:

- Computers and storage devices: computer platforms running on operating systems (e.g., Windows, Unix, Dos, Macintosh), servers, hard drives, and CD-ROMs
- Connections and service providers: modems, dial-in and dedicated services (e.g., phone line, ISDN, 56 kbps, T1)

- Internet tools: communications tools (e.g., e-mail, listservs, newsgroups, chat, MUD, Internet telephony, Internet video conferencing), remote access tools (e.g., Telnet, File Transfer Protocol (ftp)), Internet navigation tools (e.g., Web browsers, Gopher), and search and other tools (e.g., search engines such as Altavista or Google, logging tools)
- Servers: HTTP servers, HTTD software, common gateway interface (CGI)
- Browsers and other applications: text-based browsers, graphical browsers, links (e.g., hypermedia link, hypertext link), and other applications that can be added to web browsers (e.g., plug-ins)
- Multimedia components: text and graphics, audio streaming (e.g., Real Audio), video streaming (e.g., Quick Time), Graphical User Interface (GUI), and compression technology (e.g., Shockwave)
- Content development: learning and instructional theories, instructional design, and curriculum development
- Authoring programs: programming language (e.g., Hyper Text Markup Language (HTML), Virtual Reality Modeling Language (VRML), Java, JavaScript) (Khan, 1997)

Many institutions have deployed online education either by developing their own system or by buying a software package. Several online education packages are on the market nowadays, for example, Blackboard, WebCT, TopClass, Lotus Notes, and First Class. These packages vary considerably in terms of their design and functions, as well as cost. Some institutions decide to deploy a package, but many others develop online education using more basic tools (e.g., programming their own websites from scratch). This decision may depend on their needs, budgets, technical and educational support and services.

McCormack and Jones (1998) identify five main functions of online education, as follows:

- *Storing information:* many educators and students can use online education for storing course materials or research papers in document format so that they can use, reuse, or refine them. They also can better manage their materials such as syllabi, schedules, handouts, assignments, or their research so that they can access or update documents easily.
- *Information distribution:* online education can help educators distribute materials such as class materials to their students. These materials include articles, Powerpoint lectures, audio, video and animation. Moreover, it will enable links to other related locations.
- *Communication:* online education assists students and educators in communicating with each other by providing facilities that support various methods of communication. There are four such modes of communication:

- One-to-one (e-mail);
- One-to-many (online announcement, broadcast e-mail);
- Many-to-one (feedback); and
- Many-to-many (bulletins boards, mailing lists, interactive chat, audio and video conferences).

- *Student assessment:* There are many ways of assessing students, such as quizzes, essays, and evaluation. Online education allows students to assess their own learning so that they can evaluate their progress and better direct their own learning.
- *Class management:* Online education allows educators to perform tasks such as timetabling, tracking attendance, recording progress, calculating grades, and identifying the learning needs of students.

To make online education work, educators need to carry out a variety of tasks, for example, creating materials, designing the learning experience, setting up computers for students to use, preparing web pages, converting existing computer-based material, creating on-line quizzes, setting up mailing lists, drawing or scanning pictures, digitizing video, etc., and have material stored in the computer so that it can be searched, archived, indexed, and converted easily and quickly (McCormack & Jones, 1998).

Different educators may adopt online education in different ways. Some educators only adopt online education for distributing information. Some educators distribute information and communicate on the web. Some educators adopt all five functions mentioned above for their class. The way that educators adopt online education may depend on their needs, their skills, their budgets, their attitude towards online education, and their teaching and learning culture.

Online education can be used in every level of education from primary school to tertiary level. The objectives at each level may differ because the learning process at each level is different. Educators must design online education to suit each level. This chapter focuses on tertiary education. In tertiary education, there is an expectation that a majority of students possess analytical thinking skills and ability to use technology. Thus, online education can be used not only as a teaching aid but also as an aid to course management. Instructors can post information and their course materials such as course meeting, syllabi, reading, and assignments on the web. They also can use online education for testing learners at the beginning of the class in the traditional classroom so that they can adjust their lecture plan. Students can review their lessons or discuss with other students or their instructors by using e-mail or discussion boards at any time and at any place where there is an Internet access. As a result, they can share knowledge and information with others at their convenience. Also, they can ask specific questions to their instructors or to experts in the field. In addition, their assignment can be submitted through the online education and get response more quickly. Some instructors provide useful links to other related websites such as the library, student learning support centers, or have a particular focused website for their subject (Tetiwat & Igbaria, 2000).

THAI CULTURE AND VALUES

Thailand is a country of approximately 514,000 square kilometers, located in Southeast Asia. Thailand was established in the mid fourteenth century. It was known as Siam until 1939. Unlike other countries in Southeast Asia, Thailand has never been colonized by any other country. The Thai government is a constitutional monarchy. The population of Thailand is approximately 61,800,000 people. The ethnic groups are Thai (75 percent), Chinese (14 percent), and other (11 percent). Ninety-five percent of the population are Buddhist. Other religions are Islam (3.8 percent), Christianity (0.5 percent), Hinduism (0.1 percent), and other (0.6 percent) (The World Factbook, 2001). Thus, Buddhism exerts a strong influence on the way of life of the Thai people. The behavior and attitude of most Thais follow the stages of life cycle that are part of Buddhist rites and rituals. Some aspects of Buddhism that affect the Thai worldview include:

- Hierarchy—the majority of Thais are concerned with hierarchical ranking. Thus Thais are aware of age and seniority in their everyday life. Each Thai individual seen as higher or lower ranking, older or younger, senior or junior, superior or subordinate. Younger people attitude and behavior toward older people is important.
- "Kam"—meaning actions that have happened in the past and have an affect on this present life.
- "Bun Khun"—meaning that other people such as parents or teachers help or favor one. The recipient should be grateful and there is obligation to reciprocate.
- "Cool-heart"—is a characteristic of a stable personality. In social interaction, Thais place a strong value on explicit calmness. It is not proper to express dislike or anger in public. Also most Thais try to avoid open conflict because cool-heart can be considered as an intelligent social response as well as a commendable act (Podhisita, 1998).

Like other countries, Thai has its own culture and values. Hofstede (1980), a foundational theorist in the field of intercultural communication, defines culture as the collective programming of the people's mind that differentiates members of one group from other groups. Culture is learned and cannot be inherited. It actually reflects the ability of humans to feel, communicate and learn. It requires compliance with certain values, rules and practices for society.

Hofstede's research on national culture used IBM employees from countries around the world as his primary focus. In his research he has studied more than a hundred thousand participants. This research is widely accepted as a major breakthrough in social science studies. In the findings of his study, Hofstede identifies four dimensions of national culture, which are power distance, individualism, masculinity, and uncertainty avoidance. These dimensions represent the mainstream attitude, expectations, values and behaviours for members of over 50 different countries (Hofstede, 1980, 1991).

From Hofstede's research findings, Thais are categorized as a group that has a large power distance, a low level of individualism, a weak level of masculinity (cooperative) and strong uncertainty avoidance (see Table 1). This group is described as a fairly risk-averse market. Hofstede also states that members in a large power distance and low individualism society are willing to follow those in charge with little desire to participate or direct. This indicates that institutions from this group tend to wait to adopt new technology when a large group of other institutions has already adopted it. This may lead to a low level of technology adoption, which may in turn result in a low level of online education trial and adoption.

Hofstede's research has been formally verified by this study during the interview of key informants. Also, it is informally verified by local people in Thailand. They were asked whether they believe Hofstede's classification to be accurate. The majority of these interviewees and local people agree that Hofstede's findings were considered valid, especially in the first two categories – large power distance and low individual, although there were some minor variations of opinion in each dimension.

Holmes et al. (1996) also agrees that the Thai system is considered as a hierarchical system (large power distance), which means that Thais always values

Table 1: The Four Dimensions of National Cultural Framework of Thailand (From Hofstede, 1991)

Dimensions of National Culture	**Thai Ranking**	**Thai Score**
Power Distance	21/23 (large)	64
Level of Individualism	39/40 (low)	20
Level of Masculine	44 (weak)	34
Uncertainty Avoidance	30 (strong)	64

seniority in relation to age, birth, merit, wealth, power, and professional rank. One can see that the ranking system is established in most Thai organizations. This is due to the hierarchical system that has an impact on each Thai organizational structure. It is also a backbone of Thai governmental and private organizations. Hierarchical systems provide guidelines, which are recognized to be a part of a person's working behavior. People in different status know their duties toward each other. The senior people are expected to guide, control, protect, support, and look after thc needs of their juniors or employees like fathers do for their children. There is also a power distance gap between people in society. This is due to the nature of the hierarchical system in Thailand. Communication in Thai society tends to be from the top-down, so most junior people are more likely to absorb things instead of initiate things. Thus, most Thais are not experienced in expressing themselves in an assertive way. Similarly, the principle of egalitarianism, common in western societies—that all people are equal (or at least have equal opportunities)—is not the case in Thailand. Thus, equality in areas such as communication and information sharing is not common in Thai organizations.

Educational systems differ from one country to another (Kandel, 1933). In particular, the Thai educational system differs from those of other countries. In addition, the way that teachers interact with students and the way that students interact with other students is also different. This difference may affect the way that they adopt online education, as well as the factors influence the online education adoption.

Hofstede (1986) applied four dimensions of national culture, which represent the mainstream attitude, expectations, values and behaviours for members in the educational environment. Table 2 presents teacher/student interaction and student/student interaction in the group of large power distance, low level of individualism, weak level of masculinity and strong uncertainty avoidance.

Other important values that are applied to all level in Thai society are "gratitude and indebtedness" ("Katanyoo Rookkhun," which means that most lower rank people appreciate those higher rank people who have done favors for them), and "merciful and kind" ("Metaa Karunna," which means that higher rank people behave kindly to those lower rank people). These values are applied to most components of Thai society, such as family, school, work, business or government sectors. For example, students should feel gratitude and indebtedness to their teachers, children to their parents, and employees to their employers. Also, teachers should be generous with their effort and time to assist their students, parents to their children, employers to employees, and wealthy people to poor people (Vichit-Vadakan, 1990)

Table 2. Teacher/student interaction and student/student interaction by various societal types (Hofstede, 1986, p. 312 -314).

Large Power Distance Societies
Stress on personal "wisdom" which is transferred in the relationship with a particular teacher (guru)
A teacher merits the respect of his/her students
Teacher-centerd education (premium on order)
Students expect teacher to initiate communication
Students expect teacher to outline paths to follow
Students speak up in class only when invited by the teacher
Teacher is never contradicted nor publicly criticized
Effectiveness of learning related to excellence of the teacher
Respect for teachers is also shown outside class
In teacher/student conflicts, parents are expected to side with the teacher
Older teacher are more respected than younger teachers

Collectivist Societies: Low Individualist
Positive association in society with whatever is rooted in tradition
The young should learn; adults cannot accept student role
Students expect to learn how to do
Individual students will only speak up in class when called upon personally by the teacher
Individuals will only speak up in small groups
Large classes split socially into smaller cohesive subgroups based on particularist criteria (e.g., ethnic affiliation)
Formal harmony in learning situations should be maintained at all times (T-groups are taboo)
Neither the teacher nor any student should ever be made to lose face
Education is a way of gaining prestige in one's social environment and of joining a higher status group
Diploma certificates are important and displayed on walls
Acquiring certificates, even through illegal means (cheating, corruption) is more important than acquiring competence
Teachers are expected to give preferential treatment to some students (e.g., based on ethnic affiliation or on recommendation by an influential person)

Another important value is "Kreng Jai," which means that an individual is expected to control his own desire or interest when in a situation that is uncomfortable or conflicting, or when in a situation where there is a need to maintain a pleasant and cooperative relationship (Holmes et al., 1996). It also means "being aware of another person's feelings, saving the face of others and respecting them" (Niratpattanasssai, 2001). This attitude or behavior appears frequently in everyday life and is practiced by individuals from all levels of society. Examples of this attitude include trying to comply with another's request, reluctance to interrupt or disturb others, avoiding asserting one's needs or opinions, or reluctance to ask questions when one has not understood someone.

In traditional Thailand, most organizations are authoritarian in operation, with a variety of social and education levels in their staff. The supervisor is "an

Table 2: (Continued) Teacher/Student Interaction and Student/Student Interaction by Various Societal Types (Hofstede, 1986, pp. 312 -314)

Feminine Societies (Weak Masculine/ cooperative)
Teachers avoid openly praising students
Teachers use average student as the norm
System rewards students' social adaptation
A student's failure at school is a relatively minor accident
Students admire friendliness in teachers
Students practice mutual solidarity
Students try to behave modestly
Corporal punishment severely rejected
Students chose academic subjects in view of intrinsic interest
Male students may chose traditionally feminine academic subjects

Strong Uncertainty Avoidance Societies
Students feel comfortable in structured learning situations: precise objectives, detailed assignments, strict timetables
Teachers are expected to have all the answers
A good teacher uses academic language
Students are rewarded for accuracy in problem-solving
Teacher are allowed to behave emotionally (and so are students)
Teachers interpret intellectual disagreement as personal disloyalty
Teachers consider themselves experts who cannot learn anything from lay parents and parents agree

authoritarian figure and independent decision-maker, whom subordinates must regard with unquestioning obedience. The cultural ideal is a superior who asserts authority graciously and with benevolence, attaining the loyalty and respect of all subordinates" (ExcutivePlanet, 2001). Most managers have a lower level of confidence in their subordinates' capacity for leadership and initiative than would be commonplace in a western organization. They also do not like to share information with their staff or involve them in decision-making.

Another aspect of Thai culture is the agrarian value. Thais normally work in a group where they share their responsibilities; there is no requirement for accountability in the individual sense. Consequently, it is not easy to make staff to take responsibility. Staff members would normally prefer that the supervisor dictate changes and take responsibility for their implementation (Holmes et al., 1996). Holmes et al. (1996) states, "The Thai culture does not encourage all its people to dare, to make mistakes, to take initiative. It encourages only a few at the top."

When staff of Thai organizations do have good ideas, they are often afraid that the ideas may not be seen as worthwhile in the eyes of others, so they would be embarrassed to express or initiate the ideas. Also, most Thai supervisors do not expect to be informed by subordinates or juniors of events going on within the organization; being the supervisors, they believe that they should know everything, and would become aware of the events on their own.

Thais use the Thai language in daily use and also for official purposes. A majority of Thai students study English, however they only really learn English grammar. They rarely practice listening or speaking English in school or university. Nor are their teachers normally fluent in English; English is normally a second language for them as well. Thus, many Thais face obstacles when they have to use English - for example, when they have a meeting in English (Holmes et al., 1996).

EDUCATIONAL SYSTEM AND ONLINE EDUCATION IN THAILAND

The Educational System in Thailand

According to the Ministry of Education (1999), the Thai educational system is intended to provide an opportunity for individuals' development according to their ages and offers continuous and life-long learning, as well as employing various forms of education (e.g., in a school-related system of education and through the learning process from the ways of life). Education in a school-related system is categorized into five levels: pre-school education, primary or elementary education, lower secondary education, upper secondary education and higher education.

Thai education is administered by several government ministries depending on the level of education. The Office of the National Education Commission under the Prime Minister administers the long-term policy formulation and planning for development in all levels of education. The Ministry of Interior oversees primary education that is directed by municipal authorities. The Ministry of Education supervises all other primary institutions, and oversees the nation's secondary schools (which include teacher education and vocational training up to a tertiary level) non-formal education, as well as matters relating to religion and culture. The Ministry of University Affairs administers public and private universities and institutions of higher learning.

As mentioned above, this research focuses only on higher education, especially at the university level. Thai higher education is classified into three levels: lower than bachelor's degree level, bachelor's degree level, and graduate level. Thai universities can be categorized into two groups: public universities and private universities. Currently, there are 23 public universities and 15 private universities. A majority of these universities are located in and around Bangkok. There are only nine regional universities: *Chiang Mai University* and *Naresuan University* (in the north), *Khon Kaen University, Mahasarakham University, Suranaree*

University of Technology, and *Ubon Ratchathani University* (in the northeast), *Burapha University* (in the east) and *Prince of Songkla University* and *Thaksin University* (in the south). Most universities offer a bachelor's degree in general areas such as arts, commerce, and science. However, some universities specialize in certain areas and offer postgraduate level. For example, *Mahidol University* specializes in the areas of medicine, pharmacy, dentistry, and nursing. *Kasetsart University* offers courses in agriculture, food technology, and veterinary science. *Silpakorn University* specializes in architecture. *Thammasat University* offers courses in laws, public administration and social work. *Ramkhamhaeng University and Sukhothai Thammathirat University* are two open universities that provide an effective and economical way to respond to the growing public demand for access to higher education. Some universities offer graduate level (e.g., *National Institute of Development Administration (NIDA)* is a graduate institution specializing in administrative and national development. *Asian Institute of Technology* is an autonomous international graduate school that offers sciences and engineering to students from all over Asia and beyond (the Ministry of University Affairs, 2001).

The Thai education system has long "emphasized 'chalk and talk' pedagogy, rote learning, placed an importance on school education with teachers as the center of teaching-learning activities" (Kaewdang, 2001). Only few Thai teachers encourage their students to speak out or comment or express their own ideas. If students ask questions or speak out, their teachers will think those students lack respect for the teacher. Also, Chatturachinda (2001) states, "Thai Education is not favorable to the life long learning process. Cultural behavior of most Thai educators is protective, preventing learners from learning for themselves. It focuses on content of subject, not the learning process of learning."

Currently, advanced information technology is widely available, and global competition is a fact of life everywhere. Therefore, education should not be limited only to the classroom, and teachers are not the only knowledge source. Education should focus on "cultivating within students the skills of searching knowledge through self-learning so that they can learn continually at any time and any place throughout lives" (Chatturachinda, 2001).

The recession of 1997 created a need for a thorough re-examination of the country's human resource development system, and set the stage for across-the-board reform of Thai education. Actually, the financial crisis did not have a direct impact on education, but nonetheless resulted in substantial education reforms, creating an opportunity for concerted action (The World Bank, 1999). In order to speed up Thailand's economic recovery and competitiveness, Thailand needed to consider education reform. Thus, the National Education Act, 1999 was established for education reform in Thailand. The main objective of the Act is "to ensure that education aims at the full development of the people in all aspects - physical and mental health, intellect; knowledge; morality; integrity; and the pursuit of a desirable lifestyle in accordance with society and in harmony with other people." The Act will "encourage Thais to develop towards more analytical and independent thought. The knowledge-based and learning society will help find new solutions for the global era" This Act consists of nine chapters. The last chapter of the Act focuses on the technologies for education and transitory provisions (The Nation, 1999).

Online Education in Thailand

As mentioned above, the final section of the National Education Act (1999) focuses on technology for education. The Thai government has established many policies that support the education reform. One educational policy is to expand the study area so that it is no longer limited to traditional classrooms. Everyone can stay connected anywhere, any time. Thus, the government has introduced many IT projects for these institutions, for example, SchoolNet (for the schools), UniNet (for universities), and IT Campus. The University Network (UniNet) focuses on the infrastructure and framework necessary for the information networking so that all the higher education institutions nationwide can employ information technologies for academic and administrative purposes. The Information Technology Campus (IT Campus) introduces IT (e.g., videoconferencing system) into the instruction process so that remote campuses can access information. This will allow "remote campuses to have improved system of virtual instruction environment to improve quality and maximize effectiveness" (Ministry of University Affair, 2001).

According to Nectec (2000), there are 12.5 telephone lines per 100 people, and 2.4 personal computers per 100 people in Thailand. The number of Internet users in Thailand is 3.7 percent or 371.4 users per 10,000 people. Of these, 55.2 percent are in Bangkok, 14.4 percent are in areas surrounding Bangkok, 8 percent are in the north region, 10.9 percent are in the middle region, 5.7 percent are in the north east region, 4.7 percent of users are in the southern region, and 1.2 percent are in foreign countries). The Thai government has made information technology a national priority. The plan is that every district (both urban and rural) in Thailand should have at least one Internet connection, and its goal is to have ten million Thais able to connect to the Internet by 2004.

Many government policies are in progress now, including: Internet for Tambon (District), universal health care system, IT for education, and free or low cost Internet access for schools and universities in order to promote the use of Internet. Also, some of the wealthier private and public universities have established an IT infrastructure, such as Internet connectivity and a wireless campus. However, many institutions that are not in Bangkok or around Bangkok still have little or no IT infrastructure.

Many Thai institutions have deployed some aspects of online education for their teaching. However, online education is still in an early stage. As Crispin (2001) points out, Thailand currently has basic IT infrastructure, such as Internet connectivity and fiber optic cable, in place, but only 2 percent of Thai users are on-line while the global average use is 5 percent of populations. Thus, it is important to better understand the factors that influence the acceptance of online education in Thai institutions, and the ways in which Thai cultures and values impact the acceptance of online education.

THEORETICAL FRAMEWORKS FOR UNDERSTANDING TECHNOLOGY ACCEPTANCE

To examine the factors that influence Thai educators in accepting online education, three theories concerning the adoption and diffusion of IT were deployed. These theories have been widely used and accepted in many disciplines. These three theories are the Diffusion of Innovation theory (DOI) developed originally by Everett Rogers in 1962, the Technology Acceptance Model (TAM) by Davis in 1989, and the Theory of Planned Behavior (TPB) by Ajzen in 1985.

The Theory of Diffusion of Innovations (DOI)

An innovation is something that is perceived as new by an individual. Innovation diffusion is the process in which new ideas are spread from the source of invention or creation, through information channels, to their adopters or users within a social system. Adoption is the process by which people in a social system decide to acquire and utilize the technology.

Four major elements of DOI that have an effect of the adoption rate of innovation are characteristics of innovation, communication channels, times, and social system (Rogers, 1962). The DOI theory is relevant to many disciplines and topics,, for example, medical sociology, geography, public health, anthropology, communication, marketing, education, and information technology. It offers a theory for conceptualizing the introduction and adoption of new technology. Many studies of the adoption of innovations have found that innovation characteristics exert an important influence the acceptance or adoption of those innovations (Bussey et al., 2000; Karahanna et al., 1999; Cooper & Zmud, 1990; Huff & Munro, 1989). The key characteristics of innovations include:

- *Relative advantage:* the degree to which it is perceived to be better than what it supercedes
- *Compatibility:* consistency with existing values, past experiences and needs
- *Complexity:* difficulty of understanding and use
- *Trialability:* the degree to which it can be experimented with on a limited basis
- *Observability:* the visibility of its results

Rogers (1962) also states that it is not easy to adopt new ideas into an organization although people in the organization see the obvious advantages. Like other adoption of new ideas, success in adopting new educational technology like online education is not easy although many educators agree that it provides benefits. Also, Cuban (1999) points out that the availability of computer access and Internet connectivity in many institutions have increased, but many educators and students are still slow to adopt them into the classroom.

The Technology Acceptance Model (TAM)

The Technology Acceptance Model (TAM) is widely used and well recognized in studies of the adoption of technology in the information systems field (Gefen & Straub, 2000). It was adapted from Theory of Reasoned Action (TRA), which was developed by Fishbein and Ajzen in 1975. Many IS research studies have applied TAM in their studies of technology acceptance and adoption (Gefen & Straub, 2000; Agarwal & Prasad, 1999; Compeau et al., 1999; Igbaria et al., 1997).

TAM focuses on two key variables: perceived ease of use (users' beliefs that using the system will be free from effort) and perceived usefulness (users' beliefs that using the system will enhance their job performance). Perceived usefulness is also influenced by perceived ease of use. These two variables, together with other external variables (for example, training, system characteristics and development processes) are proposed to impact attitude towards use of the technology, which leads to behavioral intention to use and then actual use of information technology.

The Theory of Planned Behavior (TPB)

The Theory of Planned Behavior (TPB), another theory useful for understanding acceptance and use of information technology, was also derived from the Theory of Reasoned Action (TRA). A limitation of TRA is that individuals may not actually perform a behavior even though they may be highly motivated to do so, according to their attitudes and prevailing subjective norms. This may be because of an intervening environment condition (Godin & Kok, 1996). TPB is a modification of TRA, specifically designed to predict behaviors of people who have incomplete volitional control.

Ajzen (1985) added a third determinant, perceived behavior control, to the TRA model. If people have strong beliefs about the factors that will facilitate a behavior, then they will have highly-perceived control over behavior. However, if they have weak beliefs about factors that will hinder behavior, then they will have a low perception of control. Two factors that determined perceived behavior control are control beliefs and perceived power.

According to Ajzen (1985), there are three kinds of beliefs that guide human behaviors. These three beliefs are:

- *Behavioral beliefs:* beliefs about the likely outcomes of the behavior and the evaluations of these outcomes. They produce a favorable or unfavorable attitude towards the behavior.
- *Normative beliefs:* beliefs about the normative expectations of others and motivation to comply with the expectation. They result in perceived social pressure or subjective norm.
- *Control beliefs:* beliefs about the presence of factors that may influence or hinder performance of the behaviors and the perceived power of these factors. They create the perceived behavioral control.

The combination of these three variables, attitude towards behavior, subjective norms, and perceived behavioral controls, lead to the intention of an individual to perform the behavior. The more the favorable attitude and subjective norm, and the greater the perceived control, the stronger the intentions of the individual prefer to perform the behavior. With sufficient degree of control over the behavior, individuals are expected to carry out their intentions. Thus, this will lead to the behavior.

This research study derives an integrated research model, drawing from these three theories (DOI, TAM, and TPB), of the factors influencing the acceptance of online education. Figure 1 displays the integrated model, which forms the basis for interpretation of findings from the field study discussed later in this chapter.

RESEARCH METHODOLOGY, RESEARCH FINDINGS AND DISCUSSION

Research Methodology

This study use both quantitative and qualitative methods. A field study involving twelve institutions in Thailand is conducted using the semi-structured interview method and questionnaires during December 2001 to February 2002. First, the researcher investigated who offered online education courses in Thai institutions by

Figure 1: Integrated Research Model of the Factors Influencing the Acceptance of Online Education

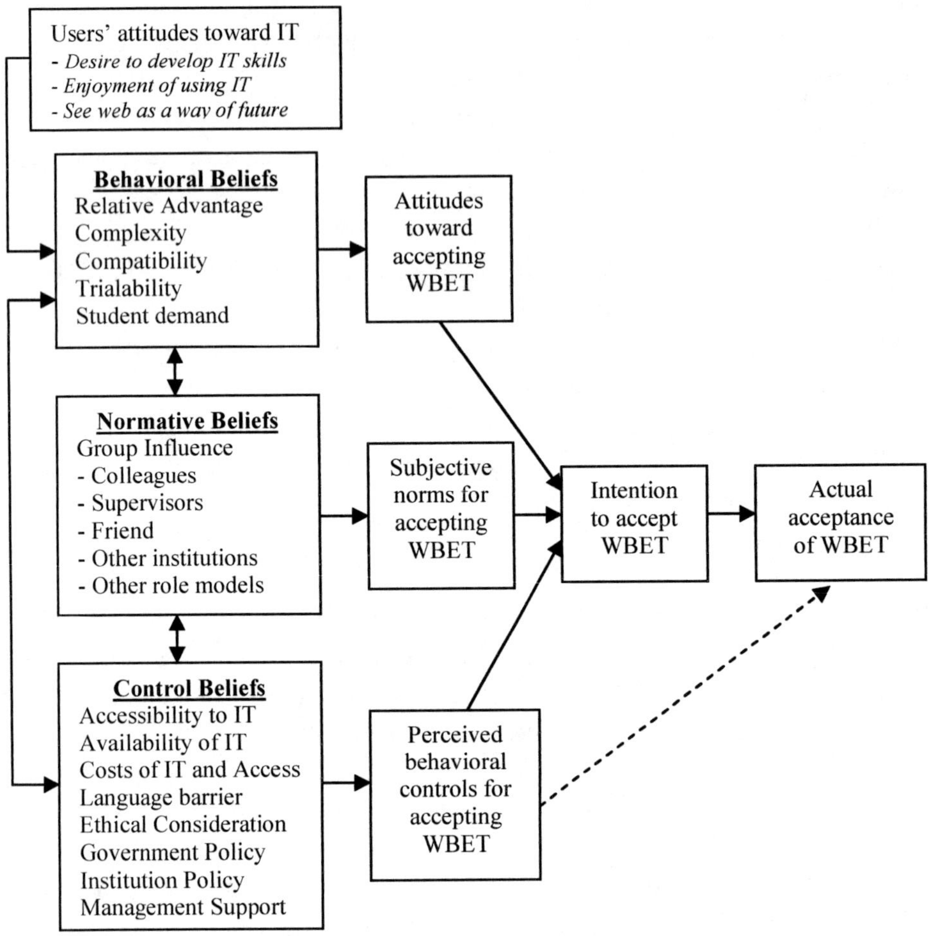

examining governmental education departments and university websites, as well as university prospectus. Then, those lecturers, Heads of Department, and the directors of the information technology involved in either adopting, managing, promoting or setting the educational and technological policy of their institutions were contacted for interviews.

At the beginning of the interview, the purpose of the study was explained, a questionnaire was given to each key informant. Each was asked to complete the questionnaire, then return it to the researchers by mail or e-mail. Then, a telephone or face-to-face interview was conducted with each informant, posing a series of open-ended questions related to the adoption of online education. Most of the interviews were conducted in the Thai language because many Thai educators requested this so that they could more fluently express their opinions, concerns, and experience. Each interview took up to an hour and was recorded on tape with the permission of the person interviewed. The names of the educators and their institutions are confidential; case numbers such as Th_A1 are used in the data coding. Data from the interviews were analyzed in accordance with the theories presented in the literature review to identify the factors which the informants perceive to be influencing the adoption of web-based educational technology in Thai institutions.

Respondent Profile

Of the 22 key informants from twelve universities in Thailand, 36 percent are male and 64 percent are female; as well, 91 percent are users and 9 percent are management and administrative staff. Their ages vary from 26 to 60 years old. The majority of key informants (59 percent) are 31 to 50 years old. All informants have some computer experience, which varied from 2 to 20 years; 64 percent have computer experience of more than ten years. The Thai key informant profile is shown in Table 3.

Research Findings and Discussion

To analyze the data, each interview was first transcribed, then translated into English. Colleagues of the researchers who were fluent in both Thai and English

Table 3: Thai Key Informants' Profile: Gender, Role, Age, and Computer Experience

GENDER

	Frequency	Percent
Male	8	36.36
Female	14	63.64
Total	22	100.00

ROLE

	Frequency	Percent
Users	20	90.91
Mgt & Admin	2	9.09
Total	22	100.00

AGE

Ages	Frequency	Percent
26 – 30	3	13.64
31 – 40	**9**	**40.91**
41 – 50	**4**	**18.18**
51 – 60	6	27.27
60 +	0	0
Total	32	100.00

COM_EXP

Years	Frequency	Percent
2 - 10	8	36.36
11 –20	**14**	**63.64**
21 - 30	0	0
30 +	0	0
Total	22	100.00

were asked to check the accuracy of the transcriptions. Then the transcriptions were analyzed using latent contents analysis. Comments made by each informant were coded into appropriate categories corresponding to the various influencing factors, as derived from the research model (Figure 1). Then the interview data and the questionnaire responses (submitted following each interview by the informant) were compared to check for consistency and expand on the interview findings.

Using the questionnaire data, the average score was obtained within each category of factors. Then, these scores were ranked from the highest to the lowest. The most influential factor had the highest score and the least influential factor had the lowest score. The results are shown in Table 4.

According to the Thai key informants, the most important factors (top five ranking – shown in bold in Table 4) are control beliefs concerning *availability of technology, cost of computer technology and Internet access,* and *accessibility to technology,* and behavioral beliefs concerning *compatibility* and *relative*

Table 4: Ranking of Influential Factors of the Acceptance of Online Education for Thai Tertiary Educators

Rank	Factors	Average
1	Control Beliefs -- Availability of technology (infrastructure, all required functions, and high quality)	4.11
2	Control Beliefs -- Cost (computer technology and Internet access)	3.93
3	Control Beliefs -- Access to technology (convenient of use and access to IT)	3.86
3:4	Behavioral Beliefs -- Compatibility (suitability to subject, teaching style, and work, as well as suitability to students' learning)	3.86
3:5	Behavioral Beliefs -- Relative advantage (enhancing of image, output quality, result demonstrability)	3.86
6	Users' Attitudes toward IT (enjoyment of using IT, desire to develop technological skills, seeing the web technology as a way of the future)	3.81
7	Behavioral Beliefs -- Student demand	3.64
8	Behavioral Beliefs -- Complexity (of online education)	3.59
9	Behavioral Beliefs -- Trialability (availability to test run adequately, no need to spend much effort, opportunity to try and use online education)	3.52
10	Control Beliefs -- Institution's policy	3.40
11	Control Beliefs -- Government's policy	3.09
11:12	Control Beliefs -- Management support (encouragement, availability of training, rewards)	3.09
13	Control Beliefs -- Ethical considerations	2.86
14	Control Beliefs -- Language Barriers	2.68
15	Normative Beliefs -- Group influence (colleagues, friends, supervisors, other institutions, and other role models)	2.36

advantage. Other important factors (ranking from six to ten - in bold-italic) include the user's attitude towards IT, the behavioral beliefs regarding *student demand, complexity of online education and trialability,* as well as control beliefs regarding *institutional policy.* Less influential factors include control beliefs concerning *government policy, management support, ethical considerations,* and *language barrier,* as well as the normative beliefs concerning *group influence.*

The highest-ranking influencing factor of online education acceptance is the control belief regarding the availability of technology. Most Thai informants agreed that the existing IT infrastructure was the most important factor that affected their decision to use online education. If there were appropriate infrastructures, functionalities, and quality of technology as well as convenience of access to technology, then Thai educators are more likely to adopt it. Although the Thai government has tried to promote this by establishing networks around the country such as UniNet (for universities), SchoolNet (for Schools), which are in place now, there is still limitations on connection and access. Many Thai educators are concerned that the IT infrastructure in Thailand is still not reliable and the quality of technology access is still poor, especially when accessing from the small cities and rural areas. Examples of Thai lecturers' comments were:

> ***The speed of the Internet is very slow if we access from home by using the phone line****. We have to wait for a while to access the website. It takes time to upload the website. Also, many Thai websites like to put a lot of graphics in their websites in order to draw attention...* ***We need to set up good infrastructure around the country*** *such as ISDN, broadband so that the quality of accessing the Internet is better.* ***It is important factors that affect lecturer's decision to adopt or use it.***

The second most influential factor is cost of IT and Internet access. Many Thai educators agree that the cost of computers and Internet access have an effect on their decision to adopt online education. Some Thai lecturers stated that their universities have provided appropriate computer access to faculties and students such as computer labs. However, they could not come to the campus to access it, so they have to have access from home. Many educators are still concerned that the cost of computers and Internet access are still high for the majority of Thais, especially for students. The majority of Thai people have a low income. It is costly to use computer and Internet access from outside. If they do not have their own computer, they have to go to the Internet café and pay a fee. Internet technology is still new to many Thais. It is not a common tool yet for the majority. This could be a problem if Thai educators adopt online education. One Thai lecturer stated,

> ***Another barrier factor is the cost****. The majority of Thais* ***have low income****. The average earning income per capita of Thais is very low.* ***To use computer and Internet access from home is costly*** *unless the institution provides enough access to all students and free connection access from home. Although the cost of Internet access is reduced now, it is still costly for most users.*

The third most important factor influencing the online education acceptance is the accessibility of technology. Many lecturers agreed that if online education is easy to access and convenient to access, they intend to adopt it. If it is not convenient for them to access, they will not use it. As one educator stated,

> *If it* ***easy to access and convenient to access,*** *I will use it. If it is not convenient for me to access, I have to travel to use the computer, I may not want to use it because it take times to travel to get there and also, it may cost money for travelling to that place. Also, I have limited time in one day and I have many thing to take care, so I may be lazy to go out to find computer to access the online education.*

The fourth factor is the behavioral belief in the compatibility of the technology, which includes compatibility with the individual's work, suitability to subject, suitability to teaching style, and suitability to students' learning culture. One educator commented,

> *I think this also* ***depends on type of subject****, and* ***approach of teaching and learning****. I think online teaching suites well in subjects such as information technology or science because this online education is related to what they study. Many institutions have adopted online education now. And If it is* ***not match with my work and my life style, it is no use for me****.*

Another important factor influencing the acceptance of online education is relative advantage or perceived usefulness. Many faculties have adopted online education because of its benefits such as accomplishing their tasks, improving quality of teaching and their image, as well as enabling students to access information at any time and at any place. Example of these comments were:

> *It helps* ***people to be fast and widely informed*** *(both good and bad information). It enables us to* ***open up to the outside world more effectively****. It is readily* ***accessible anywhere, anytime****. Let's say that I go to the USA and I would like to know what's happening back home, I can just log on the Internet anywhere to read the news and to contact Thailand at low cost and save time (economical and time effective). ...Nowadays, anywhere we go, we don't have to worry about writing letters. We could* ***communicate via the web very easily and conveniently.***

Additional factors that affect the acceptance of online education include user's computer experience and the user's attitude towards IT. All key informants have computer experience before they adopted online education. As mentioned earlier, of the key informants 63.64 percent have computer experience of more than ten years. Most Thai educators who have adopted online education have at least basic computer skills or enjoy working on IT and want to acquire technology skills. Comments made by study informants included:

> *I think the computer skill / experience is very important.* ***People who have computer skill will more likely to adopt it because it is easy for them to learn and develop online courses****. We can see from our staff that adopts it now, most of them has IT skill, and many enjoy using technology. Some of them may not have IT skill at the beginning, but they want to learn it so they try it. Many of them are very good now because they practice it and try to learn it. The more you do it, the more you learn and you can do it well.*

Student demand is another additional factors that many Thai educators mentioned. Many educators pointed out that they adopted online education because their students needed it. Many students see the benefits of having online courses, so they request faculties to have them. One lecturer commented:

> ***Students ask for it now... Using the online education, students can get information that they need****. Many lecturers upload their PowerPoint lectures onto the web before their class so that students can access this lecture note and they can prepare it in advance before they go to class or after class if they cannot take note in the lecture time.* ***I think many students like it and want to have this lecture note online****. We can see that majority of Thai*

> *students nowadays cannot take lecture well. They like to have the printouts and they can just take small notes on that printout.*

Complexity or ease of use of online education is another factor that affects their decision to accept online education. If online education is easy to use or operate, then they are more likely to adopt it. A comment that referred to this factor was:

> *My concern is the **ease of use of application software/courseware**. I think it is important that the courseware that we use should be **easy to use**. Many lectures do not have computer experience or skills. If it is easy to use, they will intent to adopt it. Also, many lecturers don't have much time to learn new thing. If **it is easy to use and it is not take their time for them to do it**, then they intend to adopt it. In my opinion, many lecturers are interested in adopting it. They do not resist doing it, but sometimes they do not have time to do it. They often think next day they do it, next day they do it so like this all the time.*

Another key influencing factor in the acceptance of technology is the characteristic of trialability. Faculties who have adopted technology point out that if they have a chance to try to use it and it suits them, they are more likely to adopt online education. One informant indicated:

> ***If I have a chance to try on first, it will help me to make a decision faster and better****... Now trialability of new technology is increasing available since the hardware is starting affordable among lower average income people and in most of educational institutions.*

The tenth most important influencing factor is the control beliefs concerning the institution's policy. Many Thai educators pointed out that their institutions should have a clear policy that the institution is promoting the use of online education. This will make it easier for educators to follow because it is their institution policy so educators are enthusiastic about adopting it and they will get support from the institution. This will also encourage people to cooperate in helping make it possible. When users ask for help, others will try to help if they can. This will influence others when they see that this is more effective. For example, educators can help in providing content for the specific courses that they have knowledge in. The management should have a clear policy on what and how so that they can encourage people to adopt it. Then, educators are more likely to adopt it. One lecturer's opinion was:

> *Currently,* ***the institution has a policy to promote web-based education****. Thus, the institutional* ***management provides the budget for developing the web-based courseware****. The computer center is responsible for this project. They develop fully interactive on-line web-based courses for five-basis courses that most students have to take them.* ***We will use these on-line web-based courses this coming year****.*

Factors that have less effect on the acceptance of online education for Thai key informants are the control beliefs regarding *government's policy, management support, ethical considerations, and language barriers,* as well as normative beliefs regarding group influences (colleagues, friends, and supervisors). Examples of Thai educators' comments were as follows:

> *The government policy* ***has an effect on the adoption of online education in the way of providing the budget to the institutions.*** *For example this year, the government is trying to promote e-learning. So the government is giving the budget to institutions for an online education project. When institutions receive the money, they have to use it. They try to set up the project for this funding; they try to make it happen. However, some of them may not think or consider that this is suitable for their courses, subjects, or their students. Some of them follow others because others do it.*

> *I think if we use the English language,* ***it will have an effect on the adoption because English is not our language.*** *Thai lecturers and students will not familiar with it. Most of them prefer to have Thai contents for Thais' subjects. If it is in English, they will not like to adopt it because they have to spend time for translating it. It will take time to understand the lesson in English. However, many new young generations begin to learn and try to use English nowadays.*

> *I think this depends on the individual. However, their colleagues, subjects that they teach and their roles may influence others in terms of if there is a good and interesting online courses and others see it, their colleagues may want to do the same.*

> *One thing that we should be concern is that* ***it is not easy to manage or persuade academic or lecturers to adopt or use online educa-***

***tion**. They all are teachers who teach a lot of students. Sometimes you cannot tell them what to do or use, unless you convince them or show them the real benefits that they will gain for using this. If they see the real benefits for them, then they will adopt it.*

IMPACT OF THAI CULTURE AND VALUES ON THE ACCEPTANCE OF ONLINE EDUCATION

After analyzing these influencing factors, it is apparent that Thai cultural values have an impact on certain factors, including *compatibility, group influence by supervisors, management support and institution's policy, government policy,* and *language barrier*. However, other factors are not impacted by Thai culture and values, including *availability of technology, accessibility of technology cost of technology, relative advantage, student demand, complexity,* and *trialability*. This section focuses only on those factors influencing online acceptance for which Thai culture and value have been important.

Compatibility of Online Education

Many Thai educators agree that one factor that has an effect on their decision to adopt online education is the compatibility of the online courses with their subjects, their teaching style or their students' learning culture. They indicate that online education is not widely used in Thai education because it is not compatible with Thai teaching and learning culture.

Traditionally, Thai teaching and learning culture is based around a teacher-centered model. Teachers control the environment of the classroom. 'Chalk and talk' pedagogy predominates. The process of learning is not frequently discussed. In addition, the cultural behavior of many Thai educators involves self-protection. Many Thai teachers do not encourage their students to speak out or comment or propose new ideas. If students ask questions or speak out, Thai teachers will think those students lack respect for their teachers (Chatturachinda, 2001). Moreover, many Thais lack experience in analytical thought. Unlike Western people who believe in systematic analytical thinking, Thais lack experience in this style of thinking. The question "why" is a key to understand a situation or clarify a point. Thais are brought up within a hierarchical social system. Thus, they are not encouraged to ask questions like "why," or "why not?"

There are variety of other Thai culture and values that have impact on this factor. The first value is "gratitude and indebtedness." This means that most of lower rank people appreciate those higher rank people who have done favors for them.

The second value is "merciful and kind." This means the high rank behaves kindly to those in the lower rank. These values are applied to Thai educators and students; for example, students should feel gratitude and indebtedness to their teachers. Also, teachers should be generous with their effort and time in assisting their students (Vichit-Vadakan, 1990). Thus, students do not dare to argue with teachers. Everything that teachers say is always right because teachers teach students and give them knowledge so students should respect teachers and not argue back.

Another important Thai value that impact on the compatibility is "Kreng Jai." This means the behavior or attitude of the individual that tries to control his/her own desire or interest when there is a situation that is uncomfortable or conflicting or when in the situation where there is a need to maintain a pleasant and cooperative relationship. In the educational environment, students are always reluctant to interrupt or disturb teachers in the classroom while teachers are teaching; they try to avoid asserting their needs or opinions; they are reluctant to ask questions when they have not understood someone. The same attitude would apply in Thai utilization of online education. For example, students would not feel that it was appropriate to e-mail teachers. Likewise they would be reluctant to use an online discussion forum.

Group Influence by Supervisors, Management Support, and Institution's Policy

Thai culture and values also impact on other factors, including group influence by supervisors, management support, and the institution's policy. As mentioned earlier, the Thai social system is hierarchical in nature. The senior people are expected to guide, control, protect, support, and look after the needs of their juniors or employees like fathers do to their children. The communication in Thai society tends to be from the top-down, so most junior people are more likely to absorb things instead of initiate things. Many Thais believe it is the responsibility of the supervisor or senior person to initiate. Due to the hierarchical nature of relationships in Thailand, Thai educators are more likely to adopt online education as a result of influence from exerted by their supervisors, or because of seniority. However, many Thai supervisors do not understand much about online technology, because the technology did not exist in their generation when they were young. It is new to them and many of them are old now and do not want to learn new things. This may be an obstacle for Thai educators who would like to adopt it, but do not do so because their supervisors do not initiate, support and encourage them to do it.

Another cultural value shared by Thais is the agrarian viewpoint. This value dictates that there is no requirement for accountability in individual sense. Thus, Thais always work in a group where they share their responsibilities. It is not very difficult to make individual staff take responsibility. Thus, most staff would prefer that the supervisor dictate the implementation of change, and take responsibility for it (Holmes et al. 1996). Supervisor should set up institutional policy so that staff can follow. Thus institutional policy is an important factor that influences the willingness of academic staff to adopt online education.

Another Thai value that has an impact on this influencing factor is authoritarian. Most supervisors or seniors have a low level of confidence in their subordinates' capacity for leadership and initiative. They also do not like to share information with their staff or let them be involved in decision-making. However, availability of online education might result in junior staff being as well-informed—if not better informed—than their superiors. Thus, this Thai cultural value may impede educators in the acceptance of online education.

Government Policy

Thai government educational policies also play a role in influencing Thai educators to adopt online education technologies.

Thai education is administered by several government ministries depending on the level of education. At the higher educational level, the Ministry of University Affairs administers public and private universities and institutions of higher learning. Recently, the Thai government established the National Education Act 1999. Among other things, this Act promotes the concept of "student learning centers," so as to help Thai students to learn to think analytically. In particular, analytical thinking can be promoted by online education. This is emphasized in the final chapter of the Act, which focuses on technology for education. The policies emerging from the National Education Act 1999 influences the acceptance of online education in part because educators receive support from the government in terms of budgets and infrastructure.

The Thai government has prioritized national technology such as Internet connection to every district, both urban and rural, by 2004, and free or low-cost Internet connections for schools and universities, in order to promote the use of online technology.

The Thai cultural value called "*bun khun*" means that if others help or provide support to one, then that individual should be appreciative and try to reciprocate. Because the Thai government provides support and funding to educators' institutions, *bun khun* dictates that those educators should be grateful and that there is an obligation on the part of the beneficiary to reciprocate, i.e., to follow the government's policies.

Language Barrier

Due to the fact that Thai language is the only official language in Thailand, most Thai people use only the Thai language when they study and communicate with each other. A majority of Thai students study English, which is the second language for writing and reading (but much less for listening and speaking) in most Thai schools and universities (Holmes et al., 1996).

Despite the fact that English is studied in school, most Thai students and educators perceive having to work in English as an obstacle. If online education is conducted in English (e.g., requires accessing and absorbing the content of websites that are presented only in English), educators and students may not want to access it because it takes time for them to read and understand the content. Also Thai students would not find it easy to express their ideas in a language other than Thai. Thus, language barrier is yet another factor impacting educators' decision to adopt online education.

CONCLUSION

This chapter has presented an analysis of the challenges of adopting online education in the tertiary sector in Thailand. Data was gathered via in-depth semi-structured interviews augmented by questionnaires, from 22 Thai educators. This study found that the most important influencing factors in accepting online education for Thai educators are the availability of technology, cost of computer technology and Internet access, accessibility to technology, compatibility, and relative advantage. Other important factors are the user's attitude towards IT, student demand, complexity, trialability, and institutional policy. Less influential factors include government policy, management support, ethical considerations, language barrier, and group influence. Also, Thai culture and values have an impact on the influencing factors of compatibility, group influence by supervisors, management support and institution's policy, government policy, and language barrier. Future research is planned to examine online education acceptance in other cultural settings and compare the findings to those in the Thai context.

REFERENCES

Agarwal, R. & Prasad, J. (1999). Are individual differences germane to the acceptance of new information technologies? *Decision Sciences, 30*(2), 361-391.

Aggarwal, A. & Bento, R. (2000). Web-based education. In Aggarwal, A. (Ed.), *Web-Based Learning and Teaching Technologies: Opportunities and Challenges.* (pp. 2-16). Hershey, PA: Idea Group Publishing.

Ajzen, I. (1985). From intention to actions: A theory of planned behavior. In Kuhi, J. & Beckman, J. (Eds). *Action-Control: From Cognition to Behavior. 11-39.* Heidelberg: Springer.

Bussey, J.M., Dormody, T.J. & VanLeeuwen, D. (2000). Some factors predicting the adoption of technology education in New Mexico public schools. *Journal of Technology Education, 12*(1).

Chatturachinda, K. (2001). True education is to learn how to think not what to think. [Online]. Retrieved, on June 6, 2001 from the World Wide Web: http://www.mua.go.th/educate1/kamheang.htm.

Compeau, D.R., Higgins, C.A. & Huff, S.L. (1999). Social cognitive theory and individual reactions to computing technology: A longitudinal study. *MIS Quarterly, 23*(2), 145-158.

Cooper, R.B., & Zmud, R.W. (1990). Information technology implementation research: A technological diffusion approach. *Management Science, 36*(2), 123-140.

Crispin, S.W. (2000). The debt detective. *Far Eastern Economic Review.* [Online]. Available: www.feer.com/articles/2000/0009_21/p26region.html. (September 21).

Cuban, L. (1999). High-tech school, low-tech teaching. *Education Digest, 64*(5), 53-55.

Davis, F.D. (1989). Perceived usefulness, perceived ease of use, and user acceptance of information technology. *MIS Quarterly, 13*(3), 319-340.

ExcutivePlanet (2001). Let's make a Deal!: What you should know before negotiating in Thailand. *ExecutivePlanet.* Retrieved on May 12, 2002 from the World Wide Web: http://www.executiveplanet.com/community/items/965090705266_en.asp?section=Thailand.

Fishbein, M. & Ajzen, I. (1975). *Belief, Attitude, Intention and Behavior.* Don Mills, NY: Addison-Wesley.

Gefen, D. & Straub, D.W. (2000, Oct.). The relative importance of perceived ease-of-use in is adoption: A study of e-commerce adoption. *Journal of the Association for Information Systems, 1,* 8.

Godin, G. & Kok, G. (1996). The theory of planned behavior: A review of its applications to health-related behaviors. *American Journal of Health Promotion, 11*(2), 87-98.

Hofstede, G. (1980). *Culture's Consequences: International Differences in Work-Related Values.* Newbury Park, CA: Sage.

Hofstede, G. (1986). Cultural differences in teaching and learning. *International Journal of Intercultural Relations, 10*: 301-320.

Hofstede, G. (1991). *Cultures and Organizations: Software of the Mind.* London: McGraw-Hill.

Holmes, H., Tangtongtavy, S. & Tomizawa, R. (1996). *Working with the Thais: A Guide to Managing in Thailand.* Bangkok: White Lotus.

Huff, S.L. & Munro, M.C. (1989). Managing micro proliferation. *Journal of Information Systems Management*, 72-75.

Igbaria, M., Zinatelli, N., Cragg, P. & Cavaye, A.L.M. (1997). Personal computing acceptance factors in small firms: A structural equation model. *MIS Quarterly, 21*(3), 279-305.

Kaewdang, R. (2001). Learning for the new century. *Office of the National Education Commission.* Retrieved on June 16, 2001 from the World Wide Web: http://www.onec.go.th.

Kandel, I.L. (1933). *Comparative Education.* Boston, MA: Houghton Mifflin Co.

Karahanna, E., Straub, D.W. & Chervany, N.L. (1999). Information technology adoption across time: A cross-sectional comparison of pre-adoption and post-adoption beliefs. *MIS Quarterly, 23*(2), 183-213.

Khan, B.H. (Ed.). (1997). *Web-Based Instruction.* NJ: Educational Technology Publications, Inc.

McCormack, C. & Jones, D. (1998). *Building a Web-Based Education System.* NY: John Wiley & Sons, Inc.

The Ministry of Education. (1999). *National Education Act of 1999.* Retrieved on June 16, 2001 from the World Wide Web: http://www.moe.go.th/English/edu-act.htm.

The Ministry of University Affair. (2001). *Project highlights.* Retrieved on June 16, 2001 from the World Wide Web: http://www.inter.mua.go.th/glance/index.html.

The Ministry of University Affair. (2001). *Universities at a glance.* Retrieved on June 16, 2001 from the World Wide Web: http://www.inter.mua.go.th/glance/index.html.

The Nation (1999, November 8). Thailand's education reform: The National Education Act 1999 hope for a better Thailand. *The Nation.*

Nectec. (2000). *Internet User Profile Survey.* National Electronics and Computer Technology Center (NECTEC).

Niratpattanasai, K. (2001). Pros and cons of Kreng Jai: Hiding bad news can be the least considerate approach of all. *Bangkok Post* (July 27). Retrieved on

May 12, 2001 from the World Wide Web: http://scoop.bangkokpost.co.th/bkkpost/2001/july2001/bp20010727/270701_Business05.html.

Podhisita, C. (1998). Buddhism and Thai world view. In Pongsapich, A. (Ed.), *Traditional and Changing Thai World View*. 31-62. Bangkok: Chulalongkorn University Printing House.

Rogers, E.M. (1962). *Diffusion of Innovations* (1st ed.). N Y: The Free Press.

Tetiwat, O. & Igbaria, M. (2000). Opportunity in web-based teaching: The future of education. In Aggarwal, A. (Ed.), *Web-based Learning and Teaching Technologies: Opportunities and Challenges*. (pp. 17-32). Hershey, PA: Idea Group Publishing.

The World Bank. (1999). Education in Thailand. Retrieved on October 5, 2001 from the World Wide Web: http://www.worldbank.org/eapsocial/countries/thai/educ1.htm.

The World Factbook. (2001). Central Intelligence Agency, Washington, DC. Retrieved on October 16, 2001 from the World Wide Web: http://www.cia.gov/cia/publications/factbook/index.html.

Vichit-Vadakan, J. (1990). All change for Thai values. Paper presented at a seminar, Societies on the Move: Changing Values (Cholburi, Thailand). *The Nation*, June 21 (Reprint).

SECTION V:

E-COMMERCE INTERFACES

Chapter XII

Chinese Cultures and E-Commerce

Jeffrey Hsu
Fairleigh Dickinson University, USA

ABSTRACT

The potential for the Internet and e-commerce in China and Chinese-speaking nations (including Hong Kong, Taiwan and Singapore) is huge. Many experts believe that China will have the second largest population of Web surfers, after the United States, by the year 2005 (McCarthy, 2000). Currently, the Internet population in China is doubling every six months (CNNIC, 2001). There are many issues relating to China's cultural aspects and society, which can impact the design and content of Websites that are directed towards Chinese audiences. Some of these issues include basic differences between Chinese and American/Western cultures, family and collective orientations, religion and faith, color, symbolism, ordering and risk/uncertainty. Attention is given to the differences between the cultures of China, Hong Kong, Taiwan, and Singapore, as well as addressing issues brought up by related theories and frameworks. A discussion of important considerations that relate to using Chinese language on the World Wide Web (WWW) is also included. Finally, insights are gained by examining Websites produced in China and Chinese-speaking countries. This chapter will focus on many of these issues and provide practical guidelines and advice for those who want to reach out to Chinese audiences, whether for e-commerce, education, or other needs.

INTRODUCTION

The revolution of the Internet and the Web has radically changed the way that we live, work, and play, to the extent that for many, using electronic means has become the norm rather than the exception. It may be assumed by some that English-language sites, or perhaps those in European languages or Japanese, make up the majority of what is on the Web. However, one enormous, yet perhaps less recognized emerging market for the Web is the Chinese-language population, well over a billion of them in mainland China alone, spread out throughout China, Taiwan, Hong Kong, and Singapore, with many more "Overseas Chinese" living throughout the world.

In fact, the Chinese market can be considered as potentially one of the largest in the world, even though currently it is in the early stages of development. Even so, in 2000 there were close to 9 million computers connected to the Internet in China (CNNIC, 2000), and the number of users exceeded 22 million (CNNIC, 2001). All of this growth occurred since 1996; China is now considered one of the top five nations in terms of Internet use. Some experts predict that China is making strides towards having the second largest population of Web surfers in the world. Clearly, there is a vast potential market that has yet to be expanded and tapped to its fullest potential.

It should be noted that while there is a very potential market in terms of total Chinese and Chinese-speaking population, the type of user who would be using the Internet actually forms a kind of subculture within the general population, with characteristics including higher income and educational levels, and more users in urban and metropolitan rather than rural areas. This is generally true for most Chinese-speaking nations.

While there are a number of issues and impacts that relate to the use of the Internet in China and in Chinese-speaking nations, culture is the area on which this chapter focuses. Culture is an important part of a successful Website or e-commerce business, since instead of working within the cultural confines of a single nation, such as that of the United States, cultural boundaries are crossed.

Consequently, there are frequent diverse issues and considerations that come into play.

Culture is a man-made part of the human environment. This definition includes not only the material features of the human environment, but also the conceptual features—the beliefs, science, myths, religions, laws, and other tenants held by a group of people. The importance of culture cannot be over-emphasized since it was found that cultural programs will not work if crucial steps are omitted, which happens when people unconsciously apply their own rules to another system. A widely used definition of culture is derived from Hofstede's book (1991), in which culture is likened to mental programs, or "software of the mind," using the analogy of computer programming.

Factoring in the effect of culture is important, since in many cases the goal of a Website is to market something – a product, service, or idea. According to Mooij (1998), culture is a fundamentally important aspect of marketing. Moreover, it is important for marketers of one cultural system to understand and adopt the cultural strategy of the system/nation it is attempting to market to (Penazola, 1998). Several cultural aspects need to be addressed, whether they are attitudes, behavior, or values. Marketing strategies and tactics that may work effectively in one culture could result in dismal failure in another.

While these will be discussed in greater detail later in this paper, some of the important considerations include properly targeting the local culture, the use of effective symbols and meanings, managing social relations, and understanding cultural identities and ethnicity (Penazola, 1989; Bouchet, 1995). In addition, when focusing on the Chinese market, such aspects as family orientation, importance of Confucianism, and group orientation make up a unique approach to life and viewing the world, which results in important differences from Western cultures (Scarborough, 1998; Lai, 2001).

The organization of this chapter is as follows: to start off the chapter, there will be a discussion of some technical issues, including those relating to Chinese language, fonts, and the display of Chinese on Websites (from browsers). This is followed by a discussion of the characteristics of the average Chinese Web surfer, with an attempt to identify some important characteristics of which Website creators should be aware.

The next section examines Chinese culture in more detail, starting from the perspective of certain theoretical frameworks, followed by a review of some of the key cultural factors which would impact the marketing of products and services (e-commerce) to Chinese audiences. From here, the chapter turns to an examination of some of the specific issues and differences which are present when it comes to Websites being directed towards Chinese audiences in China, Hong Kong,

Taiwan, and Singapore. The chapter concludes with some general conclusions gained from the concepts and principles discussed throughout the chapter.

CHINESE LANGUAGE SITES: LANGUAGE AND FONT ISSUES

One of the first issues that comes to mind when discussing Chinese sites is the issue of language. Chinese differs from Western languages in that "words" are not represented by groups of alphabets, but rather by complex characters that are displayed pictorially rather than as text. In addition, there are differences in terms of the appearance of characters: simplified characters are generally used in China, while traditional characters are used in Taiwan.

There are different ways of representing Chinese, depending on whether it is based from a PC, or from the Internet through a Web browser. From the earlier days of computing when computers could only work with English and had difficulty with foreign languages and characters/alphabets, computers have made great strides in being able to handle Chinese. Most computers are able to handle Chinese in one of three ways: Localization for Chinese is the first approach. The operating system comes with Chinese fonts and allows for the input and display of Chinese characters. The user sees all of the text and commands in Chinese. In general, these kinds of systems are best for people who communicate mainly in Chinese and do not understand English, as in China and Taiwan. Generally speaking, this requires the use of a specialized operating system such as Microsoft's Traditional or Simplified Chinese Windows.

Another method is to use a Chinese language add-on program that works in conjunction with the operating system. Using software such as TwinBridge's Chinese Partner for Windows or the Chinese Language Kit for Macintosh, it is possible to display and write Chinese on a computer. They would support the display and usage of Chinese characters using applications software, such as for word processing or Web browsing.

As technology and software sophistication advances, it is now possible to work with Chinese characters directly. The characters are stored using a universal computer encoding method called Unicode and can be readily displayed as Chinese text, provided that the appropriate Chinese fonts are loaded into the system and software. Software such as Microsoft Office, Internet Explorer and Netscape Navigator, and many programs written in Java are examples of such software. Currently, among the computing systems that can handle Chinese characters are DOS, Windows, Macintosh, and Linux.

As stated, it is now possible to have a computer operating system that operates in Chinese, and even English language-based computers can work with Chinese characters, using various font sets and software add-ons that display the characters in a variety of styles. In terms of the Internet, Web browsers have become equipped with the ability to understand Chinese character encoding and to display characters to the screen.

In fact, there are two main ways that Chinese can be displayed on a Website: as an encoded character using either *Big5* or *GuoBiao*, or as a graphic. In the case of encoded characters, the specialized software must be available or installed so that the appropriate characters can be displayed. Often this requires nothing more than setting up a certain configuration or downloading and installing some add-on software. The other option, to display it as a graphic, is simpler for the user, and does not require any additional effort on the part of the viewer, but may take time to load and be slower. Other available options include the ability to display pinyin (Romanizations) of the Chinese language in an English-like alphabet, and also to display Chinese in the traditional vertical rather than horizontal format. Please see the Websites listed at the end of this chapter for further information.

CHINESE WEB PAGE: TECHNICAL ISSUES

From the preceding general introduction, it would be useful to examine some of these issues in more detail.

Chinese Character Encoding

As mentioned, two major Chinese character encodings are Big5 and GuoBiao (GB). Big5 encodes traditional characters and is used in Taiwan and Hong Kong, while GB encodes simplified characters and is used in Mainland China. Another encoding, Unicode, can be used for both simplified and traditional Chinese. Unicode is supported by both Netscape and Internet Explorer browsers. Since using a different encoding will bring up different characters, some Websites offer the same information in several different encodings. The alternate option is to display characters as graphic images so that they can be viewed on different browsers. This approach has the advantage of ease of use, but has two major disadvantages: it can be more difficult to update the content of a page; and the graphics can take extra time to download.

Encoding Chinese on the Web

The two major Web browsers both have the ability to display Chinese themselves, as long as a Chinese font is loaded into the system. They can also read the type of encoding to use from the Web page itself. The browser can then use this information to properly display the Web page. Knowing which encoding to use is important since a browser that tries to display a page in Big5 as if it were GB will not display the characters properly.

It is possible to set up an automatic means of choosing the character set by adding a META tag to the HTML of the Web page. It is placed with the header, between <HEAD> and </HEAD>, in the same general place where the TITLE goes. This tag will specify the encoding in the charset entry, such as charset=big5.

Managing Chinese Fonts

In general, one can specify the desired Chinese font by using the HTML FONT tag with a FACE attribute. The page can specify what font to use in displaying the tagged text. In cases where the specified font does not support Chinese text or the font itself does not exist on the user's system, this can cause the browser to incorrectly display the Chinese characters. This problem can be alleviated when using Internet Explorer, as the browser may substitute other similar fonts, but certain versions of Netscape Navigator will not. To make Web pages viewable on the maximum number of browsers, it is recommended to not specify what font to use on pages with Chinese text, but to instead let the browser use its default Chinese font.

Earlier versions of Netscape and Internet Explorer did not include support for Asian languages, including Chinese. These early browsers used blank spaces to locate where one word ended and the next one started. Since Chinese does not use spaces, the browser could possibly break up the Chinese text in inappropriate places, including in the middle of a double-byte character, or not break the line at all, allowing the text to run off the side of the page or window. Some Web pages would add a space in between each character to attempt to alleviate this problem. As a result, even if the browser did not know how to handle Chinese, it would still find appropriate places to break it into lines.

With the newer Web browsers that can understand how to properly display Chinese text, the use of spaces is no longer critical. But users creating Web pages that may need to be displayed on older browsers or English-only browsers should be aware of this issue.

Ruby Annotations

Aside from Chinese characters, it is sometimes desired to add annotations to the Chinese characters. This could include the use of Pinyin or Wade-Giles Romanizations to accompany the characters, or the use of Zhuyin Fuhao (*bopomofo)*, which is a set of symbols resembling a kind of alphabet that can be used to "spell" Chinese characters. It was developed as a tool for learning to read and pronounce Mandarin Chinese. These kinds of annotations are known as Ruby Annotations, and accompany a set of Chinese characters in the main body of the text. It can also be used to add pinyin above a Chinese character or in conjunction with vertical text support to add *bopomofo* next to a Chinese character. MS Internet Explorer 5.0 and above supports the use of the RUBY tag.

Vertical Text

Western languages typically display text horizontally, from left to right. However, traditionally, Chinese is displayed vertically from top to bottom. It is possible, based on the specific browser and version used, to specify whether the text is to be displayed horizontally or vertically. Starting with MS Internet Explorer 5.5, Web pages will have the ability to display vertical text in the traditional format formerly used in China and still currently used in Taiwan.

WEB PAGE CREATION SOFTWARE

Specifying Page Language

When using special Web design software design Web pages, it is possible to specify what language the Web page is in and what language it should be displayed. The language specification helps the browser to properly display your Web page.

Avoiding Ampersand Escapes

Another problem that can occur when creating Chinese Websites is a result of the fact that Chinese characters are encoded outside the normal ASCII range used by English letters, numbers, and symbols. When interpreting these symbols, some Web editor programs can confuse the character bytes used for Chinese for other bytes used to create special characters and then do strange things such as generating special ampersand escape sequences that can affect the display of the Chinese text. Even though pages created this way may be viewable to the end user, Web page creators should make sure their pages do not encode the Chinese bytes in this way.

Viewing Chinese Web Pages

Most recent versions of Internet Explorer and Netscape Navigator can support Chinese without the use of additional software. Only the correct font is needed, and there are many fonts you can download for free. Microsoft, for example, offers downloadable language packs for Simplified and Traditional Chinese.

Installing these language packs will automatically set up Internet Explorer to display Chinese. Netscape generally requires one more step. From Netscape's main menu, select "Edit," then "Preferences." In the window that appears, select "Appearance" and "Fonts." First select "Simplified Chinese" for the encoding, and choose "MS Song" or "MS Hei" for the proportional and fixed length fonts. For the "Traditional Chinese Encoding," select "MingLiU" as the font.

As you surf to different Chinese Websites, two issues should be noted. Some Web pages "know" that they are in Chinese, and the browser will automatically use the available Chinese fonts to display the characters. For Web pages that do not have this information, you can manually change to Chinese. On Netscape, this is done from "View" and then "Character Set" on the main menu. On Internet Explorer, this can be done from "View" and then "Fonts". These fonts will also allow you to read (in Netscape Messager and Outlook) and write (in Outlook) Chinese in e-mails.

THE CHINESE WEB SURFER

What are some of the characteristics of the Chinese Web surfer? As mentioned earlier in this chapter, despite difficulties in gaining access to the Internet, whether it be the cost, restrictions placed by the government, slow access speeds, or the lack of availability in certain areas, the Chinese are very enthusiastic about getting onto the Information Superhighway. In fact, according to CNNIC (2001), the number of users is increasing by 33% per year, while the total number of Websites has increased dramatically.

Most of the users of the Internet in China are from the major cities, including Beijing, Shanghai, and Guangzhou. While the majority of China population is found in rural areas, there is a strong tendency for users to be concentrated in cities and urban areas. A strong focus on urban issues, concerns, and interests should therefore be taken into account when designing a Website for a Chinese audience.

Generally, more (roughly twice as many) males than females are online, and most of they are young. The majority of Internet users are under 25 years of age. Many have a college education, are students, and/or have a professional employment in government or industry.

DESIGNING FOR CHINESE: WEB DESIGN FOR CHINESE SITES

As a starting point, it would be useful to examine what are some of the distinctive aspects of Chinese culture, especially those that could relate in some way to the marketing and effectiveness of Websites. Chinese culture is unique, and two commonly used terms express this: *Zhong Guo*, the Chinese word for the country itself, means "the center of the world," expressing belief that China is unique and an important force in the world. In addition, *Guo Qing* reflects the fact that China is a special, important country that has its own distinctiveness and uniqueness.

In general, culture was characterized by Nathan (1998), as the traits that define the uniqueness of a culture, which differentiate it from others. In the case of Chinese versus Western (American) culture, these differences are described by Xing (1995) in Table 1.

HOFSTEDE'S DIMENSIONS OF CULTURE

The Dutch cultural anthropologist Geert Hofstede conducted detailed interviews of hundreds of IBM employees from 1978 to 1983. Through statistical analysis, he was able to determine patterns of similarities and differences among the

Table 1: Chinese Versus American Culture (Adapted from Xing, 1995)

Chinese	American
Intuitive	Rational
Aesthetic	Scientific
Introverted	Extroverted
Self-restrained	Aggressive
Dependent	Independent
Procrastinating	Active
Implicit	Explicit
Patient	Impatient
Group-oriented	Individualistic
Continuity	Change

employees. From this analysis, he formulated a theory that world cultures vary along a series of dimensions. Since his subjects were all from one multinational corporation's worldwide employees, and thus to one company culture, he attributed their differences to the effects of their national cultures. In the 1990s, Hofstede published his research in *Cultures and Organizations: Software of the Mind* (Hofstede, 1997). His focus was on highlighting essential patterns of thinking, feeling, and acting. These cultural differences are found in a culture's choices of symbols, heroes/heroines, rituals, and values (Marcus & Gould, 2000; Hofstede, 1997).

Hofstede identified five dimensions in his research. His five dimensions of culture were as follows:

- Power-distance
- Collectivism versus individualism
- Femininity versus masculinity
- Uncertainty avoidance
- Long versus short-term orientation

Power Distance

Power distance (PD) refers to the extent to which certain less powerful members expect and accept unequal power distribution within a culture. High PD countries tend to have centralized political power, and exhibit hierarchies in organizations with large differences in salary and position. Subordinates may view the "boss" in a more benevolent manner, and have no problem doing as they are told. Parents and teachers are respected. Inequalities in status are not interpreted in a negative way. Low PD countries tend to have flatter hierarchies in organizations and smaller differences in salaries and status. Parents and children, and teachers and students, may view themselves more as equals.

Hofstede believes that these PD differences can be attributed to cultural traditions hundreds or even thousands of years old. These may not disappear quickly from traditional cultures, even with the increased influence of global communications. Power distance may influence the following aspects of user-interface and Web design:

- Access to information: High PD cultures exhibit more structure, with low PD cultures exhibiting less structure. In addition, there are more complex hierarchies and "taller" ones for high PD cultures than for low PD cultures.
- There is also a greater emphasis on the social and moral order (e.g., nationalism or religion) and its related symbols for high PD as opposed to low PD cultures. This same emphasis applies to symbols that relate to expertise, authority, experts, certifications, or logos. The leadership of a nation is emphasized and prominently displayed.

Other characteristics might include an emphasis on security (restrictions to access) in the site, as well as the expression of social roles (manager's private section as opposed to those for general users). In general, it could be stated that the Chinese tend to exhibit more of a tendency towards high PD, and that the use of appropriate symbols and expressions of power and authority would be appropriate (Marcus & Gould, 2000; Hofstede, 1997).

Individualism Versus Collectivism

Individualism implies that individuals are expected to look after one's self for immediate family but no one else. Hofstede found that individualistic cultures value personal time, freedom, challenge, and such extrinsic motivators as material rewards at work. In family relations, they value honesty/truth, talking things out, and maintaining self-respect. Their societies and governments place individual interests over the group, value privacy, emphasize voting and freedom of the press, and profess the ideologies of self-realization and freedom.

Collectivism differs in that it implies that people form strong, cohesive groups that offer protection in exchange for loyalty. Collectivist cultures value training, physical conditions, skills, and the intrinsic rewards of mastery. In family relations, they value harmony more than honesty/truth, and strive to maintain "face." Their societies and governments place collective interests over the individual, favor laws and rights for groups over individuals, exercise control over the economy and press, and profess the ideologies of harmony, consensus, and equality. The characteristics of Chinese society imply a leaning towards collectivism.

Therefore, collectivism may influence the following aspects of user-interface and Web design:

- Motivation based on personal achievement is underplayed in favor of group achievement.
- Success is demonstrated through achievement of group agendas.
- Rhetorical style includes the use of official slogans and a desire to reduce controversy.
- Prominence is given to wise leaders and states of being.
- An underlying sense of social morality, with an emphasis on relationships.
- Marked emphasis on tradition and history (Marcus & Gould, 2000; Hofstede, 1997).

Masculinity Versus Femininity (MAS)

Hofstede focuses on the traditional assignment to masculine roles of assertiveness, competition, and toughness; and to feminine roles an orientation towards home and children, people, and tenderness. In masculine cultures, the traditional distinctions are strongly maintained, while feminine cultures tend to collapse the distinctions and allow the overlapping of gender roles. Traditional masculine work goals include recognition, advancement, and challenge. Traditional feminine work goals include good relations with supervisors, peers, and subordinates, good living and working conditions; and job security.

China tends to exhibit the characteristics associated with a high masculinity (MAS) index value, which seems to indicate an emphasis on dominant masculine roles. Since Hofstede's definition focuses on the balance between roles and relationships, it is believed that masculinity and femininity may be expressed on the Web through different emphases. High-masculinity cultures would support the following user-interface and design elements:

- Traditional gender/family/age distinctions
- Work tasks and roles, with quick results desired
- Navigation oriented towards exploration
- Gaining attention through games and competitions
- Use of graphics, sound, and animation (Marcus & Gould, 2000; Hofstede, 1997)

Uncertainty Avoidance (UA)

People can feel anxiety about uncertain or unknown matters, which is different from the feeling of fear caused by known or understood threats. Cultures can vary in their avoidance of uncertainty, with different rituals and values regarding formality, punctuality, and tolerance for ambiguity.

In general, cultures with high uncertainty avoidance tend to have high rates of suicide, alcoholism, and accidental deaths, and higher numbers of prisoners per capita. Businesses may have more formal rules, require longer career commitments, and focus on tactical operations rather than strategy. People in high UA cultures seem active, emotional, aggressive; dislike ambiguity; and want to help make events clearly interpretable and predictable. In high UA cultures, what is different may be viewed as a threat, and what is "dirty" (unconventional) is often equated with what is dangerous.

By contrast, low UA cultures tend to have higher caffeine consumption, higher heart-disease death rates, and more chronic psychosis per capita. Businesses may focus more on long-range strategic matters than day-to-day operations. These cultures tend to be less expressive and less openly anxious; people behave quietly without showing aggression or strong emotions. In these cultures, what is different may be viewed as curious, or even ridiculous.

Based on this definition, uncertainty avoidance may influence various aspects of user-interface and Web design. High-UA cultures would tend to emphasize the following:

- Simplicity, with clear metaphors, and limited choices
- Navigation schemes that help prevent users from becoming lost
- Mental models and help systems that focus on reducing "user errors"
- Redundant cues (color, typography, sound, etc.) to reduce ambiguity

Low UA cultures would emphasize the following:

- Complexity with many content and choices
- An acceptance or encouragement of wandering and risk
- Less control of navigation
- Mental models and help systems that focus on understanding underlying concepts rather than tasks
- Coding of color, typography, and sound to maximize information (Marcus & Gould, 2000; Hofstede, 1997)

Long Versus Short-Term Orientation

Hofstede developed an additional dimension to his original set, as long-term orientation seemed to play an important role in Asian countries that had been influenced by Confucian philosophy over many thousands of years. Hofstede found such countries shared these beliefs:

- A stable society requires unequal relations.
- The family is the prototype of all social organizations; older people (parents) have more authority than younger people, and men more than women.
- Treat others as you would like to be treated.
- Acquiring skills and education, working hard, and being frugal, patient, and persevering.

Western countries, by contrast, were more likely to promote equality, individualism, and finding fulfillment through creativity and self-actualization. When Hofstede developed a survey specifically for Asia and reevaluated earlier data, he found that long-term orientation cancelled out some of the effects of masculinity/femininity and uncertainty avoidance. It was concluded that Asian countries are oriented more towards the search for virtuous behavior while Western countries are oriented to belief and the search for truth. China was found to have a very high long-term orientation.

Based on this definition, high LT countries would emphasize the following aspects of user-interface design:

- Content focused on practical value and issues
- Relationships should function as a source of information and credibility
- Patience in achieving results and goals (Marcus and Gould, 2000; Hofstede, 1997)

Aside from Hofstede (1997), there is also Appadurai's (1991) Five Dimensions of Cultural Flow, and King's Towns and Landscapes (1991), all relevant theories of globalization. Appadurai attempted to capture the ways in which cultures relate to and influence each other. These include the following five dimensions:

King (1991) claims that the Internet allows "the global diffusion of information, images, professional cultures and sub-cultures, supported by international capital flows." Both of these models support the concept that culture exists on, and is an important component of, the Internet, and should be taken into account whenever a Website is intended to be globalized.

Combined with this are some specific characteristics of the Chinese which are important to consider when targeting sites for e-commerce and related purposes.

First, there are elements of traditional Chinese culture, which even in our modern-day society still carry weight in Chinese societies. These include the influences of Chinese philosophy, including Confucianism, Taoism, and Buddhism. The influences of these helped to create a sense of practicality, together with philosophical views of life, in Chinese culture.

Some of the traditional values which are important to be aware of when interacting with Chinese culture include respect for the elderly and social status, "face," the use of color, and various traditions which are associated with various aspects of life. These traditional values and profiles below in the table.

Table 2: Appadurai's Five Dimensions of Global Cultural Flow (1991)

Ethno-scapes	Flows of people—users and the Internet
Finanscapes	Currency and stock exchanges – Internet and e-commerce
Ideo-scapes	The distribution and proliferation of state and counter-state messages over the Internet
Mediascapes	Images of media and information
Techo-scapes	Technological products and equipment for the Internet

Unlike the United States and other Western cultures, the culture is influenced by Confucianism, in which the notions of societal harmony, and of respect for family and elders. As discussed by Xing (1995) , many Chinese attach a sense of importance to being a part of a group, rather than emphasizing their own individuality. In addition, Confucianism emphasis the moderate, "middle" path to things, instead of being to one or the other extreme.

In addition, there are a number of other characteristics of Chinese culture which are of importance when examining commerce in China. These include the conservative nature of Chinese society, the respect for conformity and authority, brand loyalty, and resistance to new products and ideas. In general, compared to Western societies, the Chinese are generally more conservative, and tend to avoid uncertainty, while preferring continuity and a more conservative view of the world (Scarborough, 1998; Jing, 1993).

Also, the attitude towards marketing and advertising differs in that authority is respected, and when a respected figure is seen promoting a product, it tends to improve effectiveness of the promotion. Social aspects such as conformity to norms and worries about the opinions of others are more a factor than in the West (Jing, 1993; Yau, 1988). Also, brand loyalty seems to be rather strong in Chinese cultures

Table 3: Chinese Cultural Traditions (Adapted from Lee, 1986)

Cultural Tradition	Description
Respect for Elders	Elderly people are respected in Chinese culture.
Respect for Social Status	Gender, age, job status, government authority, law.
"Face"	Importance of "saving face"; avoiding embarrassment
Education	Education is highly valued in Chinese traditional culture.
Dragon	An important symbol in Chinese culture.
Color	Red symbolized "happiness" White and black symbolize "mourning"

(Yang, 1989). In connection with this, tradition seems to be considered more important than innovation, and some new products and services may be met with some resistance and skepticism, especially if it is viewed as being "socially unacceptable" at that early stage (Yang, 1989). It would also be possible to generalize these tendencies to the fact that the Chinese are more concrete and traditional in their thinking, as opposed to the West, where there may be a stronger influence of abstract thinking and imagination (Li, 1998).

Other interesting insights include the important of emphasizing the geographical areas in which Chinese users are residing and accessing the Internet, the role of language, and transitional aspects of Chinese culture. According to a study conducted by Lai (2001), many Chinese Internet users are more interested in and concerned with the news and information which relates to their immediate geographical area. For instance, if someone resides in Beijing, he or she would have greater interest in Internet delivered content if it is focused on Northern China and the Beijing area rather than Guangzhou or Jiangxi, for example. Local services, or those which focus on a certain region, and deliver information such as local news, weather, or chat would have the most appeal. For instance, in the Sina.com site, the highest hit rates were reported on the Beijing and Shanghai local news and information, and also "city union" chat services (Sina Survey in Major Cities of China, 2001).

Language also appears to be a key factor. While many of the sites which currently existing on the Internet are American-culture oriented, and presented in English, many experts predict that the Internet will become increasing global-oriented in the coming years, and that the influence of China will contribute to a major shift in this current trend (Gupta, 2001). Language is an important part of China's cultural tradition, and therefore the effective use of Mandarin Chinese in Chinese Websites appears to be of critical importance (Woodfield, 1995)

This is particular true in mainland China (People's Republic of China), where Mandarin is considered the official and main language, unlike Hong Kong or Singapore, where there is a much stronger bilingual emphasis, and many people are well versed in both Chinese, English, and other languages. While it is true that many Chinese, especially those who are younger and college-educated, have studied and can communicate effectively in English, it appears that overall, the preference and emphasis of communications is in Chinese. This could be attributed not only to the ease of communicating in the native language, but also due to a sense of tradition and pride in using Chinese. In addition, there are expressions, phrases, nuances and shades of meaning in Chinese that cannot always be expressed in the same way in English.

THE ISSUE OF TRUST

No discussion of the Internet and e-commerce would be complete without a discussion of the issue of trust. Since e-commerce is in fact a new form of doing business, the cultural aspects of Chinese society as they relate to business and trust are important to examine.

While the market in China for the Internet is indeed huge and many Chinese are eagerly getting online every day, only a small percentage (roughly 20 percent) have done any shopping online. Part of this is the limited use of credit cards in China, which contributes to making e-commerce transactions more difficult than in the United States and Europe.

A larger issue is the notion of trust. For good relations, especially those relating to business, it is important to maintain good *guanxi* ("relationship" in Chinese). The definition of *guanxi* could be expressed as the existence of connections in order to secure favor in personal relations (Brunner, Chan & Zhou, 1989). While important in interpersonal relationships, *guanxi* is especially critical in business, where having guanxi can considerably improve how well a firm can do. Clearly, this is one aspect of a business relationship which is not the most easily accomplished when using the Internet.

In addition, in Chinese business there is often a need, or expectation for face to face contact in order to build up a sense of trust. This relates back to the earlier discussion of Hofstede's notion of individualism-collectivism, where Chinese culture, based on the underpinnings of Confucianism, is generally collective. Confucianism also is in favor of the evaluating a partner's past and present behavior, which is a prerequisite for trust. Therefore, when dealing with uncertainty, which is the case of business, the need still exists for some kind of face-to-face contact. This is further supported by the connection between collectivism and high power-distance, which is contrary to the expectation that e-commerce is a low power-distance activity. Clearly, one of the problems that e-commerce is facing in China may be due to a lack of trust both in the online retailers and in the concept of buying something without face-to-face contact and without *guanxi*.

REGIONAL CULTURAL ISSUES FOR CHINESE WEB/E-COMMERCE SITES

In the previous sections, discussions were focused on the effective use of cultural aspects to improve Websites for e-commerce and other purposes in China. In this section, some of the differences between the major Chinese-speaking regions are discussed.

China. Users in Mainland China generally are young, college-educated, and reside in the major cities. They generally prefer to surf and use the Internet in Mandarin Chinese, and currently there are emphases on more traditional and risk-adverse products and services. However, the markets are changing and the situation may be different in a few years. The use of simplified Chinese throughout China would require the use of GuoBiao (GB) or Unicode encoding.

Hong Kong. Because of its cosmopolitan nature and British influence (a former British colony), the use of English is more widespread in Hong Kong as compared with China, and more Western influences have taken hold. Therefore, the use of both Chinese and English on the site, or having two language versions for the same site, might be appropriate. In addition, Hong Kong being in the South of China, and having as its native dialect Cantonese, has its own written version of Cantonese that is combined with Mandarin. The interpretation of this language requires both a knowledge of spoken Cantonese and written Mandarin (Chang, 2000).

Taiwan. While considered by China to be one of its provinces, but a separate nation from its own perspective, Taiwan uses traditional Chinese characters, and users there would likely not only have difficulty understanding simplified characters, but there would be a negative reaction to the use of these. The use of traditional characters is strongly recommended.

Singapore. Singapore is more like Hong Kong in that its orientation is more inherently global. A former British colony, it has been on the forefront of the Internet revolution, and currently has not only a well-developed Internet infrastructure, but a nation with the largest numbers of Internet surfers in Asia. It is also the fourth-most information-driven economy in the world. Web surfers, like those in other Chinese-speaking countries in Asia, are generally, young (29 or younger). A typical example is most likely male, with at least a secondary school education. The types of applications most favored and used in Singapore include many of the same which Americans favor—e-mail, chat, news, games, and obtaining information for various needs. Much like the U.S., books and computer products appear to be the top purchases online, however surfers in Singapore tend to purchase more food and grocery products online than Americans.

Singapore, because of its unique mix of multiculturalism, influence of technology, and Westernization, has somewhat different orientation than China, for example. There is a much stronger influence of modernization, Westernization of the youth, a predominantly masculine culture, and a stronger influence of individualism.

Another interesting phenomenon that is unique to Singapore is the concept of "kiasuism" (Milakov, 1995), which is described as being "going for one's own interest, at the expense of the common good." This could be captured more concisely as being "success-driven," or as being "extremely competitive." The fast-moving nature of Singapore and the desire to succeed is one of the traits that have become engrained into Singapore culture, and perhaps can be captured in terms of success and advancement oriented products and services via the Web.

Also, there are subtle language issues to be considered for Singapore as well. People in Singapore, because of the multitude of cultures and nationalities, have developed their own kind of slang called "Singlish." This combines English with words and expressions from languages including Malay, Mandarin Chinese, and from various Chinese dialects. The result is a mixed language that is generally unique to Singapore. While not an official language by any means, it has been reported by some various business persons from outside Singapore that an understanding of "Singlish" was important to their success of their projects and business endeavors (Milakov, 1995).

CHINESE WEBSITES

Of course, there is no better way to examine Chinese Websites than by examining some of these sites themselves. Several different Websites have become dominant in the Asian and the Chinese-language community, and these are profiled briefly below:

- Sina.com (www.sina.com). This in an important Chinese language portal, and one that bills itself as a "Chinese community online." In fact, the site actually is composed for four sites, each one targeting a certain group or market: China, Taiwan, Hong Kong, and overseas Chinese. In China, www.sina.com.cn is one of the top visited sites.
- Netease.com (www.163.com). Another major Chinese language site. China-oriented audience, simplified characters.
- Sohu.com (www.sohu.com). The site name means, "search fox." Sohu.com is another leading portal in China, which includes search engine services (Chinese and English), e-mail, chat rooms, news, etc. It is designed to appeal to China's younger generation.

Other important portals and sites include 163 e-Post Office (www.163.net), Capital Online (www.263.net), China.com (www.china.com), Yahoo! China (www.yahoo.com.cn) and Eastnet (www.east.com.cn).

SUMMARY AND CONCLUSION

In this chapter, a number of issues and considerations with relation to Chinese cultural and Website/e-commerce design were discussed, and clearly, there are a number of important considerations and issues which should be noted when creating a Website or e-commerce site for Chinese audiences.

To start, the Chinese value using their language. Whether it be simplified or traditional Mandarin Chinese, the use of the language implies respect and understanding of Chinese culture. Because of technology developments, it is not difficult technically to display Chinese, although it may require the services of an effective translator in order to be certain that the language being presented is correct. There is currently the option either to display Chinese using encoded Big5, GB, or Unicode, or to create the characters as graphics images and it display them as pictures. The advantage of graphics is that they do not require any additional effort or software on the part of the users. However, the use of graphics often would result in slower download and page load times. There are many resources that are available to assist firms and individuals in managing translations, fonts, and related issues. There are also the differences that are attributed to which location you are attempting to target. If you are targeting the Chinese mainland, the use of the simplified characters is called for. Taiwan uses traditional characters. Hong Kong and Singapore, for example, could have a bilingual site with both Chinese and English.

Cultural traditions, while not quite as strong as in the past, still exist, and Web designers need to be sensitive to the many complexities of a civilization that has developed over thousands of years. The social aspects of *guanxi* and its role in business are also important to understand. In conclusion, marketing to or communicating with Chinese audiences over the Internet is a complex task, but one which can yield great benefits and opportunities.

REFERENCES

Appadurai, A. (1999). In King, A.D. (Ed.) (1991). *Culture Globalisation and the World-System*, Macmillan Press Ltd., SUNY-Binghampton.

Bouchet. (1995). *Marketing and the Redefinition of Ethnicity.* In Costa, J. & Balmossy, G. (Eds.) *Marketing in a Multicultural World*, London: Sage Publications.

Brunner, J.A., Chan, C.S. & Zhou, N. (1989) The role of guanxi in negotiation in the Pacific Basin. *Journal of Global Marketing*, *3*(2), 58-72.

Chang, S.F. (2000). *A Study of Cultural Influences on Singapore-Chinese Use of e-commerce*, Major Thesis, RMIT.

CNNIC (2000). *Semi-Annual China Internet Report.*

CNNIC (2001). *Semi-Annual China Internet Report.*

Gupta, A.F. (2001). *Internet and the English Language.* Retrieved on July 14, 2002, from the World Wide Web: http://www.fas.nus.edu.sg/staff/conf/poco.paper6.html.

Hofstede, G. (1997). *Cultures and Organizations: Software of the Mind.* Mc Graw-Hill.

King, A.D. (ed.) (1991). *Culture Globalisation and the World-System.* Macmillan Press Ltd., SUNY-Binghampton.

Jing, L.B. (1993). The influence of Chinese culture on marketing management. *Economics Studies*, July, 10, 36.

Lai, J. (2001). Marketing Web Sites in China. *Minor Thesis*, RMIT.

Lee, S.M. (1986). *Spectrum of Chinese Culture.* Pelanduk Publications (M), Selangor Darul Ehsau.

Li, C.H. (1998). China: *The Consumer Revolution.* NY: Wiley.

McCarthy, T. (2000) China's Internet Gold Rush. *TIME Magazine*, Feb 28, 20-23.

Marcus & Gould. (2000). Cultural dimensions and global Web user-interface design. *Proceedings of the 6th Conference on Human Factors and the Web.*

Milakov. (1995). *Asian Games*, Coolum Beach: Gull Publishing, 19.

Mooij, M. (1998). *Global Marketing and Advertising*. CA: Sage Publications.

Nathan, A. (1998), *China's Transition.* NY: Columbia University Press.

Penazola, L.N. (1998). Immigrant consumer acculturation. In Srull (Ed.) *Advances in Consumer Research*, Provo, UT: Association. for Consumer Research.

Scarborough, J. (1998). Comparing Chinese and western culture roots. *Business Horizons*, November.

Sinai, (2001). *Survey in Major Cities in China.*

Woodfield, A. (1995). The conservation of endangered languages. *CTLL Seminar of University of Bristol.*

Yang, C.F. (1989). A conception of Chinese consumer behavior. In *Hong Kong Marketing Management at the Crossroads*. Hong Kong: Commercial Press, 317-342.

Yau, O.H. (1988). Chinese culture values: Their dimensions and marketing implications. *Journal of Marketing,* 22, 44-57.

Xing, F. (1995). The Chinese Cultural System. In *SAM Advanced Management Journal*, 60, 1, 14-20.

CHINESE LANGUAGE COMPUTING LINKS

http://www.sinologic.com/ChinaLinks.html, SINOLOGIC, select "Computing."
http://www.gy.com/www/ch.htm, Chinese Software Digest.

About the Authors

Theerasak Thanasankit earned his Ph.D. in Management Information Systems from the University of Melbourne. He is currently a Senior Lecturer in the School of Information Management and Systems at Monash University, Australia. Dr. Thanasankit has taught at many universities in Australia, New Zealand and Thailand. His research focuses on the influence of indigenous cultures and values on the use, adoption and implementation of information systems, especially in e-commerce. Dr. Thanasankit also conducts researches in requirements engineering and creativity and IT policy.

* * * * *

O. Chieochan has a Bachelor of Science (first class honors) degree from Rajamangala Institute of Technology, Thailand, a Master of Computing degree from Griffith University, Australia, and a Ph.D. in the School of Information Studies, Charles Sturt University, Australia. His research interests focus on information technology and electronic commerce in agricultural businesses and rural development in developing countries, especially in Thailand.

Brian J. Corbitt is Professor of Information Systems and Head of School in the School of Information Systems at Deakin University in Melbourne, Australia. He specializes in Electronic Commerce policy development, analysis and implementation and in Business Modeling and Electronic Commerce trade relationships, and knowledge management in tertiary institutions. He is currently responsible for the development of e-learning and KM initiatives at Deakin University as Pro Vice Chancellor. His published research includes reports to public and private agencies on Smart Cards, implementation of Electronic Commerce in SMEs in Australia, on Intranets and on Electronic Commerce policy implementation. He has a great deal of experience in the implementation of e-Commerce solutions in developing countries especially Thailand and Malaysia and in the implementation of EC in Singapore and New Zealand.

Jacob L. Cybulski is a Senior Lecturer in the School of Information Systems at Deakin University (Melbourne), Australia. His professional interests include requirements engineering, domain analysis and web-based business systems. Jacob works as a consultant with organizations willing to introduce novel approaches to their business, e.g., e-commerce and web technologies, UML development methods and design patterns. Jacob's past projects range from mechanical engineering and telecommunications applications to developing software productivity environments and toolkits. Jacob also acted as an expert witness in the area of software development methodologies and process quality. His current work involves investigation of novel methods and tools for e-commerce and web development.

T. Dunn has a Master of Agricultural Science in Extension from the University of Melbourne. He is a Senior Lecturer in Extension and Agricultural Systems in the School of Agriculture at Charles Sturt University, Australia. His research interests are in rural social sciences including the application of qualitative methodologies to improve agricultural use of natural resources and the social condition of rural people. His particular specialties include the application of methodologies like Soft Systems Methodology and Rapid/Participatory Rural Appraisal to assist change in rural social systems.

Amnuay Ekasdornkorn has a master's degree in Information Technology from King Mongut's Institute of Technology (North Bangkok) in Thailand. He is an IT professional and has been working extensively in IT security in banking industry.

Donal Flynn is a Senior Lecturer in the Department of Computation at the University of Manchester Institute of Science and Technology, UK. His research interests include Interpretivist approaches to empirical studies of IT-organizational interaction, the associated social shaping of IT with a particular interest in the fit between social and technical factors.

Sid L. Huff is Professor and Ericsson Chair of Information Systems at Victoria University of Wellington, New Zealand, and is the Head of the School of Information Management. He has been teaching and researching in the information systems field for over 25 years. His current research focuses on electronic commerce, IS strategy, and senior management roles in IT. He has taught at universities in the US, Canada and New Zealand, and has published extensively in the leading information systems journals. He has also written over 50 teaching cases, and is the lead author of *Cases in Electronic Commerce*, the second edition of which was recently published by Irwin/McGraw-Hill.

Jeffrey Hsu is an Assistant Professor of Information Systems at the Silberman College of Business Administration, Fairleigh Dickinson University, USA. His research interests include electronic commerce, human-computer interaction, groupware, distance learning, and data mining/business intelligence. He is the author of six books, including numerous papers and articles, and has professional experience in the IT industry. Hsu holds a Ph.D. in Management Information Systems from Rutgers University, three master's degrees, and several professional certifications. In addition, he is an active member of FDU's Chinese-American Business Institute (CABI), which seeks to develop educational partnerships and exchange opportunities with China. Dr. Hsu is always interested in discussing opportunities for research and other scholarly activities, and can be reached via e-mail at jeff@fdu.edu.

Arunee Intrapairot is a Lecturer in Management Information Systems, Faculty of Business Administration at the Rajamangala Institute of Technology, Thailand. She received her master's and Ph.D. from Curtin University of Technology, Australia. Her research focuses on Decision Support Systems, System Dynamics, Multiple Criteria Decision Making, e-commerce, and e-learning.

Joseph Kabalimu is an academic at the University of Dar es Salaam. He completed master's degrees in Information Sciences and Information Systems from that University and Victoria University of Wellington in New Zealand.

Wei-Chang Kong is an IT professional working in Singapore. He earned his Bachelor of Information Systems from the University of Melbourne. He received his undergraduate degree with first class honors and his honors dissertation focused on IT implementation policy in Singapore. His current research is in the area of IT policy, IT implementation and e-commerce.

D. Lindley has degrees in computing and information management and a Ph.D. from the University of New South Wales, Australia. He has approximately 15 years of industrial experience and is presently an academic in the School of Information Studies, Charles Sturt University, Australia. He is also the Chief Examiner of the Australian Computer Society and a consultant to IDP Education Australia. His principal research interest lies in the use of information technology for national economic and social development, especially in the countries of South and East Asia.

Gary S. C. Pan is a doctoral candidate in the Department of Computation, University of Manchester Institute of Science and Technology, UK. His current research focuses on the abandonment of IS development projects – the contributory factors and the prevention strategies.

Konrad Janusz Peszynski is a graduate from the Victoria University of Wellington in New Zealand. Konrad has received first class Honors in Information Systems as well as a Bachelor of Science with a major in Psychology from Victoria University of Wellington. He has an interest in the social areas of electronic commerce, specifically cultural factors. Konrad is currently undertaking his Ph.D. at Deakin University in Melbourne, Australia, where he is also employed as an Associate Lecturer in the School of Information Systems.

Utomporn Phalavonk is currently Dean of the Faculty of Applied Science at King Mongut's Institute of Technology (North Bangkok) in Thailand. She has a Ph.D. from the University of New South Wales.

Pradipta K. Sarkar is a Ph.D. student in the School of Information Systems at Deakin University (Melbourne, Australia). His research aims at improving current methods of requirements engineering for web-based application development to better service the diverse needs of a global user. In the past, Pradip also worked in India, Thailand and Australia in both software industry and academe, which gave him a unique opportunity to have first-hand experience with software development practices across national, language and cultural boundaries. He was a Lecturer in Computer at Assumption Business Administration College University in Thailand from 1998-2000.

Anongnart Srivihok received a Master of Science in Engineering Science-Computer Science from the University of Mississippi, USA, and a Ph.D. from Central Queensland University, Australia. She is an Associate Professor in the Department of Computer Science, Kasetsart University, Thailand, a deputy director of the Office of Computer Service, and a consultant at Institute of Promotion Science and Technology, Thailand. She regularly presents at international IT conferences, teaches both undergraduate and postgraduate classes in Computer Science and Information Systems. Her research interests are Decision

Support Systems, Executive Information Systems, e-commerce, e-learning and e-CRM.

Orasa Tetiwat is a lecturer in Faculty of Science at Naresuan University, Thailand. Currently, she is working on her Ph.D. in Information Systems at Victoria University of Wellington, New Zealand. Her educational background includes an EMBA (2000) from the Peter F. Drucker Graduate School of Management and an M.S. in MIS (1999) from School of Information Science at Claremont Graduate University, Claremont. She also received MS in Computer Science (1989) from DePaul University, Chicago, a Post Graduate – Higher Diploma in the Graduate Volunteer (1984) from Thammasart University, and a Bachelor in Economics (1983) at Ramkamhaeng University, Thailand. Her research interests are in the areas of technology in education, organizational learning, and electronic commerce.

Chia Yao Lee is a Ph.D. candidate in the Department of Information Systems at the University of Melbourne, Australia. He received his Bachelor of Engineering (Electrical and Electronic) from the University of Melbourne. His research interests include strategies for the implementation of electronic business and interorganizational information systems. His current focus is on understanding the business value of business-to-business electronic markets.

Index

I

K

L

M

N

O

P

Journal of Electronic Commerce in Organizations (JECO)

NEW! NEW!

The International Journal of Electronic Commerce in Modern Organizations

ISSN: 1539-2937
eISSN: 1539-2929

Subscription: Annual fee per volume (4 issues):
Individual US $85
Institutional US $185

Editor: Mehdi Khosrow-Pour, D.B.A.
Information Resources
Management Association, USA

Mission

The ***Journal of Electronic Commerce in Organizations*** is designed to provide comprehensive coverage and understanding of the social, cultural, organizational, and cognitive impacts of e-commerce technologies and advances on organizations around the world. These impacts can be viewed from the impacts of electronic commerce on consumer behavior, as well as the impact of e-commerce on organizational behavior, development, and management in organizations. The secondary objective of this publication is to expand the overall body of knowledge regarding the human aspects of electronic commerce technologies and utilization in modern organizations, assisting researchers and practitioners to devise more effective systems for managing the human side of e-commerce.

Coverage

This publication includes topics related to electronic commerce as it relates to: Strategic Management, Management and Leadership, Organizational Behavior, Organizational Developement, Organizational Learning, Technologies and the Workplace, Employee Ethical Issues, Stress and Strain Impacts, Human Resources Management, Cultural Issues, Customer Behavior, Customer Relationships, National Work Force, Political Issues, and all other related issues that impact the overall utilization and management of electronic commerce technologies in modern organizations.

For subscription information, contact:

Idea Group Publishing
701 E Chocolate Ave., Ste 200
Hershey PA 17033-1240, USA
cust@idea-group.com
URL: www-idea-group.com

For paper submission information:

Dr. Mehdi Khosrow-Pour
Information Resources Management Association
jeco@idea-group.com